D0722497

OUT OF
THE
CLOUDS

OUT OF
THE
CLOUDS

The Unlikely Horseman and the Unwanted

Colt Who Conquered the Sport of Kings

LINDA CARROLL AND

DAVID ROSNER

NEW YORK   BOSTON

Hachette Books
Hachette Book Group
1290 Avenue of the Americas, New York, NY 10104
hachettebooks.com
twitter.com/hachettebooks

First Edition: May 2018

Photo credits can be found on page 303.

Hachette Books is a division of Hachette Book Group, Inc. The Hachette Books name and logo are trademarks of Hachette Book Group, Inc.

The publisher is not responsible for websites (or their content) that are not owned by the publisher.

The Hachette Speakers Bureau provides a wide range of authors for speaking events. To find out more, go to www.hachettespeakersbureau.com or call (866) 376-6591.

Library of Congress Cataloging-in-Publication Data

Names: Carroll, Linda, 1956– author.
Title: Out of the clouds: the unlikely horseman and the unwanted colt who
    conquered the sport of kings / Linda Carroll and David Rosner.
Description: First edition. | New York : Hachette Books, 2018. | Includes
    bibliographical references and index.
Identifiers: LCCN 2017049734| ISBN 9780316432238 (hardcover) |
    ISBN 9781549168468 (audio download) | ISBN 9780316432214 (ebook)
Subjects: LCSH: Jacobs, Hirsch. | Racehorse trainers—United States—Biography. |
    Horsemen and horsewomen—United States—Biography. | Race horses—United
    States.
Classification: LCC SF336.J33 C37 2018 | DDC 636.1/2092 [B]—dc23
LC record available at https://lccn.loc.gov/2017049734

ISBNs: 978-0-316-43223-8 (hardcover), 978-0-316-43221-4 (ebook)

LSC-C

10 9 8 7 6 5 4 3 2 1

*For all the underdogs, longshots, and outsiders
striving to realize their American Dream*

CONTENTS

Contents

AT FIRST SIGHT

On a beautiful New York spring afternoon in 1943, Hirsch Jacobs stood in the tree-shaded paddock at Belmont Park, elbows leaning on the wrought-iron fence that rimmed the walking ring, as he watched the horses being saddled for the first race. A regular fixture in the bucolic saddling area just behind the stately brick grandstand of America's grandest racetrack, he blended right in with the spectators who trickled through the nearby turnstiles seeking a diversion, if only for a few fleeting hours, from the unremitting stress of a world at war.

A short, stout man in his late thirties with a round, ruddy face and bright red hair, Jacobs sported a conservative three-piece suit and tie that made him look more like a button-down businessman than the hardened horseman he was. While the racegoers around him casually sized up the field in hopes of picking a winner for their $2 bets, he was hard at work scrutinizing the dozen entrants with his discerning eye in search of a bargain to add to his successful stable of modest Thoroughbreds that had all been bought on the cheap.

Despite operating on a shoestring budget in a rich man's pastime fittingly dubbed "The Sport of Kings," Hirsch Jacobs had managed to establish himself over the past decade as America's winningest trainer. He did it by scooping up the discards of prominent high-society racing stables at bargain-basement prices and somehow transforming them into winners. He would buy those cheap and often-unsound nags out of claiming races—the lowest-level competitions in which any horse entered can be purchased, or "claimed," shortly before post time at a preset price—and promptly diagnose their problems and work his magic with a combination of home remedies and equine psychoanalysis. The strategy had worked so well that he'd saddled more winners annually than any other trainer for a record-smashing nine of the previous ten years.

For all his achievements, though, the old-money racing aristocracy, galled at being beaten by the very horses they had recently discarded as worthless, haughtily dismissed Jacobs as nothing more than a "claiming trainer." To them, he was the ultimate outsider: a commoner in The Sport of Kings, a Jewish immigrant tailor's son who grew up dirt poor on the streets of Brooklyn and never gave horses a second thought until his late teens, a greenhorn who owed everything he knew about training them to his youthful passion of raising and racing pigeons. At a loss to rationalize the incomprehensible success of a New York City street kid in a pastoral pastime whose ingrained traditions had been passed down from English royalty and nobility to Kentucky Bluegrass gentry, they were sure Jacobs must have been doing something underhanded and even went so far as to hire private investigators to surveil his barn round the clock for proof of illicit practices or "voodoo" potions. When they could find no hints of any wrongdoing, they continued to snipe about how he only ever won the most ordinary races by running his cheap claimers "like a fleet of taxicabs" and wouldn't know what to do with the Thoroughbred equivalent of a Rolls-Royce—a high-class horse with the talent to enter the big-purse stakes from the Kentucky Derby on down—if he ever got his hands on one.

As much as the blue-blooded swells resented him, Jacobs reigned as the favorite of all the blue-collar horseplayers who could trust him with their hard-earned $2 bets because they knew that any horse he sent to the post would be ready to race. In a larger sense, he was a working-class hero to all the downtrodden common folk who could identify with his Horatio Algeresque rise from impoverished outcast to the realization of the American Dream: the city boy who never even rode horses now climbing the ladder, one cheap claimer at a time, past all the hardboots from Bluegrass pastures and cowboys from Western plains. Thus did he bond with the masses of working-class fans who made horse racing America's most popular spectator sport and who viewed the racetrack as a source of affordable entertainment where a lucky bet could make their dreams come true. They rooted for longshots, for underdogs, for castoffs like the common claimers that populated the majority of all races run each day and that popularized Hirsch Jacobs as "The Pigeon Man" and a "Miracle Man" in headlines nationwide.

On this mild and sunny Saturday of a Memorial Day weekend made more meaningful for a nation in the throes of World War II, Jacobs had come to the Belmont Park paddock on the lookout for his next project horse. Which is why he was joined there by his partner in their public stable of cheap claimers: Isidor Bieber, a Runyonesque high roller who, as a first-generation Jewish immigrant with shared Eastern European roots, was as much an interloper as Jacobs. Their unlikely partnership—Bieber providing the bulk of the start-up bankroll, Jacobs all the horse sense and training savvy—had for two decades been shaking up the racing establishment.

Standing against the paddock fence, this pair of New York city slickers presented the most incongruous Odd Couple: Bieber, a flamboyant dandy notorious as a high-stakes gambler and Broadway ticket hustler who looked in his clashing stripes and checks as if he'd stepped right out of a Damon Runyon short story (and who had in fact served as both source and model for some of his famous writer friend's colorful characters), towering over the much-younger Jacobs, a devoted family man who acted as modestly as he dressed and never even played the ponies. While the bombastic Bieber would hold forth quoting everyone from Shakespeare to Voltaire and espousing provocative opinions that he often backed up with his fists, the soft-spoken and mild-mannered Jacobs quietly went about his business with guarded privacy, parsing his words and pausing only to greet fellow racetrackers with an easy smile and amiable "Hiya" in his high, nasal voice. All they seemed to have in common, besides their shared outsider status, were the cheap claimers they invested in together and the other horses they managed for a handful of small-scale owners like their mutual friend Damon Runyon.

As the dozen two-year-old Thoroughbreds now paraded past them in the Belmont paddock, one caught Jacobs's keen eye. Where other observers saw just a small, ordinary-looking chestnut, Jacobs alone saw potential. Although no single feature of the shiny copper colt stuck out, the trainer realized that was because all the parts melded together in perfect balance. The colt was sturdy and well muscled, with good bone, a powerful hind end, and a broad chest with a well-angled shoulder. He was a solid chestnut except for the irregular streak of white that began wide between his eyes and thinned to a faint trace as it meandered to the tip of his nose. Though he measured only a shade over 15 hands, he looked much taller because of the way he proudly puffed himself up. Jacobs was particularly struck by how high the little chestnut held his head, a regal carriage that reminded the trainer of the incomparable Man o' War and hinted at a high-strung and headstrong temperament that could prove hard to handle. Watching the high-headed colt walking past and exiting the paddock, Jacobs looked hard to find flaws in conformation.

The trainer then turned to Bieber and flashed a knowing smile. "I got a feeling about that colt," Jacobs said matter-of-factly. "I like the way he walks. He's a proud little thing."

As the twelve horses slowly made their way from the paddock toward the tunnel leading under the massive grandstand to the track for the post parade, Jacobs noted the Number 1 on the coppery colt's saddlecloth and the distinctive brown and white silks of the majestic King Ranch, America's largest farm sprawling over a million Texas acres. He borrowed Bieber's *Daily Racing Form*, thumbed to the entries for the first race, and looked up the Number 1 horse. He learned that the chestnut's name was Stymie; that he too was an outsider, obscurely bred of unaccomplished parentage in Texas far from the Kentucky Bluegrass most celebrated for producing Thoroughbred champions; and that he had been a well-beaten seventh by eight lengths in his only previous start, a cheap claiming race three weeks earlier in which he had no takers at a price tag of $2,500. This time the colt would be trying his luck in a maiden race—just one rung up from the lowly claiming races in the hierarchy of events capped by the marquee stakes—against green two-year-olds that likewise had never won anything.

Jacobs did not follow those maidens to the track to watch the afternoon's first race. So he would not see Stymie run to form as a prohibitive 78-to-1 longshot, lagging far up the straightaway through the short sprint and trudging home sixteen lengths off the pace in second-to-last place. Instead, the trainer had already turned his attention back to the paddock where he would get down to the business of saddling a cheap claimer of his own for the second race—but not before he made a mental note committing Stymie's name to his famously photographic memory of all things equine.

Little could Hirsch Jacobs imagine that this moment would change both of their lives.

Like every other horseman, from the lowliest claiming trainer to richest high-society owner, Jacobs had a dream of someday getting his hands on that one great horse. Even though he saw the glimmer of something special in Stymie, Jacobs couldn't know that both he and the little horse would come to inspire a generation coming home from World War II—with a real-life Horatio Alger story showing that no matter how far down you started, you could make it to the top by dint of sheer determination and hard work. He couldn't know that this cheap claimer could someday develop into that one great champion he had been searching for his entire career, the one that would prove his ability to cultivate a racing legend, the one that would finally win him the acceptance and respect that the racing elite had long denied him. He certainly had no reason to believe that this might be the beginning of a rags-to-riches Cinderella story the likes of which no one—not even Jacobs himself—dared dream.

Chapter 1

"THE PIGEON MAN"

Among bird fanciers, there's an old saying: "If horse racing is the sport of kings, then pigeon racing is the sport of the common man."

By that bit of conventional wisdom, Hirsch Jacobs was made to race pigeons. He was, after all, born a commoner in New York City at the dawn of the twentieth century just as pigeon racing was taking off as "the poor man's horse racing." It was a place and a time that fostered the sport as a popular urban pastime, as an ingrained part of life for the masses of working-class stiffs who flocked to rooftop coops after long days toiling in sweatshops, and as a fresh-air escape from the confining grit and mundane monotony of the immigrant experience.

For Hirsch Jacobs, the dirt-poor son of European Jewish immigrants, growing up in America's largest city meant sharing overcrowded environs with, as the old saw goes, "one pigeon per person." With the mass immigration of the early twentieth century swelling the city's population past 5 million, New Yorkers had to cohabit with all those pigeons drawn to the asphalt jungle by building ledges that evoked their Eurasian natural habitat of coastal cliffs, which had given their species its formal name: the "rock dove," or "rock pigeon." Many city dwellers, of course, found less complimentary names to call those feral cliff dwellers roosting in their buildings: "rats with wings," "flying street rats," and worse.

It wasn't those "rats of the sky," as the reviled street pigeons were also branded, that struck young Hirsch Jacobs's fancy. Rather, he was smitten by the elite subspecies of rock doves revered as the "Thoroughbreds of the sky." These were the racing pigeons—that is, homing pigeons as well bred and well conditioned as the Thoroughbreds that had made horse racing America's most popular spectator sport. While thousand-pound racehorses got all the glory galloping 40 mph once around a mile-long track, these one-pound racing pigeons were routinely flying hundreds of miles in a single day at average speeds approaching 80 mph. Some 75,000 of these avian Thoroughbreds graced New York—bursting from roofs into the air like fistfuls of thrown confetti, soaring in swirling flocks above the city like gray puffs of chimney smoke, then diving back home to their own appointed coops.

The pigeon coops that dotted the rooftops were as much a part of the developing New York City skyline as the newfangled skyscrapers then sprouting up in Lower Manhattan (from the distinctively triangular Flatiron Building to two edifices that each reigned for years as the world's tallest, the Metropolitan Life Tower and the Woolworth Building). In Brooklyn, where the Jacobses lived in an ethnic working-class neighborhood crammed with rowhouses and tenements, almost every rooftop sported a coop—a sign that the raising of pigeons had become the prevailing hobby of both men and boys. If horse racing was America's oldest sport and baseball its "national pastime," pigeon racing was cementing itself, in contrast to those pastoral pursuits, as a uniquely urban passion. In the New York metropolitan area alone, almost 3,000 fanciers made pigeon racing the city's fastest-growing recreation. Watching those enthusiasts exercise their flocks at twilight each day, young Hirsch would become hypnotized by the birds flying laps round and round over the roofs while their owners kept them from landing in their coops by repeatedly scaring them back into the air with long bamboo poles.

The wide-eyed youngster couldn't wait to possess pigeons of his own. Like many street kids who felt caged in New York City's confining neighborhoods, he longed to embrace a vicarious escape on the striped wings of homing pigeons. "It was quite the fad in those days to raise pigeons and develop them," he would explain years later to anyone intrigued by his youthful hobby. "Almost every kid in the neighborhood was interested in keeping pigeons when I was growing up."

Small wonder his fondest childhood memory was acquiring his first one. At the time, he was all of eight years old.

It's easy to see how a young boy like Hirsch would become so taken by those "dinosaurs of the sky" that had been roaming the earth for 30 million years and had been domesticated for 10,000. He found himself seduced by a species that was revered by the great civilizations and empires, adored as a universal symbol of peace and purity, and worshipped in religions from Hinduism to Christianity. The Bible offered him a romanticized introduction: the white dove released from Noah's Ark in the Genesis flood narrative returns with an olive twig signifying that the floodwater has ebbed enough to make the land habitable again, and the white dove at Jesus's baptism descends as the very embodiment of the Holy Spirit. Beyond biblical tales, history books traced pigeons' more concrete contributions as messengers dating back to Mesopotamian cuneiform tablets carved in the cradle of civilization itself.

What fascinated the boy most was the very trait that made mankind's earliest domesticated bird invaluable to all civilizations: the innate homing instinct that had originated with the pigeon's need to find its way back to its nest after foraging over long distances for food and then intensified through natural selection. It was the study of the pigeon's mystical homing instinct, in fact, that had led the pioneering natural scientist Charles Darwin to devise his theory of evolution. Devoting the first chapter of his seminal 1859 book *On the Origin of the Species* to the evolution of pigeons, Darwin demonstrated how natural selection had transformed the humble rock dove into a homing machine that combined uncanny navigational skill and athletic ability.

Like Darwin, an avid fancier of homers who had joined two London breeding clubs and used his own pigeon loft as a lab to prove how man could enhance their superior traits through artificial selection, Hirsch Jacobs "found in them quite a study." Making a science of them himself on Brooklyn rooftops, the youngster eagerly soaked up everything the neighborhood fanciers could impart about breeding, housing, nurturing, training, and racing them.

It didn't take long for him to expand his own pigeon stock from that first slaty-blue homer into what was said to be the healthiest and happiest flock on his block. He prized all his pigeons, naming each one and learning its idiosyncrasies. He loved everything about caring for them year-round: feeding them the most nutritious grain, dropping a rusty nail in their water dish to boost their iron, scrubbing their coop clean to encourage a speedier return home. He could often be found standing on the rooftop of the rowhouse where his family lived in a tiny apartment, releasing them into the air for "training tosses," watching them circle overhead on those daily exercise flights, and eventually waving a long bamboo pole with a flag on the end of it to signal them back home at dusk.

From the moment he first tossed them skyward, it was clear that Hirsch Jacobs was a natural. By the time he was twelve, he had already demonstrated a remarkable memory for detail that would serve him well with racing pigeons and eventually with racehorses.

"I could identify one hundred pigeons by sight—while they were flying," he liked to point out with a proud smile but not a trace of braggadocio.

So exceptional was his eyesight that, without the aid of binoculars, he could focus on someone else's flock of forty pigeons soaring 200 yards above his head and suddenly pick out a stray. "Hey, there's one of ours," he would exclaim with furrowed brow. "What's he doing with that outfit?"

When asked how he could possibly distinguish his own bluish-gray homer from the rest of the bluish-gray flock in full flight, he would explain with a shrug, "It's just having an eye for it."

Not to mention a passion for it. He enjoyed nothing more than simply raising them and would have been happy if that proved an end in itself. But the true measure of his acumen as a pigeon fancier, he realized, would involve putting them to the test in a race. These were, after all, avian athletes—all speed, power, grace, and pedigree, born and bred to race in much the same way Thoroughbred horses were. Millenniums of natural and artificial selection had crossed many of the rock dove's hundreds of breeds to create a superpigeon: a feathered rocket built for speed and endurance, powered by an aerodynamic muscular body capable of flying a thousand miles at 60 mph and an enhanced radar homing system adept at finding its way home from a unfamiliar place over an uncharted course without stopping for food or water.

That peerless combination had made pigeons the consummate messengers since the dawn of civilization, uniquely qualified to deliver posts far faster than couriers on foot or horseback. Pigeons carried news to ancient Egyptians of a pharaoh's ascension to the throne, results to ancient Greek city-states from the first Olympic Games in 776 B.C., military dispatches to commanding warriors ranging from Julius Caesar to Genghis Khan. They became big business in the nineteenth century when the Rothschild banking family utilized them as the fleetest financial couriers to amass history's richest private fortune, inspiring a fellow German entrepreneur named Paul Julius Reuter to parlay his own pigeon posts into the world's largest news-gathering service on the wings of 200 feathered messengers.

Those same mythic homing powers that launched the Reuters News Agency and the House of Rothschild dynasty also made pigeons world-class racers. Pigeon racing can be traced back to the Roman Empire as well as to the ancient Hebrews in the Talmud, the book of Jewish law that forbade all such competitions and barred anyone who bet on them from bearing witness in court. Sixteen centuries later, by the 1800s, pigeon racing had become not only an accepted sport, but also a budding pastime among European lower classes that welcomed the affordable diversion of watching—and betting on—the birds. With pigeons gradually being replaced as postal messengers by the advent of the telegraph and the steam-powered railroad, the Belgians concocted the idea of racing them for pure sport. Pigeon racing soon emerged as Belgium's national sport, its prize purses prompting fanciers to crossbreed messenger homers and create hybrids for greater speed and endurance. By the mid-1800s, Charles Dickens was reporting to his equine-obsessed British readers across the Channel that "pigeon racing is as fashionable an amusement in Belgium as horse racing in England." That avian amusement soon spread to Dickens's Victorian England, where fanciers nurtured the superior-bred Belgian imports in castle-like dovecotes befitting the British monarchs who would famously race their prized pigeons out of their royal lofts.

Around that same time, in the mid-1870s, pigeon racing landed on America's Atlantic shores along with the latest wave of European immigrants and emerged as the sport not of royalty but of the common man. While racehorses were beyond the means of a New York workingman or schoolboy, a good pair of Belgian-bred homers could be bought for sixty cents and housed cheaply in a rickety soapbox perched on a rooftop. The pigeon game began gaining momentum after the first-ever U.S. race dangled a winner's purse of $100 in gold, a king's ransom for a commoner in 1878 New York. With coops popping up on urban rooftops and with local clubs starting up to organize races, the then-still-independent city of Brooklyn ranked third nationally in the cultivation of the fledgling sport (behind only New York and Philadelphia). The *Brooklyn Daily Eagle*, a civic institution whose masthead boasted "the Largest Circulation of any Evening Paper published in the United States," covered it like horse racing with regular stories on pigeon races, pigeon clubs, pigeon sales, even pigeon thefts.

Lured by its ever-growing cachet, Hirsch Jacobs couldn't wait to throw himself into what seemed the ideal sport for a twelve-year-old pigeon lover.

Pigeon racing had become as much a part of immigrant New York as the cramped tenements, the stifling sweatshops, and the teeming ghettos. For countless workingmen, it provided a brief respite from the unrelenting struggle that was the immigrant experience. For a boy like Hirsch Jacobs, it offered more than an escape from the poverty that defined his daily existence—the flight of the pigeons stoked dreams of freedom and a brighter future.

The path to that future was laid out for him in the Horatio Alger dime novels so popular among adolescents at the time. There, he could imagine himself the protagonist in all those success stories glorifying the rags-to-riches rise of impoverished boys from humble beginnings to middle-class respectability through hard work, sheer determination, and noble values. As much as Alger's young-adult novels had inspired a Gilded Age generation when they were published in the latter third of the nineteenth century, their universal theme would resonate even louder with youngsters coming of age in the immigrant New York of Hirsch Jacobs's youth. The idea that any American, even the poorest, could rise to the top became known as the "Horatio Alger myth." Later on, it would become renowned as the "American Dream." Call it what you will, the pursuit of that American Dream was something that inspired not only Hirsch, but also his immigrant parents and grandparents.

All four of his grandparents had fled the oppressive living conditions and anti-Semitic persecution sweeping through Eastern Europe, first finding refuge in England and then, in the 1870s, emigrating to the New World in search of the economic opportunities it promised. Like so many others arriving at the time, both of his grandfathers joined the multitude of Jewish immigrants drawn to the needle trades that were flourishing in New York. Each man found low-paying tailoring work and cheap housing in Brooklyn, then still an independently incorporated municipality whose roughly 1 million inhabitants made it the nation's fourth-largest city in its own right (behind only New York, Chicago, and Philadelphia).

At the time the two families immigrated, both of Hirsch's parents, Jack Jacobs and Theresa Singer, were young enough to easily assimilate into American culture. By his early twenties, Jack felt financially secure enough as a tailor to marry the teenaged Theresa in 1893 and to support the family they planned to start building right away.

With the flood of Eastern European immigrants sparking a boom in the needle trades, Jack decided he could improve his lot by moving to Manhattan, whose Lower East Side had emerged as the bustling center of the nation's garment industry. There, the vast majority of factories and sweatshops were owned by German Jews who had come in an earlier wave of immigration. Jack landed a job with one of those German Jewish immigrants, the well-known custom clothier Marks Arnheim, who ran what he billed as "The Largest Tailoring Establishment in the World" out of his handsome five-story building on Broadway in Greenwich Village. Arnheim's innovative tailoring house prided itself on fine custom-made clothes at "panic prices," its 500 workers fitting and manufacturing suits on the premises while promising home delivery within four hours after a customer got measured. It was a far cry from the stifling sweatshops that left laborers like Jack physically and emotionally drained, improving his working conditions if not quite his living conditions.

Jack settled his wife and four children in East Harlem, the Upper Manhattan neighborhood that had been expanding into a Jewish ghetto large enough to rival the infamous Lower East Side slum as an immigrant magnet crammed with squalid five-story tenements. It was there, in the dank and dingy bedroom of a tiny tenement flat on Second Avenue between 111th and 112th Streets, that their fifth child was born on April 8, 1904, and named Hirsch Wolf Jacobs.

Despite the better-paying job in an industry notoriously built on cheap nonunion labor, Jack soon realized he could not afford to keep his fast-growing family in Manhattan. Moreover, with Hirsch still in diapers and a sixth child on the way, it was becoming impossible to squeeze everyone into a claustrophobic tenement apartment devoid of sunlight and ventilation. Desperate to escape the clamor and congestion of East Harlem, the Jacobses gravitated back to the familiar borough that promised more light, air, space, and affordability. So they joined the mass exodus of Jewish immigrants then migrating from Harlem to eastern Brooklyn.

The family settled for good in the East New York section of Brooklyn, a predominantly Jewish and Italian neighborhood where the streets were lined with identical two- and three-story rowhouses punctuated by the occasional tenement. They rented a narrow railroad apartment just large enough to accommodate a brood that now included six kids and counting. The four Jacobs boys would have to sleep like sardines in the same bed while their two sisters shared another one, and it wasn't uncommon to be awakened by a rat nibbling on toes.

If the family's living quarters remained tight, at least their horizons were rapidly expanding. Since the 1898 annexation of Brooklyn into the City of New York, transportation innovations had been opening up the world to the outer borough's formerly isolated residents. Where once they had to rely on the Fulton Ferry or the Brooklyn Bridge to carry them across the East River to Manhattan, the first decade of the new century saw the grand opening of two additional suspension bridges and, more relevant to the poor workingman, of train tracks beneath the river. The New York City subway system, which had opened to great fanfare on Manhattan Island the same year Hirsch was born there, would expand its rapid-transit rail to Brooklyn through the East River tunnel four years later. The subway's 1908 connection with Brooklyn significantly shortened Jack's daily commute, even if the nickel fare still seemed something of an extravagance.

By then promoted to foreman by Marks Arnheim, Jack was now joined on that Manhattan commute by his firstborn, Harry. As soon as Harry had finished elementary school and was old enough to get his working papers at age fourteen, Pop had secured him a job at Arnheim's as an entry clerk taking orders for tailoring and alterations. It was understood that Harry's younger siblings would be expected to likewise drop out of school and enter the workforce as soon as they turned fourteen—a rite of passage for immigrant families needing the added income.

Enviously watching his father and big brother head off for work every morning, young Hirsch couldn't help feeling that Manhattan—just ten miles west as the pigeon flew—might as well have been a million miles away. His world was circumscribed, his day-to-day existence confining.

He would later call his upbringing "a strenuous life" in which a boy "meets and sees many sidelights, bright and drab and rough with life." While a keen observer of that tough street life, he was careful to avoid getting mixed up in the gangs of idle children that were spiking the city's juvenile crime rate. With a cherubic face topped by a wavy shock of flaming red hair that earned him the nickname "Red," he stood apart from the wilder street kids. He would earnestly hustle for spare change, running errands around the neighborhood for pennies and nickels as well as hawking newspapers on the corner.

For the most part, though, Red Jacobs often filled his idle hours with the kinds of pastimes that kept many street kids out of trouble: playing pickup baseball and its urban cousin, stickball; contesting sidewalk games of handball and stoopball; and, during the dog days of summer, swimming in the city's thronged public pools until he was old enough to take advantage of Brooklyn's many beaches. But more than anything, pigeon racing was the sport that captivated the boy's imagination.

By the age of twelve, Red decided the time had come to begin racing his birds for sport as well as for prize money and side bets to defray the cost of their upkeep.

The logistics of pigeon racing when he started out in 1916 had remained essentially unchanged from ancient times. The objective, as ever, was to ship the competing birds to a starting point far away, release them en masse, and see which ones flew home fastest. As the ancient Hebrews had discovered when they held the earliest known competitions in the third century, pigeon races were far more complicated than any of the horse races that had been staged for five millenniums already, mainly because the course in the sky was invisible and the fanciers could never see their birds in flight except at the finish.

For starters, the pigeons had to be transported to a "liberation point" anywhere from 100 to 1,500 miles away from the city. That meant pigeon fliers like Red Jacobs had to cart their flocks to a railroad station and pay the fare for the long trip to the race's starting liberation point. On the eve of each weekend during racing season, which ran in the spring for older birds and from the summer well into the fall for younger ones, fanciers would bring their homers to the train station in wicker baskets and pay a railroad conductor a couple of dollars to pack them in wooden cages and ship them to the destination. The fanciers, or the local club organizing the race, would arrange for the baggage master or a baggage clerk to liberate all the pigeons the following dawn when the train reached the starting point. For big events like the one later dubbed "the Kentucky Derby of pigeon racing," the Pennsylvania Railroad would run special trains of baggage cars crammed with thousands of crated pigeons accompanied by a New York club official whose title was "convoyer-liberator" and whose responsibility was to release them at the start for their daylong flight homeward.

Pigeon racing has been called "the sport with a single starting gate and a thousand finish lines." That's because, unlike all other contests known to man and beast, each bird is racing to reach its own home coop. After dropping their pigeons off at the train station, fanciers had to head home and wait patiently by their coops for them to return. The fanciers would spend the afternoon anxiously scanning for specks on the horizon, well aware that a quarter of the homers would be lost to faulty navigation or to predators and never make it back. As soon as one did return home, its owner grabbed it and removed the rubber band called a "countermark" that had been attached to its leg before the race for identification. In bygone days, the owner or his designated "runner" had to then dash through cobblestone streets with pigeon in hand to get to the race organizer's clubhouse fastest; by Red Jacobs's time, the advent of a special manual clock meant that each owner could simply place the countermark into that device at home to stamp it with the time of arrival. Because home coops were all varying distances from the liberation point, the winner would be determined by computing each bird's average flying speed.

Red Jacobs may not have won his debut race, but he was instantly hooked nonetheless. He could now call himself a full-fledged pigeon racer.

Thus was born the legend of "The Pigeon Man." That nickname would forever follow Hirsch Jacobs around racetracks and across headlines, his life story as inextricably linked with pigeons as it was with horses. No matter what he would go on to achieve on the track, his humble beginnings as a pigeon fancier remained integral to the myth positing the quaint theory that he learned to train racehorses by first learning to fly pigeons.

It's no coincidence that he would one day give a Thoroughbred racehorse the exact same name as his all-time favorite racing pigeon: Featherfoot. By then, he himself would attribute some small measure of his success with racehorses to what he picked up from homers like Featherfoot. "Maybe it was noting their peculiarities, their individual traits, that has helped me to train horses," he mused at the time. "Training pigeons is about the same as training horses. It's all a matter of condition. A flying pigeon has to be in top shape; so does a running horse." To be sure, pigeon racing involved everything from breeding to training to competing—all endeavors that would come in handy for horse racing. But none of that constituted the most significant boost that homers would provide his career. "The importance of pigeons in my case was that they put me in touch with people who were also interested in horses," he would later conclude. "One of the people I met this way was Charlie Ferraro."

Charlie Ferraro lived just three blocks from the Jacobses while Hirsch was growing up in the Jewish and Italian enclave of East New York. Ferraro was a builder, a family man, and, not incidentally, a pigeon fancier. Hirsch palled around with Ferraro's sons but spent most of his time hanging out with their father on neighborhood rooftops. Ferraro took the kid under his wing, first being a mentor and then becoming, in Hirsch's eyes, "one of my pals—in fact, my chum."

Seeing something in Hirsch's passion for pigeons, Ferraro got him into the East New York Homing Club. Hirsch made enough of a first impression that the members elected him the club's racing secretary and treasurer—even though he still was not yet a teenager.

Like many street kids of his generation, Hirsch Jacobs had to grow up fast. His formal education ended just two months past his thirteenth birthday when he graduated from Public School 140. Following the example set by his eldest sibling, Harry, Hirsch got right to work to bring money in to help support a family that now included ten children. Of the six boys and four girls, Hirsch's other elder brother, Irving, would be the one chosen to continue beyond eighth grade and become the first Jacobs to earn a high school diploma. Irving's career path was charted based on his aptitude and aspirations: he had recently enrolled at City College of New York, the nation's first free public institution of higher learning, with dreams of becoming a doctor. Hirsch's path was less clear. Upon dropping out after elementary school, he performed various odd jobs around the neighborhood. Once old enough to get his working papers at fourteen in 1918, he took a menial job in downtown Brooklyn at the Sperry Gyroscope Company, which manufactured navigation equipment for a military then gearing up for America's inevitable entry into the Great War raging in Europe since 1914.

Not long after that, he landed a better job with Charlie Ferraro's brother Frank, who owned and operated a steamfitting shop that was closer to home. There Hirsch could learn a trade, much as his father had with tailoring. He went to work as a steamfitter's assistant, cutting and bending pipe.

A fringe benefit of the job was that Charlie Ferraro kept his pigeon coops on the rooftop of his brother's shop. Ferraro invited Hirsch to do likewise and suggested they merge lofts. Now, rather than having to hurry home to exercise his pigeons after a long day cutting pipe in the shop's garage, Hirsch needed only climb the stairs to the roof.

Ferraro, who as a successful building contractor always seemed to have a good deal of spending money, soon suggested the pair form a pigeon racing partnership in which he would spring for the birds and Hirsch would train them. Until then, whenever Hirsch needed a longer training toss to enhance his pigeons' natural homing abilities, he had to splurge for the nickel fare to cart them by ferry across New York Harbor and release them on the Staten Island side for the short flight home. Now, whenever he wanted to step up their training tosses incrementally, he could simply load them into Ferraro's jalopy or pay the railroad to ship them as many as 500 miles away. The enhanced training regimen quickly began to pay off, putting the Ferraro-Jacobs racing loft on the map.

All of that would be interrupted by World War I. In 1918, the year after the United States entered the war, pigeon racing was banned to ensure all homers be available for military service. That was a measure of how vital pigeons had been to warfare ever since ancient armies began relying on them as the chief carriers of battlefield intelligence. After besieged Parisians used them in the Franco-Prussian War of 1870 to messenger news of the city's encirclement by the enemy, the rest of Europe's modern armies launched pigeon forces of their own. By the time the Americans joined the European Allies in World War I, pigeons had already saved thousands of lives by carrying messages through barrages of artillery, machine guns, targeted rifle fire, and poison gas attacks. With nearly half a million homers serving in what was then known simply as the Great War, U.S. Army Signal Corps "pigeoneers" hurriedly trained a force of a thousand winged messengers that American doughboys would haul to the muddy trenches of the Western Front.

During the Battle of the Argonne Forest in the fall of 1918, when a U.S. Army battalion was trapped behind enemy lines without ammunition or food while under friendly fire, the besieged Americans sent out several pigeons carrying pleas for help.

After the Germans shot them all down, the desperate soldiers of the "Lost Battalion" released their last remaining pigeon, a small slaty-blue racing homer named Cher Ami. As the little bird ascended through a massive barrage of enemy fire, all hope suddenly seemed lost when German sharpshooters shattered his right leg and blasted a quarter-size hole through his breastbone. Covered in blood and blinded in one eye, Cher Ami somehow managed to keep flying the twenty miles to U.S. Army headquarters in twenty-five minutes and deliver the message in a silver canister still attached to a leg that was hanging by just a tendon: "We are along the road parallel to 276.4. Our own artillery is dropping a barrage directly on us. For heaven's sake, stop it." Credited with thus saving the lives of 194 infantrymen on his twelfth and final mission, Cher Ami was himself saved by a team of surgeons and awarded the Silver Star by the famed commander of the U.S. forces, General Black Jack Pershing.

With that bloodiest of battles ending "the war to end all wars" the following month, Cher Ami became as illustrious as any human war hero. Immortalized by taxidermy and permanently displayed at the Smithsonian Institution, the brave bird brought his entire breed of racing homer a new level of glory and appreciation. And when pigeon racing resumed in the United States, the sport likewise soared to new heights of popularity, especially in the Lost Battalion's base of New York.

In that heady time the following summer, the Ferraro-Jacobs loft would enjoy unprecedented success, winning most of the major sweepstakes on the East Coast along with eight silver cups. Over the next few years, they could have filled a scrapbook with *Brooklyn Daily Eagle* clips heralding their triumphs in races ranging from 500 to 800 miles. Jacobs also served as racing secretary for the Brooklyn Concourse, an umbrella organization for the borough's neighborhood clubs. Although that volunteer job meant hours su-pervising races and enforcing rules, it didn't detract from the time he devoted to his own pigeons.

Marveling at Jacobs's passion for the pigeons, Ferraro wondered if the kid might also enjoy another kind of racing. One day Ferraro asked if Jacobs would like to go to the racetrack with him.

Chapter 2

FROM PIGEONS TO PLATERS

On a sunny Saturday morning in the spring of 1922, Charlie Ferraro pulled in through the Jamaica racetrack's backside entrance and parked next to the barn where his horses were stabled. He turned off the engine and nodded to the eighteen-year-old boy sitting next to him. As Hirsch Jacobs swung his door open, he took in the new sights and smells. Here was something very different from the city streets he was used to. The low-slung barns didn't block the light like the taller buildings in his neighborhood, and though there were clearly people at work, an air of serenity surrounded the stables. He picked up the sweet scent of recently baled hay and even a whiff of the horses themselves. The barns may have been plain and utilitarian, but there was something homey and comforting about them.

As Ferraro and the boy approached the stall doors, the horses briefly looked away from their hay to focus on the humans walking toward them. Jacobs was instantly drawn to the massive creatures. He could sense the paradox of powerful, muscly beasts that were at the same time sensitive and fearful. He was struck by the expressiveness of their faces and their dark, soulful eyes. And, inexplicably, he felt as if they were somehow speaking directly to him.

Ferraro handed Jacobs some carrots and suggested offering them to the horses, who took them politely, crunching them with relish. Ferraro noted how Jacobs focused on the horses and seemed to connect with them. He had thought it might be possible that the boy would be drawn to horses given his close relationship with the birds, but there was no guarantee that the kind of bonds that Jacobs had forged with pigeons would translate to another species.

Besides, the only horses the boy had ever seen before now were those drawing drays through city streets. Born in an era when the trolley and the newfangled automobile still shared Brooklyn streets with the horse and buggy, he had grown up regularly seeing horse-drawn wagons deliver milk, ice, coal, and wood. But he had never walked up to a horse before and stared it in the face. He had never seen a horse running, let alone watched one galloping gracefully at a racetrack. He had never even seen a glistening, sleek Thoroughbred, only the sturdy draft horses that drew carts, carriages, and firewagons.

He certainly had no family connection to horses. He knew that his father had once liked to occasionally bet on them, but that was back when Brooklyn boasted three racetracks and prided itself as "the mecca of horse racing." Through the latter two decades of the nineteenth century, southern Brooklyn had reigned as the capital of what was then America's most popular spectator sport. At the height of the Gilded Age, large crowds regularly streamed seaward to the three Brooklyn racetracks located within a mile of each other: Brighton Beach, Gravesend, and the one hailed in homage to England's royal racecourse as "America's Ascot," Sheepshead Bay.

All that ended with the coming of the Progressive Era's temperance movement when New York State, spurred by antigambling reformers and by race-fixing scandals involving unsavory bookmakers, outlawed betting on horses in 1908 and shuttered all the tracks in 1910. That could have permanently killed horse racing throughout the state if not for a New York Supreme Court appellate decision that legalized "oral betting," in which nothing could be written down and no cash could be exchanged until after a race. The legal loophole may have lifted the state's racing ban in 1913, but Brooklyn's tracks would never rebound or reopen after the sport's return. Ironically, that left the borough called Kings County totally without The Sport of Kings—"the sport," as the *Brooklyn Daily Eagle* had declared around the turn of the century, "for which Brooklyn is most famed."

As horse racing struggled to regain its footing at a time when pigeon racing was actually more popular in New York City, a boy like Jacobs wouldn't have been inclined to venture to the nearest remaining tracks in neighboring Queens County: Aqueduct, which had opened in southwestern Queens in 1894, and Jamaica, which in 1903 was carved into what the *New York Times* described as "the wooded wilds" of central Queens. Both were near enough to Brooklyn that grooms used to walk their horses over several miles of city streets from the Gravesend, Brighton Beach, and Sheepshead Bay tracks every morning, race them at the Queens tracks in the afternoon, then lead them back home again at night. Jamaica was only ten miles from his East New York neighborhood in Brooklyn, but to Jacobs it might as well have been a world away. Without someone like Ferraro to give him entrée, Jacobs could have no idea what horse racing was about.

It was only fitting that Jacobs's introduction to horse racing would be at Jamaica. Of all the New York racetracks, Jamaica was by far the most proletarian. Dubbed "the people's track," it was always the favorite of the common folks, the working-class fans, the $2 bettors. All wood, steel, and concrete, the no-frills track stood drably in antithesis to that grandest of racing palaces just six miles east: Belmont Park. Right from its gala opening only two years after Jamaica's, Belmont reigned as America's most majestic racetrack, sprawling over 650 bucolic acres that straddled the city line from Queens into Long Island. Built by the financiers August Belmont II and William C. Whitney, scions of aristocratic dynasties, the track dubbed "Beautiful Belmont Park" stood as a plush playground for all their high-society friends. In stark contrast, Jamaica had been built by the infamous Tammany Hall political machine that controlled New York City and ran the racetrack like a gambling den for everyone from notorious gangsters to raucous blue-collar bettors. Big Tim Sullivan, the corrupt and charismatic Tammany boss who lorded over racing at Jamaica, would eschew his clubhouse box to sit in the cheap grandstand bench seats with the "regular folks." With those masses feeling more at home there, Jamaica regularly enjoyed higher attendance than its swanky new neighbor Belmont as well as its old neighbor Aqueduct, which fell in the middle of the three local tracks in terms of the class of race-goers it drew and the amenities it offered.

Since Jacobs didn't have either Belmont or Aqueduct to compare this experience with, Jamaica instantly struck him as the biggest and most breathtaking facility he had ever seen. He would spend the day absorbing all the diverse sights covering its 107 acres: the back-side barns housing the horses, the cantilevered steel grandstand and wooden field stand seating a total of 10,000 fans, the clubhouse accommodating another 1,500, the betting shed that was manned by more than sixty bookmakers but was off-limits to minors and women, the glass-roofed saddling paddock, and, at the center of it all, the one-mile elliptical dirt track that was shaped like an egg rather than the standard oval.

Ferraro hadn't said anything to Jacobs other than to suggest a fun day at the races, but it was a chance to see if his young friend would connect with horses. As he watched the boy interacting with them, it dawned on Ferraro that there might be some innate talent in Jacobs that would make him one day as successful at training racehorses as he had been with pigeons.

Ferraro, after all, had followed a similar path to horse racing. He had been introduced to it a few years earlier by a fellow pigeon fancier named Theodore Smith. A member of the same homing club as Ferraro and Jacobs, Smith often passed the time on Brooklyn rooftops regaling his fellow pigeon racers with stories about the Thoroughbred horses he owned and trained. Whereas Ferraro was a full-time builder and part-time pigeon flier who was only now just starting to dabble in horse racing, Smith had long made his living as a Thoroughbred trainer whose brother George was a millionaire New York book collector who spent as lavishly on racehorses for his Brighton Stable as he did on rare first editions of Shakespeare. Whenever Ferraro stopped by the backside barns to see the two or three horses he owned at any one time, he would make a point of looking up Smith, who based the public stable he operated as well as his own horses at Jamaica.

While Jacobs was communing with the horses, Ferraro tracked down his groom to check in and make sure all was well with his charges. Once he had ascertained that they were eating fine and seemed fit and content, he asked the boy if he would like to grab some lunch and then head over to the backstretch where they could watch some races standing by the rail.

At the sight of Thoroughbreds hurtling down the track right past him, Jacobs sucked in a breath and gripped the rail, his heart racing. It was such a different experience from the hours he whiled away next to his coop waiting for a racing pigeon to come home. In this first flush of exhilaration, he could immediately see horse racing's unique excitement and appeal. Now he understood why Ferraro, whenever they were hanging out on the rooftops with their pigeons, was always talking about how much he loved horses.

On the drive back home to Brooklyn after Jamaica's last race, Ferraro asked if the boy might want to come back again and maybe spend more time on the backside, helping around the barns and learning how things were done there. Jacobs jumped at the chance.

Over the next couple of years, Jacobs often went to the races with Ferraro at the various New York tracks. Mostly they wound up at Jamaica, where Ferraro based his horses.

Whenever possible, Jacobs made time in the mornings to drop in at the track before he went to work at the steamfitting shop for Ferraro's brother. He walked out horses hot from morning workouts, helped around the barn, and learned the basics from Ferraro and anyone else willing to share knowledge. He learned how much horses needed to be fed and how often, how to tell if a horse was fit and ready for racing, how to spot when one was starting to colic. He learned how to trim horses' hooves and how to nail on shoes. He learned how to put a saddle and bridle on a horse and to make sure the girth was tight enough that the saddle wouldn't slip during a race. He learned how far to gallop a horse to get it fit for a particular distance. He learned which injuries could be easily treated, which would need time to heal, and which might mean the end of a racing career.

All the while, Jacobs was also observing how other trainers brought their charges along. In the same way he had learned about pigeons by hanging out on the rooftops and observing the fanciers, so would he "pick up a smattering of horse education" from studying the methods of the trainers and picking their brains whenever they had a few moments to spare. He learned as much as he could from Ferraro, even more from Theodore

Smith, and still more from one of the nation's most respected trainers, George Odom.

Jacobs spent as much time as he could hanging around the stable that Odom ran at Jamaica. He would listen spellbound as Odom held forth with tales from his Hall of Fame career as a jockey riding for such Gilded Age owners as Diamond Jim Brady, William C. Whitney, and August Belmont Sr. What Jacobs was most interested in, however, was Odom's transition from riding horses to training them at the age of just twenty-three shortly after piloting Delhi to victory in the 1904 Belmont Stakes. Odom ran a public stable training horses first for George Smith and years later for the likes of Louis B. Mayer, W. Averell Harriman, and Marshall Field III. The more time Jacobs spent there, the more he felt himself "drifting into the game." After absorbing everything he could from Odom as well as all the other trainers, Jacobs concluded that this was a game in which he could excel.

One day, he went up to Ferraro and said, "Charlie, this is easy."

Ferraro's eyebrows arched as he looked to his young friend for an explanation. Jacobs reminded Ferraro of the many times they'd seen a lot of the trainers and their stablehands sitting around drinking and playing cards rather than tending to their horses. "If these guys are making good money, I could do even better running it like a real business," Jacobs said. "It looks like a business I could have a lot of fun with and do good at."

Jacobs's timing couldn't have been better. Between 1922 and 1924, while he had been learning the ropes at the Jamaica track, American horse racing coincidently was starting to make a comeback as both a sport and a business. The revival was driven by a confluence of forces both on and off the track. In the aftermath of World War I, the nation had entered a new era of prosperity and optimism, sparking the cultural revolution known as the Roaring

Twenties. At the same time, the puritanical bent of the anti-gambling crusaders that had almost killed horse racing was giving way to the hedonism and indulgence that characterized the Prohibition era. The resulting boom in the sport's popularity was evidenced by huge increases in race cards, purses, attendance, and headlines that made household names of horses like Man o' War and stakes races like the Kentucky Derby. Many Americans, flush with profits from business ventures, the stock market, and Prohibition bootlegging, decided the time was ripe to jump into this resurgent sport.

Charlie Ferraro was one of them. He began to expand his racing interests beyond merely a couple of cheap claimers. While still shopping in claiming races, he was now aiming for a higher-caliber horse. In the summer of 1924, he picked up a few young horses, placing each with a different local trainer. When one of them went on to win him a piece of the purse in a few claiming sprints, it just whetted his appetite for more. Early that October at Jamaica, he shelled out $1,000 to claim Demijohn, a four-year-old bay gelding bred by Sam Riddle at the same time the astute owner was campaigning Man o' War through the greatest career any Thoroughbred has ever had. Unplaced in most of his claiming races all year, Demijohn trudged home dead last in the one from which Ferraro claimed him. Even as Ferraro slipped the halter onto his new acquisition minutes after that disappointing finish, he remained confident that the right handling could turn the claim into a profit. He also saw it as a chance to let his young protégé, who had recently turned twenty, try his hand at training. So he approached Jacobs and asked, "How would you like to be the one to train this horse?"

That fall and winter, Jacobs had some success with Demijohn in claiming races, finishing in the money several times. In December, Ferraro invited Jacobs to take a few weeks' vacation from his job and go with him to New Orleans for the winter race meeting at Jefferson Park, where they would run Demijohn and a couple of other horses. All Jacobs had to do was arrange the time off, which was no problem since he was still working for Ferraro's brother in the steamfitting shop.

While they were in New Orleans, Ferraro asked his young friend to join him in a racing stable. Jacobs wasn't about to give up his day job on a lark for something he viewed as a hobby. But Ferraro was persistent. Having seen Jacobs work wonders with the pigeons and then watched as the kid threw himself into horse racing, Ferraro was ready to make a surprisingly generous offer: he would match the salary of the steamfitting job and sweeten the deal with a percentage of any profits the stable made. Jacobs was stunned. Although it would mean giving up the job security afforded by Ferraro's brother at the steamfitting shop, this offered a chance to do something he had come to love and get paid for it. He nodded and extended his right hand to shake on it.

What Ferraro was proposing to Jacobs was that they put together a small claiming stable. That was the only way they could afford to get into the racing game at all. There was certainly no way they could compete with the so-called society stables, where the wealthiest owners bred, bought, and nurtured the best stock to run for big purses in stakes races. For aspirants with limited resources in a rich man's game that was dubbed The Sport of Kings for a reason, claiming races were the great equalizer.

"The claiming game," as the low-budget horsemen call it, has remained essentially unchanged since Jacobs and Ferraro began playing it. Claiming races are the lowest-level competitions in which any horse entered can be purchased, or "claimed," shortly before post time by any licensed party at a set low price. The claimed horse belongs to its new owner from the moment the starting gate (or, in those days, barrier) snaps open, though any purse money won in the race goes to the previous owner. A claiming horse enters the starting gate belonging to one owner and leaves it belonging to the claimant who had put down the required amount of cash in the racing secretary's office. Right after the finish, the claiming trainer must collect his acquisition, slipping a halter over the horse's head and walking it by an attached lead shank to its new stall. That's how claiming trainers came to be called, in the racetrack parlance of Jacobs's day, "haltermen."

Haltermen operated in a separate sphere entirely from the prominent trainers who saddled the well-bred stakes champions for the society stables. In the class hierarchy of events topped by stakes and followed by handicap and then allowance races, claimers subsisted at rock bottom, beneath even maiden races.

Jacobs noticed that many old-timers eschewed the common term "claiming race" in favor of its antecedent: "selling race." Though the terms were often used interchangeably, a selling race was technically a claiming race in which the winning horse had to be put up for auction immediately after the finish. The selling race, tracing back to the 1689 running of the Basingstoke Plate in England, caught on in the United States following the Civil War. The term "selling plater" was coined in the 1880s to define, specifically, a horse that is only good enough to compete in a selling race or, more generally, an inferior horse of limited ability or value. That term was shortened to simply "plater," meaning a cheap claiming horse.

The most fabled of the Progressive Era platers was Roamer, a commonly bred little gelding who had been dropped into a $1,000 selling race at Belmont in 1914. After he won the $380 first-place prize and thus had to be put up for auction, his owner found himself in a bidding war, shelling out $2,005 to keep a horse he wound up selling a few days later for $2,500. Roamer went on to lead the nation with $29,105 in earnings that year and to total $98,828 in a Hall of Fame career distinguished by twenty-four stakes wins and eleven track records.

Around that time, the selling race gave way to the claiming race. Gone was the auction loophole that owners commonly exploited to enter a class horse in a selling race for an easy purse and then buy it back in the postrace bidding. What remained in the claiming game were the cheap horses and the pejoratives employed to brand them.

Call them what you will, claimers or platers, they typically possess less raw talent than the class horses bred and conditioned to run at the top of the racing game in stakes races. While the stakes capture the attention of even the general public, it is the claimers that constitute the lifeblood of Thoroughbred racing. For owners and horseplayers, these most common of races are the backbone of the sport, making up more than half of all events run in the nation every day if only a fraction of the overall purses. Most Thoroughbreds run in claiming competitions simply because there are many more cheap horses than class ones.

The invention of the claiming race as a vehicle for filling the daily card was ingenious. Claiming races were designed to ensure that all the horses in a given competition are of similar ability, leading to closely fought battles and thus fostering heavier betting volume. Within the claiming division, there is a hierarchy: the higher the price and the purse, the better the quality of the horse entered. It's up to owners and trainers to determine the value of their horse and, therefore, what level claiming race the horse is qualified for. Back in the 1920s, claiming races ranged from under $1,000 to over $5,000 (compared to, say, $60,000 for top-grade stakes like the Kentucky Derby). A horse that a trainer believed was worth $1,000 would be entered in a $1,000 claiming race against a similar class of horses. The incentive for the trainer not to enter a better-class horse—say, one he deems worth $5,000—in that cheap race for an easy win purse was that any entrant was at risk of being claimed for purchase at the bargain-basement $1,000 price tag.

A claiming trainer had to be a special breed of horseman. The most successful ones had the knowledge and skill to detect subtle faults and weaknesses—as well as hidden strengths—in their own and rival stables' horses. They demonstrated the uncanny instinct to spot the untapped potential in other stables' claimers and then the uncommon ability to quickly develop it.

During his initial visits to the Jamaica racetrack back in 1922, Jacobs had a chance to see one of the most successful claiming horses that ever raced. An awkward-looking brown colt known as "The Ugly Cripple," Morvich was the talk of the backside that spring as he trained at Jamaica for the upcoming Kentucky Derby. As a 30-to-1 longshot in his debut claiming race the previous spring, he had romped home by ten lengths. When trainer Fred Burlew ran him back in another claimer as the even-money favorite, Morvich remarkably still had no claims from shoppers who were scared away by his crooked forelegs. Minutes after the colt won that one by six lengths, Sam Hildreth, the nation's leading trainer, warned Burlew, "If you ever start that horse in a claiming race again, it'll be the last you'll see of him." Looking over the gangly colt with the badly conformed knees, even a neophyte like Jacobs could understand how Morvich could have run two claiming races at Jamaica during his undefeated two-year-old season without any takers. The following month, when Morvich wired the field to win the Kentucky Derby easily, Jacobs had learned a valuable lesson about seeing potential where others didn't.

By the same token, he had been counseled by hardened horsemen not to expect to find a claimer like Morvich. The odds against finding a Derby horse, or any diamond in the rough, in a claiming race were over a million to one. A far more likely scenario was ending up with a worn-out claimer whose owner was trying to dump a worthless nag on an unsuspecting buyer. Even worse, sometimes a seemingly sound horse would suffer a career-ending injury or would catastrophically break down during the very race from which he was being claimed, leaving the new owner with the cost of euthanizing the animal and disposing of the remains. Between the extremes, the successful halterman stayed ahead of the game if he could buy a horse at a bargain and then "step up" to win at a higher claiming price.

By definition, claiming stables were always in a state of flux. Their barns might as well have been equipped with revolving doors, since horses were constantly being lost and added through claiming races. In a sport predicated on betting, the claiming game represented the ultimate gamble. Like a poker player discarding unwanted cards in anticipation of drawing better ones, haltermen dumped poor performers in hopes of replacing them with horses that had more potential. They weren't claiming horses as long-term investments, and they certainly couldn't afford to become attached to any of them. They were running each horse several times a week, sometimes vanning one to nearby tracks for another claiming race every two or three days. With claiming purses as meager as they were, a small stable could subsist only if its horses were running as often as practicable.

It occurred to Jacobs that he and Ferraro for years had been operating their loft of racing pigeons much like a stable of claiming horses. Whenever someone expressed surprise over Jacobs's success transitioning from pigeons to platers, he would explain, "We used to sell some of the pigeons from one nest and keep the others.

Other people couldn't do anything with their pigeons, but ours went good. It's been the same way with me with horses."

Over the winter of 1924, Jacobs and Ferraro began building their modest claiming stable, which they naturally continued to base at Jamaica. Through the 1925 season, they ran their small string of claimers at big meetings in New York and Maryland as well as smaller tracks in the South, the Midwest, and Canada. While apprenticing with some of the public trainers that the stable was still using, Jacobs took the lead in conditioning a few horses for Ferraro. By year's end, Jacobs had begun to have some success, just enough to build his confidence even though he had yet to saddle a winner.

In 1926, Jacobs achieved a series of milestones. For starters, he took out his trainer's license and began officially saddling horses. Then that May he made his first purchase, tapping his pigeon nest egg for the $2,000 price tag to claim a chestnut colt named Tiger Gloss. That claim didn't pan out, but the one he made in November would give him his first breakthrough.

Jacobs had just arrived in New Orleans for the annual winter meeting at Jefferson Park when a bay named Reveillon caught his eye. Although the four-year-old gelding was a fellow son of Man o' War's sire, Fair Play, Reveillon bore no resemblance to either of his famous relatives on the track. Still, Jacobs liked the way he was put together. So the next time Reveillon's name turned up in the entries, Jacobs rushed over to the racing secretary's office, stuffed $1,500 in cash into an envelope along with the claim slip, and deposited it into the claim box on the counter. Immediately after the race, he slipped a halter over the bay's head and led him to his new stall.

Jacobs wasted no time putting his new acquisition to work, running him in two claiming races over the next four days. After giving Reveillon a few days' rest, the trainer ran him ten more times over the next month, mostly in cheap claiming races. Although Reveillon didn't win any of them, he did at least take a piece of the purse on a few occasions and closed out his New Orleans campaign with a fast-closing kick that left him just a head short of giving Jacobs his first win as a licensed trainer.

Jacobs had reason to feel optimistic when he shipped Reveillon to a brand-new racetrack that was about to open in Florida on Christmas Day. Despite laws banning all forms of gambling in Florida, Pompano Race Track had been built for $1.25 million to lure away Southern and Eastern horsemen who would normally journey to Cuba for the winter racing season. Though tiny compared to the New York tracks, Pompano represented an ambitious venture whose 6,800-seat grandstand could accommodate more than triple the entire population of the backwater South Florida farming town and whose backside barns could house 1,000 racehorses. Jacobs found himself caught up in the excitement when he arrived for the track's grand opening on Christmas Day along with 20,000 fans who had bussed in from all over the state.

Four days later, he saddled Reveillon for the thirteenth time in the five weeks since acquiring him and sent him out in yet another cheap claiming race. This time, finally, Reveillon galloped home first for him. That gave Hirsch Jacobs, at the age of just twenty-two, his first official win as a trainer—a milestone that would be commemorated by a plaque erected years later at the site of the finish line. As Jacobs made his way to the winner's circle for the first time in his career, it didn't matter that Reveillon had earned a meager first-place prize of $700 and still hadn't made back what his owner had paid for him. At least Jacobs could now close out 1926—a year in which he saddled just that one winner among mounts that earned a total of merely $1,700 in purses—on an upbeat note. During the same year, Ferraro's stable had won twenty-eight races and earned $27,515 in purses.

Both Jacobs and Ferraro were anxious to migrate north back home to New York. The whole Florida trip had been colored by the controversy and chaos surrounding Pompano. Right from the track's grand opening, the state's antigambling crusaders were trying to shut it down. Florida's governor, John Martin, branded Pompano "a center of lawbreakers" and threatened to "send the militia down there with a tractor and plow up the track and plant it in cowpeas." Soon after Jacobs and Ferraro shipped their stable back north in January, Pompano indeed was shuttered, never to be used for horse racing again.

Jacobs was happy to return home to the Jamaica track to prep for the 1927 season. He still wasn't winning much that spring and summer, but that had less to do with the quality of his training than the lack of talent among the claiming horses in Ferraro's stable. Jacobs did the best he could with what he had, his horses occasionally finishing in the money when they didn't seem to have the talent to do that well. The stocky kid with the wavy red hair was starting to draw attention.

Racetrackers around the backside began asking, "Who is this Hirsch Jacobs?"

The answer was often delivered dismissively with a shrug: "He's a kid who races pigeons."

Such disrespect merely fueled Jacobs's drive to prove himself as a real horseman. Gradually he did start making a name for himself around the racetrack, but his roots followed him in the nickname bestowed on him by everyone in horse racing: "The Pigeon Man." By now, of course, neither Jacobs nor Ferraro had time anymore to indulge in their beloved hobby of pigeon racing, so busy were they trying to make their mark in the cutthroat claiming game.

As they became more and more serious about horse racing, friction began to build up in their working relationship. That summer, Ferraro took out his trainer's license in Canada. Later in 1927, he started training horses for a pair of Canadian owners, Johnny Mascia and Louie Sylvestri, both sporting men who raced a small stable based in Ontario. Not surprisingly, that didn't sit too well with Jacobs. It didn't take long for Mascia and Sylvestri to realize that Jacobs must have been the up-and-coming talent at Ferraro's stable. So, on the eve of the winter racing season, they asked Jacobs if he would be interested in taking over the conditioning of both horses that Ferraro had been training for them. When Jacobs observed that this would effectively end his working relationship with Ferraro, the Canadians sweetened the deal by offering to let him train their other horses. Once Jacobs agreed to train for them, they went a step further and claimed a couple of the Ferraro horses that Jacobs had been conditioning.

Whenever someone would ask him about the falling out that ended his working relationship with Ferraro, Jacobs would simply shrug and say, "Oh, we just had an argument over something." For 1927, the final year of their three-year partnership, Ferraro's stable won fifty-nine races and purses totaling $51,580. Of those, Jacobs was officially credited as trainer with two wins and total earnings of $1,750.

They went their separate ways that December, Ferraro running his stable in New Orleans as usual and Jacobs heading to Cuba, where Mascia and Sylvestri liked to ship their horses for the winter racing season. Cuba represented a big step up in class for the young trainer, since Havana's Oriental Park drew an annual migration of top American horses, stables, trainers, and jockeys.

There, at Oriental Park, he would meet the man who would change everything and become his lifelong business partner: Isidor Bieber.

CHAPTER 3

RUNYONESQUE

If Isidor Bieber hadn't actually existed, Damon Runyon would have had to invent him.

At the peak of his powers as America's favorite storyteller of both fact and fiction, Damon Runyon proclaimed Isidor Bieber "one of the most colorful characters in the racing game and incidentally one of the greatest stories, if anybody ever undertakes to write his life history." Tempted to take on the task himself, Runyon ultimately realized Bieber was such a stranger-than-fiction character that no one would believe a real-life biography was indeed a work of nonfiction. "Bieber's so fantastic," Runyon mused about the prospect of a writing such a book, "but my heart couldn't stand it."

That spoke volumes coming from a storied newspaperman who regularly consorted with myriad larger-than-life personalities both as famous as Babe Ruth and as infamous as Al Capone. And it said even more coming from a prolific short story writer whose vivid imagination conjured up a colorful cast of riffraff that would be immortalized on the stage as *Guys and Dolls* and in the dictionary as "Runyonesque."

By definition, few guys or dolls were more Runyonesque than Isidor Bieber, a legendary New York eccentric who personified what became renowned through those short stories as Runyon's "Broadway characters." Runyon's love affair with Broadway had begun after he hit the big city in 1910 and landed a sportswriting job with William Randolph Hearst's newspaper empire during the heyday of New York's myriad warring dailies. When Runyon wasn't hunt-and-pecking out yarns on his Corona portable typewriter, he could be found hanging out on America's grandest thoroughfare. He centered his signature beat on Broadway between 49th and 50th Streets, where the clamorous sidewalk was a haunt for everyone from mobsters and bookmakers to the boxing and racing crowd. From his vantage point on that sidewalk littered with butts of the cigarettes he chain-smoked, he quietly observed the mob scene through owlish wire-rimmed glasses that made him look more like a bookish voyeur than a hard-boiled newspaperman.

Even amidst that flashy gathering of gangsters, gamblers, con men, showgirls, and Broadway dandies, Isidor Bieber caught Runyon's sharp eye and flinty stare. Dressed loud from his high hat and tails down to his striped trousers and spats, Bieber worked the street as a ticket speculator in a bygone era when pushy hustlers with dollar bills wrapped around their fingers swarmed under the theater marquees of all the hit Broadway shows. But as Runyon discovered, Bieber was much more than just one of the ubiquitous ticket specs. He was a dime-store philosopher blaring bellicose opinions. He was a belligerent brawler leading with his mouth and following up with his fists. Above all, he was, in the vernacular of Runyon's realm, a two-fisted "plunger"—that is, a reckless high-stakes gambler who thought nothing of betting fifty grand on a single horse race or of taking the hundred grand he had won at the track in the afternoon and blowing every penny of it on a prizefight that night.

All of which would spur Runyon to confess once in his widely syndicated column, "The writer has known Mr. Isidor Bieber over 20 years, and is rather fond of him if only for his idiosyncrasies. A man without idiosyncrasies is apt to be uninteresting. Mr. Bieber is a character right out of Dickens."

More accurately, Bieber seemed to step right out of a Damon Runyon short story. That made perfect sense, of course, because Bieber served as both a source for Runyon's noirish tales and a model for his rakish characters. The better the writer got to know him, the more it seemed Bieber was born to the Broadway that Runyon romanticized in life and mythologized in print.

In reality, Isidor Bieber had been born in a Polish shtetl near Warsaw, back in 1886. His father, Morris, emigrated from Warsaw to New York in 1890 and toiled as a tailor for five years before he could save up enough money to send for the rest of the family. Isidor was nine years old when his mother, Sarah, brought him and his two siblings to join Morris in Manhattan. Growing up poor in the immigrant Jewish ghetto of the Lower East Side, Isidor forsook classroom schooling for the teeming streets, a pugnacious kid getting into fights, running with gangs, shooting craps in alleys. When the family moved just after the turn of the century to Hell's Kitchen, the gang-infested midtown neighborhood branded the most dangerous in the nation, living by his fists and his wits became a matter of basic survival.

To escape that crime-ridden slum and his stifling tenement on Ninth Avenue just south of 42nd Street, Isidor needed only venture two blocks east to Times Square. There, trading a Dickensian childhood for a Runyonesque adolescence, he found his true calling as a Broadway hustler. He was still in his teens when he identified his occupation to a census enumerator as, simply, "Speculator." After years scuffling as a street scalper, he opened a legit office at Broadway and 42nd Street as a broker speculating in tickets for all the hit shows and big sporting events.

By the time Runyon first spotted him scalping on Broadway, Bieber had already made a name for himself up and down the Great White Way as "Kid Beebee." It was a nickname Bieber so despised that he begged Runyon and everyone else to call him Isidor, Izzy, Beeb, Beebee, anything but Kid Beebee.

"I think it was Mark Twain who said nicknames are the invention of the devil," he would grumble to Runyon and any reporter who'd listen. "Well, I got this nickname of Kid Bieber as a result of a scrap I had with a certain private detective—a house dick, I believe—named Paddy McDonald. I forget what the argument was about, but, anyway, he took a poke at me in the lobby of the Grand Opera House on Twenty-Third Street. I didn't hit him back then and there. I wouldn't stoop to such undignified conduct in a theater lobby. But I informed this bum McDonald that I would be pleased to meet him on the Hudson River docks later that night. Well, a big crowd showed up on the docks to see the fight. I gave McDonald the shellacking of his life. Some freelance reporter was there and he phoned in the story to the New York Journal. Next day the paper came out and told all about the big fight between Paddy McDonald and Izzy 'Kid' Bieber."

The headline would haunt him forever: KID BEEBEE BATTERS PADDY THE DICK. The nickname stuck, and certainly fit. Kid Beebee cut a formidable figure, from his above-average height and strapping build to his square jaw and menacing glare. He forged a reputation as a burly brawler who claimed he never threw the first punch but couldn't deny often firing the first taunt and almost always responding to the slightest provocation with a left hook and right cross.

If he didn't go looking for it, trouble easily found him anyway. One night in 1915 he was minding his speculating business in front of Oscar Hammerstein's Victoria Theatre vaudeville house in Times Square when he found himself verbally sparring with the prizefighter Frank Moran, a top contender who had recently fought for the world heavyweight championship. "If you don't like it," Moran huffed, "we can settle it on the dock." Kid Beebee led the procession down 43rd Street to his favorite dock on the Hudson, where the combatants hastily pulled on skintight kid gloves and squared off. They pounded each other for fifteen minutes until Moran, doubled over with blood streaming down his face, waved a stop to the fisticuffs. While the equally bloodied Beebee refused aid, Moran was rushed to the hospital, where he stayed for three days. A few months later, Moran got another title shot and managed to go the distance in a vain attempt to dethrone Jess Willard as heavyweight champ. "Willard didn't beat me—Beeb did," Moran declared afterward. "I've never been the same since that night on the dock. Against Willard, my ribs and jaw were still tender. I was lucky Jess had a punch like a baby's bottom."

Mike Jacobs, a rival Broadway ticket speculator who would go on to become boxing's top promoter, once actually hired a hall so Kid Beebee could settle a street argument in the ring. When someone dared suggest years later that Kid Beebee had taken a beating in one of those many fights, Jacobs threw down a fat wad of bills and shouted, "A thousand dollars to a dime that nobody ever licked Beeb in those days! Beeb and I don't like each other, but nobody ever licked him then. He could take plenty care of himself."

Kid Beebee took on all comers, from prizefighters to mobsters. He particularly liked to brag about the scrap he got into at the Hotel Metropole, whose ornate bar on 43nd Street just off Broadway was frequented by gangsters and gamblers. The scene of a 1912 gangland slaying then sensationalized as "the crime of the century," it was such a hotspot that Runyon regularly staked out a ringside roundtable with his mentor, the Wild West gunfighter turned New York newspaperman Bat Masterson. The joint was jumping as usual on the night Kid Beebee exchanged words and blows with George Considine, the notorious proprietor who ran the Metropole in partnership with Tammany Hall. "I gave him a pretty good beating," Kid Beebee boasted to reporters. "Matter of principle, involving a girl."

Never one to walk away from a fight, Beebee enlisted in the army as soon as the United States entered World War I in the spring of 1917. While serving as a machine gun instructor at the U.S. Army Field Artillery School, he fretted that Fort Sill in Oklahoma was a far cry from where he wanted to be stationed. So he reached out to his influential Tammany Hall and Newspaper Row acquaintances, hoping they could pull some strings. Chief among them were two bylines as famous as the personages they covered: Damon Runyon, whose dispatches from the underworld anchored Hearst's *New York American*, and Herbert Bayard Swope, whose war correspondence for the rival *New York World* had just earned him the first Pulitzer Prize ever awarded for reporting.

"He came to me one day during the war," the swashbuckling Swope would later recount to Runyon. "I had known him many years, and he started out by telling me I had to help him out in this war business. I somehow gathered the impression that what he wanted me to help him out in was to avoid the draft. So I told him it was out of the question and was giving him some sound advice when suddenly it dawned on Beebee what I was driving at and a look of horror came over his face. 'Say,' he said, 'do you think I'm trying to get out of the war? Why, I'm trying to get in. I've been enlisted in the regular army for six weeks. I want you to help me get to France where I can see some fighting.'"

After serving as an army private during the war, Kid Beebee reestablished his street reputation for being as fast with his fists as

Jack Dempsey, the savage heavyweight champion whose raucous reign after dethroning Willard came to symbolize the Roaring Twenties. That entailed fearlessly challenging the likes of Johnny Broderick, the legendary Broadway cop who was so tough that he routinely beat up vicious mobsters like Legs Diamond and so feared that Dempsey himself admittedly "wouldn't fight him in an alley for a million bucks." One night Beebee was operating as a ticket speculator outside the six-day bike races at Madison Square Garden when Detective Broderick sauntered up to him under its glittering Eighth Avenue marquee and threatened to punch him in the nose. "You do that, Broderick, and I'll just give you a receipt," Beebee shot back. "Go ahead and punch me, and see what happens."

If the toughest cop on the beat thought better of picking a fight with Kid Beebee, Runyon wasn't about to risk one over a nickname. "If you call him 'Kid,' you are apt to make him mad," Runyon cautioned his readers. "Those who are aware of this detestation of the nickname compromise with him on 'Beeb.'"

Pugilism may have earned Kid Beebee his hated nickname, but it was plunging that would prompt *Sports Illustrated* to remember him as "a legendary figure along Broadway." That Beeb loved nothing better than betting is also what made him a legendary character after Runyon's own heart.

Judging by the sheer number of times he wrote these words, Runyon knew of only one sure thing in gambling as well as in life: "All horseplayers die broke." The maxim so struck him that he adopted it as a mantra in his newspaper columns, as the title of one of his classic short stories, and as the moral of so many of them. He was simply following the old adage to "write what you know." For, it was said, Damon Runyon made a fortune writing about gamblers and lost one betting with the bookmakers he also chronicled. His five-figure annual salary may have made him the highest-paid newspaperman at the peak of the city's circulation wars, but that was small consolation for a betting man who could gamble away as much in a single month.

That compulsion explains why none of the many underworld figures he consorted with fascinated him more than Arnold Rothstein, the New York mob boss considered America's most notorious gambler. Most infamously, Rothstein reputedly conspired to fix the 1919 World Series by bribing the favored Chicago White Sox to throw games, then made a killing by betting on a sure thing and escaped conviction in the so-called Black Sox scandal. With the onset of Prohibition in 1920, the kingpin of the Jewish mob consolidated his organized crime empire through bootlegging, speakeasies, and the narcotics that made him America's first drug lord. For all the racketeering that inspired Runyon to immortalize him in short stories as a criminal mastermind called "The Brain," Rothstein's vice of choice always remained gambling.

Just like Runyon, if Rothstein wasn't busy conducting business at Broadway and 50th Street either from the sidewalk or from his usual booth in Lindy's star-studded delicatessen, then he could surely be found holding court in the gambling parlors of Times Square. Dubbed "The Big Bankroll" for the fat wad of C-notes he always flashed, Rothstein famously once outdrew Nick the Greek, the world's most fabled professional gambler, to rake in a $797,000 poker pot said to be the richest anyone had ever seen.

One of the gambling dens Rothstein frequented belonged to Isidor Bieber, who ran a craps game out of a rented loft on 47th Street just a dice roll from Broadway. In the early years of Prohibition, Bieber and a partner, the bootlegger Big Bill Dwyer, paid off the cops and the Tammany Hall pols to keep the city's biggest illegal dice game running for a who's who of high rollers. After Bieber backed the wrong horse in the 1925 election, however, New York's new mayor, the dashing man-about-Broadway Jimmy Walker, shut down the game so he could open up one of his own. Bieber and Dwyer went out in style on their club's last night by lighting candles on a cake, pouring lighter fluid on top, and dumping a shoebox full of IOUs onto the fire as a violin played "Auld Lang Syne."

Bieber could shrug off the closing because he much preferred being on the betting side of the action. In an era when bookmakers were legally allowed to man the clubhouse betting rings at the New York tracks so long as they took oral rather than cash wagers, he ran in that select circle of plungers who could bet twenty grand on a race with just a word or a nod. The bookmakers didn't worry that he lacked the kind of fortunes owned by fellow plungers like the oil baron H. L. Hunt, the stock swindler Charles Stoneham, and the construction magnate Subway Sam Rosoff. The bookies trusted that the ticket speculator Isidor Bieber was good for the money and let him plunge with the richest of them, sometimes as high as $75,000 on a single horse.

"Bieber bets all he can, and he will bet 'til the cows come home," Runyon marveled in his column. "Down through the years he has undoubtedly been one of the biggest plungers on the turf. He has probably won and lost millions. Bieber was widely known along Broadway long before he went into racing, and from his youth he was celebrated as a high player in all games. He would bet on anything."

As proof, Runyon needed only point to the 1916 presidential election, a race so hotly contested that the *New York Times* was reporting odds updates almost daily for weeks. The bookmakers and the Wall Street betting market had made President Woodrow Wilson, running for reelection on the slogan "He Kept Us Out of

War," an underdog against Charles Evans Hughes, the Republican challenger who as New York governor had once outlawed gambling in the state for five years. Bieber, who never forgave Hughes for having banned betting in 1908 and horse racing in 1910, strongly backed the Democratic incumbent. That spurred Rothstein, a staunch Republican, to lay him 8-to-5 odds, putting up his own $80,000 on Hughes to Bieber's $50,000 on Wilson.

On Election Day, Bieber joined the hundreds of thousands crowding Times Square to follow bulletins flashed on the lofty canvas screen that served as the public's central source of breaking news before the advent of radio. Around 9 P.M., the canvas bulletin board declared Hughes the winner to boisterous cheers, and the red searchlight atop the New York Times Building spread that projection for miles in every direction. "Oh well," Bieber said with a shrug as he followed the election returns from his ticket brokerage at Broadway and 42nd Street, "there's always something coming up where you can start a parlay going again."

As Bieber slept in the next morning, America was still awaiting the California returns that would determine the official winner. But not Rothstein. Barging into Bieber's office, he demanded, "I must speak to him. It's important." Irked to find his quarry not there yet, Rothstein telephoned the family's apartment, only to be told by Bieber's sister that Izzy wouldn't be down to Times Square until around 4 P.M. When Bieber finally strolled into his office, Rothstein was lying in wait.

"Beeb, it's all over," Rothstein pounced. "How about getting the thing settled? I really need the dough."

Bieber shook his head and said firmly, "When Wilson congratulates Hughes, you collect. Not before."

"I need the cash now," Rothstein protested. "I'll give you five thousand dollars to settle."

"Nothing doing," Bieber retorted.

"This is your last chance to save something," Rothstein fumed. "I'll give you ten thousand dollars to clear it right now."

"Arnold, get the hell out of here," Bieber snapped. "It's all or nothing, and that's final. Don't bother me again."

As the door slammed behind Rothstein, Bieber's business partner mused, "Gee, Beeb, ten grand is better than nothing."

"Barney," Bieber replied with a mischievous smile, "you don't know that guy. He's got eyes and ears all over the country and gets every bit of news. I like my chances better now than I did before the election."

As the vote counting dragged on into the next day, Rothstein again tried to call the bet off. "Nothing doing," Bieber repeated as both men slammed down their telephone receivers to punctuate their intensifying mutual animus.

On his way to his office the day after that, Bieber saw the Times Square bulletin board report the shocking news that the California tally had finally swung the election—to President Wilson. That night, Bieber collected his $80,000 in winnings from Rothstein. Five weeks later, Bieber had gambled away the whole $80,000 and was broke again.

Nothing could have better illustrated the pathology at work in Runyon's "immutable law" that all horseplayers die broke. "The only reason that can be suggested for Bieber's plunging is that it must be the one big thrill he gets out of life," Runyon psychoanalyzed in print, "because even when he has all the money he could possibly need, he keeps on betting until it is gone, then starts over again."

That vicious cycle was certainly on display in the summer of 1927. Bieber had been mired in such a prolonged losing streak that he would need to once more start all over again. He was so broke that he had to stop going to the racetrack altogether, instead spending his days at the beach.

One morning on what promised to be another beautiful beach day, he asked his kid brother Phil, "How much money do you have?"

Phil scrounged through his pockets and replied, "Six dollars."

"I've got fourteen dollars," Izzy said. "Let's go to Empire City."

When they got to Empire City Race Track just over the Bronx border up in Yonkers, Izzy bet the $20 on a 4-to-1 shot named Turkey's Neck. After Turkey's Neck romped home, he put all the winnings on a 6-to-1 shot that also came in. On a roll for the first time in longer than he cared to remember, he kept parlaying his winnings, betting it all back at 5-to-2 the next race, then at 2-to-1, then at 8-to-1. Having hit five winners in a row, he would let it all ride in the final race on the even-money favorite Red Cliff. When Red Cliff also won, his six-race parlay had netted him a cool $135,000—not a bad return on his initial $20 investment.

The next afternoon, Izzy went back to Empire City and paid off $15,000 in debts that remained from the losing streak, leaving his pockets flush with $120,000. Since the day's card was lousy with small fields and short prices, he decided against playing the ponies. That hardly stopped him from strolling up and down the betting ring placing wagers—not on the races, but rather on that night's heavyweight fight at Yankee Stadium between Jack Dempsey and Jack Sharkey. Izzy believed that Dempsey, whose seven-year reign as heavyweight champion had ended the previous fall in a decision loss to Gene Tunney, was "all through" and that the up-and-coming Sharkey should be an even bigger favorite than the bookies were making him. So Izzy approached all the bookies taking action in the clubhouse and on the track apron, laying some money with each of them on the favored Sharkey at 5-to-2 odds.

That night at dinner, he surprised his brother by pulling a pair of $27.50 ringside tickets out of his jacket's breast pocket. In a banner year when Babe Ruth was slugging home runs at a record clip for the New York Yankees, this was by far the hottest ticket that speculators like Izzy had handled for any event at the huge stadium dubbed "The House That Ruth Built."

"Come on," Izzy laughed, "let's go watch Dempsey get his head punched off."

The brothers Bieber headed to Yankee Stadium. Just before the main event, Izzy slid into his fourth-row seat, leaned over to his brother, and casually said, "Phil, the parlay is still riding. I couldn't resist two and a half to one. What an overlay! Sharkey will murder him."

Phil was incredulous. "You bet the whole one hundred and twenty grand?" he exclaimed.

"Certainly," Izzy replied matter-of-factly. "Never limit your winnings, Phil. Just your losses."

Before his speechless brother could reply, the bell rang. Sharkey dominated the early rounds, staggering Dempsey in the first and bloodying his face. The fight was so lopsided that Dempsey's nervous backers made a beeline to Bieber's ringside seat after the sixth round. Those gamblers desperately tried to hedge their bets by offering tempting longshot odds on Dempsey that would have assured Bieber a tidy profit no matter who won the fight. Bieber shook his head and said dismissively, "All or nothing."

Before they could take no for an answer, Dempsey charged out for the seventh round, stunned his foe with an apparently low blow, and, as Sharkey turned toward the referee to cry foul, knocked him down with a vicious left hook to the jaw. In the ten seconds it took the ref to count Sharkey out, Bieber had lost the whole $120,000—the biggest boxing bet that Runyon, covering the fight at ringside, had ever heard of.

On the subway ride home, both Biebers were quiet for a long time. Finally, Phil ventured, "Iz, I can't fault you for betting big. If you hadn't, we wouldn't have won a hundred and thirty-five thousand dollars in the first place. But we're horsemen, not fight people, and we've had a long bad streak. Couldn't you have bet a hundred thousand dollars and held out twenty grand?"

"Quit squawking," Izzy snapped. "We only lost twenty bucks. So what?"

The moral of this true tale wasn't much different than that of so many Damon Runyon short stories, those ironic and fatalistic morality plays in which gambling stands as a metaphor for life. Or, as one of his protagonists would famously sigh, "I long ago come to the conclusion that all life is six to five against." It was no coincidence that the Broadway character who uttered that oft-quoted line, Sam the Gonoph, happened to be a ticket speculator as well as an inveterate gambler.

Izzy Bieber traced his love of racehorses to Belmont Park's grand opening in 1905. That's when the streetwise teenager caught the racing bug—or, more accurately, the pathological passion for betting big on horses. Even after he opted to become an owner in his twenties, he still identified, first and foremost, as a horseplayer. His main interest would remain betting, frequently on his own horse but almost as often on a competitor's.

The racing bug didn't catch up with Damon Runyon until much later, at the dawn of the Roaring Twenties when he was already over forty. For the previous decade, he had been too busy covering America's most popular spectator sports, baseball and boxing. Not only did he chronicle the prodigious feats of each sport's surpassing superstar, but he also palled around with them: going hunting with Babe Ruth in the offseason and nurturing a close friendship with

Jack Dempsey, which dated to their shared Colorado roots that inspired Runyon to famously nickname him "The Manassa Mauler."

Runyon's only exposure to horse racing had come during his infrequent visits to the New York tracks, not to mention one interesting day at the races on the Mexican border as a guest of Pancho Villa. Runyon had been covering spring training in Texas when he ran into Villa and accepted an invitation to the Mexican revolutionary leader's private box at the track in Juarez. Runyon was too preoccupied keeping an eye on Villa, a cold-blooded killer who made the gangsters back in New York look like choirboys, to pay much attention to the races.

Horses didn't really engage Runyon until Man o' War stole America's heart in the wake of World War I, becoming as transcendent an athletic icon as Ruth or Dempsey and leading The Sport of Kings to once again rival baseball and boxing as the king of sports. With the so-called Golden Age of Sports now in full stride, Runyon reckoned the time had come for a pilgrimage upstate to Saratoga Springs so he could check out the mecca of horse racing and see what all the fuss was about.

On the last night of July 1922, he arrived at Saratoga's United States Hotel and moved into a luxurious $16-a-day room with trunks full of the custom-tailored $200 suits, monogramed silk shirts, and patent-leather shoes that had earned him a dapper reputation as a Broadway Beau Brummell. The next day, when he strolled out onto the mammoth hotel's white-pillared veranda, Runyon suddenly felt as if he were experiencing déjà vu.

"On awakening this morning and descending to the vaulted dining room to collect some of the board that comes with the room, we found scores of citizens that we had seen somewhere before," he wrote that day in his column. "We had a vague sense of having taken a long journey the night before that carried us back from strange parts to familiar haunts. We were back on Manhattan Island, with the same bunch you see in front of the Hotel Astor in the early evening, dapper, soft-collared, knowing-looking gentry, scattered about."

Not to mention the same bunch of Broadway plungers you see in front of Lindy's deli just up the block from the Hotel Astor. There was Arnold Rothstein. There was Nick the Greek. There was Isidor Bieber. As Runyon surveyed the assemblage of New York City horseplayers, bookmakers, and touts from the hotel veranda, it suddenly dawned on him why the Great White Way seemed a little dimmer every August. It had been transplanted to Saratoga for the annual monthlong race meeting. If he felt as if he were standing right on Broadway, that's because he literally was. The United States Hotel, the most elegant and prestigious in town, sprawled over seven acres on Saratoga's quaint main street—named, coincidentally enough, Broadway. "Saratoga's Broadway is brisk and busy with traffic," Runyon wrote that day. "Big motor cars come thundering in packed high with luggage and passengers who have disdained the slower transportation of the railroads. Perhaps the street was named Broadway to keep a little home touch for the denizens of the Big White Line who come this way each year."

No Broadway big shot made himself more at home in Saratoga than Rothstein. By night, he ran the nation's most lavish casino at his opulent Victorian mansion on the outskirts of town. By day, he was the biggest plunger at Saratoga Race Course, once scoring $900,000 on a single win bet (an unheard-of payoff in 1920 dollars and the equivalent today of over $11 million). His relationship to racing could be summed up by his first words to his bride, a Broadway showgirl he married at the 1909 Saratoga meeting, after carrying her across the cottage threshold on their wedding night: "Sweet, I had a bad day today, and I'll need your jewelry for a few days." He immediately scooped up the jewelry, hocked it, and parlayed the cash into a killing at the track.

The talk of the town when Runyon arrived for the 1922 meeting was the caper Rothstein had pulled off the previous summer in Saratoga's marquee race, the Travers Stakes. Rothstein, who liked to boast he would bet on anything except the weather because that was the only thing he couldn't fix, had the audacity to muck with racing's oldest stakes just as he had with the national pastime's World Series two years prior. After bribing a stablehand for a tip that the heavy favorite was off her feed and off her form, Rothstein realized his own longshot colt, Sporting Blood, might have a legitimate chance at winning the 1921 Travers. He promptly conspired with a rival stable's trainer to manipulate the odds so that Sporting Blood became an even longer shot, then bet $150,000 on him. When Sporting Blood pulled the upset, Rothstein scored $450,000 in winning bets, the $10,275 purse, and a place in Saratoga lore as a race fixer.

It wasn't hard to see why Runyon would quickly adopt Saratoga, making it his own in much the same way he had New York City's Broadway. Never mind the charm of the quaint spa town and the nostalgia of a timeless track founded during the bloodiest throes of the Civil War just a month after the Battle of Gettysburg, what Runyon found irresistibly alluring was "the action" that attracted all the high rollers to America's gambling paradise.

One day at the track, Runyon was chatting up Johnny Walters, who as the nation's biggest bookmaker handled $1 million in wagers a day and more than $50 million during a single monthlong meeting at Saratoga. At a time when Thoroughbred owners made much more from their win bets than their first-place prize purses, Walters was telling Runyon how he had just taken a $100,000 wager from an oil magnate who was backing his own horse in that afternoon's Saratoga feature.

"Gee whiz," Runyon exclaimed, "that guy must be the highest player in town."

"No," replied Walters, whose client list ranged from infamous gamblers like Rothstein and Bet-a-Million Gates to famous aristocrats with names like Whitney and Widener. "It is not an unusually high bet for any one of a number of individuals at this meeting. And it isn't high for that particular fellow because it means nothing to him if he loses. He has plenty more left."

"So," Runyon ventured with arched eyebrows, "who is the highest player you know?"

"A chap called Beeb," Walters said. "He will bet all he has. No man can bet more."

Runyon resolved to see for himself by following Beeb around Saratoga. At the track, Runyon would observe Beeb "go shouldering his way through the betting ring whispering his wagers to the bookies while a mob surged at his heels trying to hear what he is saying." After the last race, as the crowd streamed out of the track's main Union Avenue gate, Runyon would stalk Beeb, whose flamboyant attire made him easy to spot in his brightly clashing stripes and checks: "I noticed that on some days he walked right down the middle of the cement walks on those homeward strolls, stepping briskly and with forthrightness, but on other days he would guide his feet to the neatly clipped lawns in front of the homes on Union Avenue occupied by the higher permanent residents of Saratoga or leased to the visiting squillionaires and that he moved quite gingerly—'sore going,' the horsemen would call it. Finally I decided that the sidewalk days were days when he was winner and the grass days were days he was loser and his feet hurt, and I want to say right here that there is a definite association between a horseplayer's puppies and his betting operations."

Runyon learned that the hard way. Often he would shuffle back from the track and pull his pockets inside out to show what the horses had left him to play with that night at the casinos. One time Runyon had to take refuge in the United States Hotel when he was unable to cover a bet he had placed on a "sure thing" that wasn't, hiding out for three full days from a bookie called Gloomy Gus until one of his distress telegrams brought enough cash to relieve the debt.

Not surprisingly, Runyon recognized a kindred spirit in Beeb. "I am sure the betting with him is nothing more than a form of excitement," Runyon observed. "No man I ever knew has so little regard for money as money. He is almost frugal in his way of living. He is surrounded by none of the luxuries that usually go with money, yet he will bet more on a race than it costs a rich man for his living expenses per year."

Indeed, Beeb would bet big on a horse before post time and then double down during the race. One time, as his horse was loafing along the backstretch some thirty lengths behind the early pacesetter, Beeb was offered past-post odds of 300-to-1 and instantly took $1,000 of that proposition. His horse made up all the ground except for a short nose, losing a photo finish. Not only did Beeb shrug off the $1,000 loss, but he also actually declared it a moral victory because it confirmed his good judgment in taking the midrace bet at such a long price.

Watching him get beaten like that on a photo finish or on a disqualification, Runyon was surprised at how philosophically Beeb always dealt with heartbreaking losses. "Well," Beeb would simply sigh with a shrug, "that's horse racing."

Of all the racetrack philosophers Runyon encountered on his daily rounds of the Saratoga stables and dinner tables, he was amazed to discover that none was more interesting and erudite than Beeb. Although racing's mecca gave Runyon the chance to rub elbows with the rich and powerful on their annual summer pilgrimage to America's biggest gambling resort, he gravitated to the familiar riffraff from New York City who congregated each evening on the hotel verandas to handicap the next day's races.

Having long known Beeb for his truculence along Broadway and at the metropolitan tracks, Runyon was intrigued to find him now sitting "in the evening shadows mildly discussing Voltaire, and Shakespeare, and Balzac, and especially Shakespeare, and arguing that John Barrymore was the greatest Hamlet that ever stalked the boards." The writer loved listening to Beeb "quote Shakespeare by the yard" and wax poetic on novelists from Dickens to Dostoevsky. Runyon felt deprived of that entertainment on those nights when Beeb had suffered a losing day at the track. On those occasions, Beeb would decline dinner invitations and instead grab an apple or a bag of peanuts and retire to his room, where he would slip into bed and devour the classics.

That made Beeb just the kind of racetrack philosopher Runyon would mine for his daily columns and later for his short stories featuring darkly comic plots and seedy characters. As Runyon would famously write, "The race is not always to the swift, nor the battle to the strong, but that's the way to bet." How many racetrackers besides Beeb recognized that Runyon was paraphrasing a biblical line from Ecclesiastes?

In the early twenties, while Hirsch Jacobs was still a teenager racing his pigeons for small side bets in Brooklyn, Isidor Bieber was already a hardened horseplayer planning to start his own stable. After claiming a couple of promising prospects and choosing his colors, he christened his new venture B. B. Stable, a name he would come to regret if only because it served to reinforce the Kid Beebee nickname he so hated.

For all the dough he was willing to gamble with in the betting ring and at the betting window, Beebee was downright parsimonious when it came to investing in racing stock. He was rapidly buying up cheap claimers and losing them just as quickly. His fledgling stable generally comprised maybe half a dozen horses, but he spent so little time with his new acquisitions that he couldn't tell them apart or even recognize which ones were his once they were out of the barn. As for trainers, he was going through them as fast as he was going through the claimers.

Although his small stable of ordinary horses invariably ran in the red, Beebee was still making money, if only because his habitual betting was enhanced by the inside information to which he was now privy. The betting tips could come from unexpected sources. While racing at Belmont in 1925, Beebee loaned $5,000 to a veteran trainer whose horses were stabled in the same backside barn as his. Strapped for cash and unable to repay the debt, the trainer, Billy Garth, led Beebee to his stalls and said, "Some of these horses are mine. Pick one you think is worth five thousand dollars." Beebee chose a filly named Fatigue, who went on to win a couple of minor races for him. A few weeks later, Garth approached him in the barn and said, "Beeb, I'm happy that Fatigue turned out OK. I see you've got her in today against my Miss Midworthy. You can't beat my filly, so use your own judgment." Beebee took the hint, betting a bundle on Miss Midworthy at 6-to-1. When Miss Midworthy beat Fatigue, he walked away content that Garth had more than paid his debt.

By 1926, Beebee was getting more serious about B. B. Stable. Three times during that August's Saratoga season, a horse he had just claimed for several grand won its first race carrying the stable's colors of scarlet, white, and black. The third one, a three-year-old colt named Banco Suivi that he had claimed from the great

Kentucky breeder E. R. Bradley, romped home at 7-to-1 to win Beebee $50,000 in bets and a new kind of acclaim. The next day's *Brooklyn Daily Eagle* introduced Beebee as "the newest plunger of the season."

No claim confirmed the usually frugal Beebee's newfound seriousness that summer better than Sarapion, a three-year-old colt that the nation's leading trainer, Sam Hildreth, had entered in the Woodmere Claiming Stakes for the oil baron Harry Sinclair's Rancocas Stable. Spotting the chestnut colt's name listed atop the field for that afternoon's feature at Aqueduct, Beebee hurried to the racing secretary's office, stuffed $5,000 in cash into an envelope along with the claim slip, and deposited it into the claim box on the counter. As soon as Sarapion romped to victory as the favorite, Beebee rushed back to the racing secretary's office, only to discover the room jammed with claimants. When the box was unlocked, there were nine claims for Sarapion. A drawing was held, and Beebee won the lottery, known as a "shake." After running a few races in the B. B. colors that fall, Sarapion was shipped to winter at Big Bill Dwyer's Lakewood Stud Farm, where the colt developed pneumonia and died.

Undaunted, Beebee continued to claim a better class of horse. Now all he needed was a better class of horseman to train them. He was in the market for a trainer during the winter of 1927 when he made his annual migration to Cuba for its racing season and first met Hirsch Jacobs.

CHAPTER 4

THE ODD COUPLE

One warm Cuban afternoon in January 1928, as Isidor Bieber was strolling toward the paddock at Havana's Oriental Park, he noticed "a little redheaded lad" walking away from it. Sure that the lad was someone he recognized from back home in New York, Bieber greeted him with enthusiasm. "Hello!" he called out as if hailing an old friend.

The lad nodded back and, being an affable sort, smiled easily, responded with a "Hiya," and stopped to talk. When Bieber started addressing him by the name of Martin Harvey, however, it dawned on the young man that this middle-aged gent had mistaken him for someone else.

"No, my name isn't Harvey," said the young man. "I'm Hirsch Jacobs."

Without missing a beat, Bieber stuck out his right hand. "Pleased to meet you," he said. "I'm Izzy Bieber."

As they began to chat, it became clear why Bieber thought Jacobs looked so familiar. Bieber had often noticed this "redheaded kid" hanging around the Jamaica racetrack. In fact, the two had crossed paths once before, during the previous year's meeting at Jamaica. Moments after a race one afternoon, Bieber had been loudly bemoaning the bad luck that had just caused him to lose a big bet on a horse named Scat. Jacobs couldn't help but overhear Bieber cursing out a horse named Forecaster for swerving in the stretch and cutting off Scat. Stifling a smirk, Jacobs turned to Bieber and cracked, "What are you crying about? We had Corinth in the race, and if he don't get left at the post, he walks in."

Back then, Bieber had been in no mood to engage with some smart-aleck kid. But now, having struck up a conversation with the little redheaded lad, he found himself thoroughly engaged.

As they chatted, Bieber couldn't help but think, "This boy has such honest eyes I would trust him with my uncounted bankroll."

After a few minutes, Jacobs excused himself to get back to the horses he was training for his new clients, the Canadian owners Johnny and Louis Mascia along with their partner Louie Sylvestri. Just weeks after going out on his own as a trainer, Jacobs had journeyed to Cuba because that's where the Canadians customarily shipped their modest racing stable for the winter season. Traveling abroad for the first time, he was excited to join the annual winter migration of the leading North American horses and horsemen on the five-hour trip via steamship from Key West on the Florida coastline to the little country that billed itself the "Isle of Enchantment."

While Jacobs was all business throughout that winter meeting, Bieber had come to Oriental Park not to race his own B. B. Stable horses but "really for a rest." Meaning, he was there to do what he loved most: bet the horses.

Bieber had been religiously sailing to Cuba every winter since December 1919 when, caught up in the spirit of hedonism and exuberance that was sweeping America in the wake of World War I, he embraced Oriental Park, a grand racetrack with a glamorous casino right on the grounds, as the perfect place for a plunger like himself to vacation. He had spent much of his time in Havana that first winter hanging out with Charles Stoneham, the Wall Street stock swindler and inveterate gambler rumored to have won ownership of the New York Giants baseball franchise in a poker game.

One rainy day that winter at Oriental Park, Bieber and Stoneham got an inside tip on a "mudder" that was practically a sure thing in the featured race. "There isn't a horse in America that can beat him in this kind of gooey, sticky mud," the horse's trainer confided to them. The two American plungers exchanged a sly glance and, as soon as the trainer excused himself, began plotting their betting strategy.

Although the track did offer the pari-mutuel betting windows that were just starting to come into vogue, Bieber and Stoneham, like the vast majority of Oriental Park horseplayers, instead chose to patronize the bookmakers in the old-fashioned betting ring. Both plungers were happy that the New York State tracks had yet to adopt pari-mutuel wagering, a European system whereby all bets were placed in a centralized pool from which odds would be calculated and payouts shared among the winning ticket holders. They preferred being able to shop around for the most favorable odds among the dozens of bookmakers in the betting ring, assured that their wagers would pay out at those fixed odds rather than the variable pari-mutuel calculations beyond their control. The one hitch at Oriental Park was that you had to wager with "syndicated books" owned and operated by the track, which set and revised the odds that all the bookies would then conspire to offer.

To beat such price fixing, Bieber and Stoneham hatched an ingenious plan. Needing four bettors to pull it off, they recruited Bieber's kid brother Phil and Stoneham's right-hand man, the fiery New York Giants manager John McGraw. Each of the four stationed himself near a different bookmaker. At Bieber's prearranged signal, he and his three compatriots each bet on their "tip horse" with a different bookie at the exact same time, thus locking in the generous opening odds of 4-to-1. They put so much action on the horse that the bookies immediately dropped the odds for subsequent bettors, ultimately sending him to the post at 3-to-5. Watching that odds-on favorite leave the entire field wallowing in his muddy wake, the Biebers, Stoneham, and McGraw could barely contain their smug smiles as they cashed in at 4-to-1.

The next day, the Bieber brothers were still celebrating when Oriental Park's suspicious stewards tracked them down in the club-house and started grilling them on their killing. "Where did you get your information?" demanded one of the stewards.

"Someone told us how good the horse was doing, and I knew he was a superior mud horse," Izzy Bieber replied matter-of-factly. "Anything unusual about that?"

The head steward nodded emphatically and decreed, "We can do without you two at this track."

Bieber was about to reply in kind when he spotted Stoneham and McGraw climbing the clubhouse steps in their direction and held his tongue. When the stewards started interrogating the new-comers, Bieber half expected McGraw, the only sporting man he deemed more pugnacious than himself, to take a swing at them. Stoneham must have expected that as well, because he quickly stepped in to cut off the colorful Hall of Fame manager fittingly nicknamed "Little Napoleon."

"What in the hell is this all about?" Stoneham bellowed at the stewards. "By what right do you talk to your patrons this way? Un-less you stop this nonsense, I will make it my business to publicize your tactics, and I can assure you it won't help Cuban racing one bit."

His pudgy face turning red, he then wheeled around toward

McGraw and the Biebers. "Come on, boys," Stoneham huffed, "let's try to forget this nonsense and enjoy the races. It's evident this track could use better management. I will certainly give it plenty of thought."

A couple of weeks later, Stoneham purchased Oriental Park along with its casino known as "The Monte Carlo of the Western Hemisphere," bringing in McGraw and the New York mobster Arnold Rothstein—a longtime business associate and friend of his—as limited partners. Four years after that, baseball's first high commissioner, Judge Kenesaw Mountain Landis, crusading to clean up its tarnished image in the wake of the Black Sox scandal stemming from Rothstein's reputed 1919 World Series fix, forced Stoneham and McGraw to divest themselves of ownership in Oriental Park and its Gran Casino Nacional if they wanted to keep the reins on what was then the national pastime's most successful franchise.

Of course, no one—not the American baseball commissioner or the Cuban racing stewards—could deter plungers like Stoneham, McGraw, and Bieber from continuing to gamble every winter at Oriental Park. With its lavish casinos and luxurious hotels, Havana had long established itself as "The Riviera of the Caribbean," a favorite winter vacation destination for high society and high rollers from America and Europe. The grand opening of Oriental Park in 1915 only enhanced Havana's reputation as a tropical den of iniquity where wealthy tourists could gamble and gorge themselves on a bounty of illicit pleasures largely controlled by American mobsters. In those years before grander racetracks sprouted up in Florida and California to entice the horsey set to stay stateside, Oriental Park reigned supreme as the palm-lined place for the well-heeled to see and be seen, whether soaking in the scene from the clubhouse veranda or dancing between races on the grandstand promenade to the music of a fine orchestra. For Prohibition-parched Americans, there was the bonus benefit of free-flowing booze to go with gambling that was actually legal. For hardened horseplayers like Bieber and Stoneham, it was nothing short of a plunger's paradise.

Around the same time as Bieber's chance encounter with Jacobs during the 1928 Oriental Park meeting, he and Stoneham each bet a bundle on Cuba's most popular horse: King David, a four-year-old son of the first foreign-bred Kentucky Derby winner, the 1917 champion Omar Khayyam. Watching the odds drop precipitously as bettors made the handsome bay such a prohibitive favorite that the track-backed bookmakers stood to take a beating, Stoneham began to worry that there might be a "window wash" for King David. "Window washing" was a rigged system in which the bookies would call up to the stewards' stand whenever they thought they were going to lose big on a heavily bet favorite. The crooked stewards would respond right before post time by raising and lowering the window shade a certain number of times corresponding to the post position of the horse they wanted washed—a signal to the official starter to make sure that the specified favorite got off too slowly in the race to come back and win.

It was such a common practice at Oriental Park that Stoneham turned to Bieber during the post parade and blurted out, "Is King David in danger of a window wash?"

"Charlie, see those five men in that front box?" Bieber said, pointing to the best finish-line seats in the house. "The gray-haired guy is Gerardo Machado, president of Cuba, owner of the horse, who is the pride of his heart. The other four are senators whom he invited to see his horse win. They just couldn't be dumb enough to try any rough stuff in this race."

Sure enough, King David got the jump at the start and wired

the field to win going away. That's why Bieber always bet on King David whenever Machado was in attendance, especially if the Cuban president was entertaining prominent visitors ranging from European royalty to American aristocrats. It didn't surprise Bieber to see flamboyant New York mayor Jimmy Walker, his old Broadway nemesis, among the power brokers who frequented Machado's box. During Machado's increasingly dictatorial and corrupt reign, Havana became more of a rollicking tourist destination and Oriental Park more of a boisterous hot spot. Ever the hardened Broadway hustler, Bieber felt right at home in the racetrack's raucous environment where gunfire mingled with mariachi music near the betting ring.

By contrast, Hirsch Jacobs—the straight-arrow lad who didn't bet, drink, smoke, or carouse—found this Cuban baptism-by-fire to be a completely foreign experience. He steered clear of the corruption that characterized Cuban racing's low standards, from window washing to doping. Instead, he focused his time and energy on the horses he was saddling for his Canadian clients. For all of Oriental Park's tropical beauty, architectural opulence, and stylish spectators, the racing itself wasn't so different from what the young trainer was accustomed to back at Jamaica racetrack. Of the six or seven races on the cards that Oriental Park offered every day but Mondays from December to March, the vast majority were claimers with meager $700 purses. Which was enough to make Jacobs feel right at home. By the time the Oriental Park meeting closed in mid-March, the Mascia brothers and Sylvestri were so pleased with Jacobs's results that they enthusiastically entrusted him with the stable they were shipping back north for the spring season in Ontario, New York, and Ohio.

* * *

That summer, Jacobs was racing the Canadian stable's horses at a small racetrack in northern Ohio when he got a surprise telegram from that Bieber fellow he had met in Cuba months earlier and chatted with only briefly. Bieber said he wanted to sell four of his horses and wondered if Jacobs might be interested in handling the sale.

Jacobs was amused, having just read about one of Bieber's latest escapades in the *Daily Racing Form*, the bible of the sport since 1894. It seems Bieber had recently picked a fight in the Empire City press box with a *Racing Form* correspondent by shouting, "I think you are nothing but a cur!" In the paper's issue of July 7, 1928, an editorial took Bieber to task for his pugnacity. "In the course of the opening day at the Empire City meeting, the stewards had occasion to impose a fine of $200 on Isidor Bieber, owner of the B. B. Stable, but it had nothing to do with racing itself, and was just a kind of disciplining," the editorial began. "Bieber had offended and been punished before, so that it was no new thing for him to be placed on the carpet. On this occasion he was guilty of conduct that is not tolerated on any race course, but it would seem that it did not entirely cure him of his unruly conduct."

On a previous occasion at Empire City, Bieber had stopped one fall day to gab with a hotheaded racetrack habitué named Johnny Victor, who was accompanied as usual by his gang of gunmen. Out of nowhere, Victor sucker punched him on the jaw. Bieber, who had been warned by the Empire City stewards to refrain from his habitual disturbances under threat of suspension, shocked everyone by turning the other cheek and lumbering away. He nursed the grudge all winter until the time and place were right. When he spotted Victor the following spring at Belmont Park, Bieber pushed through the crowd, dragged him up by the lapel, and began pummeling him. As Victor slumped to the ground, five of his hoods jumped Bieber, punching and kicking him mercilessly. When one pulled a knife, Victor shouted, "Put that away!" Helping the battered Bieber to his feet, Victor draped an arm around his shoulders and said, "Beeb, nobody ever dared to come fight me alone. I love a brave man. Let's be friends." Victor then held out his right hand, which Bieber, after hesitating, prudently shook, satisfied that getting his revenge was well worth the $200 that the Belmont stewards would fine him for the fisticuffs.

Such shenanigans weren't about to scare Jacobs away from Bieber's business proposition. Still trying to make his way as a claiming trainer, Jacobs was in no position to turn down any business. He jumped at the opportunity to sell the horses for Bieber.

Bieber shipped the four Thoroughbreds to him at Bainbridge Park, a brand-new track near Cleveland where Jacobs was saddling horses in cheap claiming races for tiny purses. Jacobs handled the task with aplomb, selling all four horses in short order for Bieber's asking price at a fledgling track that attracted few well-to-do horsemen.

The best of the four was a skinny but well-bred bay gelding that Bieber had once liked well enough to claim from the Whitneys' Greentree Stable and to then rename Jack Biener after a friend of his. Still a maiden at age three, his disappointing performances had now made Jack Biener expendable. But Jacobs saw something in the bony gelding and, instead of offering him to unknown buyers, convinced Johnny Mascia to buy him.

After pocketing his sales commission, Jacobs didn't give Bieber another thought as he returned his focus to training Mascia's horses. They kept him plenty busy throughout 1928. It turned out to be a breakthrough year for Jacobs, who finally cracked the *Racing Form*'s official annual list of trainers that had saddled multiple winners. He finished the year with thirty-eight winners and purse earnings of $33,770, a twenty-fold hike in both categories.

For his part, Bieber also considered 1928 an eventful year, even if his B. B. Stable didn't enjoy as much success on the track as the Jacobs-trained Mascia Brothers Stable. That November, like everyone else in the racing world, Bieber was shocked—though hardly surprised—by the banner-headline news of his nemesis Arnold Rothstein's murder. Damon Runyon, who had been hanging out with Rothstein at their preferred Lindy's haunt when a mysterious phone call summoned the mobster to a high-stakes card game at the nearby Broadway hotel where he would be gut-shot, put it succinctly in his next column: "Life, for the average man who minds his own affairs, is about even money. That is to say, when he walks out of his door in the morning it is 50-50 that he will return safe and sound. Arnold Rothstein was the only man I ever encountered who was 'No Price.' When he stepped beyond his threshold he was 'Out' in the betting." Given Rothstein's notoriety as an underworld plunger, nobody doubted that he had been executed mob-style over a week-old poker debt he refused to pay after claiming the card game had been fixed. After a sensational trial in which the alleged hit man was acquitted because Rothstein had refused to name his shooter to the cops on his deathbed, what was then dubbed "the crime of the century" would remain unsolved.

Shortly before his untimely demise, Rothstein had been enjoying a day at the races when Grantland Rice, the heir to Runyon's claim on sportswriting supremacy during the Golden Age of Sports, ran into him in the Jamaica clubhouse. When Rice asked about the secret of his betting system for winning so big, Rothstein surprised him by candidly replying, "I go to the leading trainers. 'Tell me if your horse is right,' I say. 'If he is, I'll bet one thousand or two thousand dollars for you. But don't double-cross me.' In this way, I get the best information. Information, sound information, is what you need at the racetrack."

If only Runyon could have employed such a betting system, maybe he wouldn't have had so much bad luck. Unlike Rothstein's system of bribing and threatening horsemen for inside information, Runyon's involved getting his tips from the touts who used to populate racetracks promising "I got the horse right here." Damon Runyon short stories were populated by small-time touts like Hot Horse Herbie, so nicknamed "because he nearly always has a horse to tell you about that is so hot it is fairly smoking, a hot horse that cannot possibly lose a race unless it falls down dead, and while Herbie's hot horses often lose without falling down dead, this does not keep Herbie from coming up just as hot." In real life as in his fiction, Runyon surrounded himself with no shortage of touts. For years, he retained as his own personal "turf adviser" one Horse Thief Eddie Burke, a hustler so nicknamed because he had once been caught trying to walk out of Bowie Race Track leading a horse that didn't belong to him with a stray piece of rope he'd found on the ground.

Runyon got most of his tips from his oldest racetrack confidant, a professional tout and plunger with the unusual name of E. Phocion Howard. Phoce Howard, as he was known everywhere from Broadway to the backside, was an eccentric every bit as Runyonesque as Izzy Bieber. In fact, it was said Phoce Howard came as close to being a Damon Runyon character as anyone could in real life. Like Bieber, Howard dressed loud—from his white hat, purple plaid suit, and pink shirt with ruby studs and cuff links all the way down to his white spats and gold-headed walking stick—and talked even louder. And like Bieber, he was always spouting quotations from the classics. Mostly, though, Howard touted horses as the founding editor and publisher of the *New York Press*, a weekly rag devoted to racing and stock tips.

Too bad those tips rarely panned out for him. On the occasions when they did, he was sure to gamble away the winnings like Bieber or give them away to downtrodden horseplayers. No matter how strapped his plunging left him, Howard always managed to live in the Plaza Hotel and tool around in a vintage Rolls-Royce chauffeured by a manservant called Chicken Fry Ben, so nicknamed for the fried chicken he kept on the front seat to feed passengers who had bet away all their meal money on the horses. Every August throughout the Saratoga meeting, Howard and Runyon would share a rented Victorian house straight down Union Avenue from the racetrack. It was Howard whom Runyon always credited with first uttering the truism that the writer would co-opt for his own mantra: "All horseplayers die broke." As if to prove the point, Phoce Howard would indeed die broke. On the last day of his life, he won several grand at the Saratoga track and celebrated that night by playing faro at a local gambling house. When Chicken Fry Ben found his employer dead of a heart attack the next morning in the rented Victorian, he searched the pockets of Howard's trousers and found a grand total of $2.37. It was enough to inspire Runyon to suggest a fitting epitaph for Howard's tombstone: ALL HORSE-PLAYERS DIE BROKE.

In the spring of 1929, four years before Phoce Howard would die broke, he and Runyon traveled together from Broadway to the Bluegrass for the Kentucky Derby. On the eve of the Derby, they were standing on the sidewalk outside the Hotel Kentucky when Howard introduced Runyon to Clyde Van Dusen, the trainer who had entered a horse also named Clyde Van Dusen. "I am going to win the Derby!" Clyde Van Dusen the trainer proclaimed to them.

When it rained hard overnight well into Derby day, Howard tipped Runyon off that Clyde Van Dusen the horse, although a son of Man o' War, couldn't handle the deep mud. Upon arriving at

Churchill Downs early that afternoon, Runyon went to the jockeys' room in search of Pony McAtee, only to learn that the colt's rider didn't plan on showing up before the Derby to get a feel for the track. So Runyon resolved to check out the condition of the racing strip himself. He walked under the stands, scrounged up a pair of muck boots, and ventured out to the muddy track wearing a panama hat against the rain. When his boot sank deep into the mud, Runyon betrayed a smile at the thought of the inside tip that Howard had given him earlier.

Suddenly, Runyon's reverie was interrupted by a soft, high-pitched voice emanating from the rail nearby. "What is your object?" the voice queried.

Runyon turned toward the voice and spotted a short, stout red-headed young man he vaguely recognized as the upstart New York trainer Hirsch Jacobs. "This limestone soil certainly makes deep mud," Runyon observed.

"I think it is the rain that makes the mud," Jacobs said with a smile.

"I just wanted to see the condition of the track," Runyon explained. "The jockey doesn't want to get a feel of it. That means I have to do it myself. I get penalized for losing; he gets paid for it."

"If the jockey gets a feel of the racetrack, I would say he is in trouble," Jacobs said, "because that means he just fell off the horse."

Runyon, betraying no amusement, paused to take a drag on the cigarette in the holder clenched between his teeth. "I know I'm going to make one of the biggest bets of my life against him," he said. "I fancy the Bradley entry."

Jacobs indeed liked the looks of Blue Larkspur, the morning-line favorite as the better half of E. R. Bradley's two-horse entry, but doubted that the lightly raced colt was ready for the well-conditioned Clyde Van Dusen. "I do not want to influence you,"

Jacobs said tentatively, "but did your foot in the mud have anything to do with it?"

"Absolutely," Runyon replied. "Clyde Van Dusen can't run in deep mud. He can only run in light mud. I am going for the lump on Blue Larkspur."

Jacobs raised his eyebrows and said, "Isn't the mud just as deep for Blue Larkspur as it is for Clyde Van Dusen?"

With that rhetorical quip hanging in the dank air, Jacobs smiled knowingly and took his leave rather than risk alienating such an influential sportswriter.

Up in the press box, as Runyon relayed the conversation he had just had with Jacobs, Howard dismissed the young whippersnapper. "He is trying to sway us with racetrack terminology," Howard scoffed. "A frontrunner like Clyde Van Dusen cannot make it in the mud. Besides, the trainer is a lunatic. Having the horse named after him. Go with quality. Go with old-fashioned understatement. Colonel E. R. Bradley." To reassure themselves, they tracked down Bradley, the nonpareil Kentucky breeder, who praised Blue Larkspur as an excellent prospect that "might even have a chance today." Translating Bradley's racetrack terminology for Runyon, Howard whispered, "He means he'll win by a thousand yards." Nodding, Runyon headed straight for the $100 betting window and plunked down $2,500 in "large, coarse bank notes" on Blue Larkspur.

Returning to the press box, Runyon could only watch forlornly as Clyde Van Dusen kicked mud in everyone's face wire to wire, winning by two lengths and paying off at 3-to-1. By the time Blue Larkspur slogged home a well-beaten fourth as the 3-to-2 favorite, Runyon was already tearing up his betting tickets.

At least he had learned a valuable lesson. Next time, he would heed the advice of the expert horsemen, whether it be a seasoned breeder like E. R. Bradley or a green trainer like Hirsch Jacobs.

* * *

Jacobs had enjoyed his maiden journey to Bluegrass country to take in the Kentucky Derby, even if it was merely as a spectator. He knew he was a long way from ever saddling the kind of stakes horses that Runyon bet on and wrote about, let alone a Derby horse. He had no illusions about being any more than a claiming trainer, one still striving to make a name for himself.

Right after the Derby, he caught the next train home to New York, rushing to get back to the reality of his claimers and the familiar surroundings of Jamaica racetrack. For Jacobs, it was a hectic, eventful spring season. He was busy saddling horses for the Mascia Brothers Stable and, as a public trainer based at Jamaica, he took on a few other clients as well. One of those was Izzy Bieber, who asked if Jacobs wanted to try his hand training a couple of the B. B. Stable horses. In Bieber's mind, it was something of a test run.

Bieber was also hoping that Jacobs could orchestrate another horse transaction for him. Bieber wanted to reacquire Jack Biener, the gelding whose sale Jacobs had brokered the previous summer. Would Jacobs be interested in arranging the purchase from the Mascia brothers?

In the ten months since the original sale, Jacobs had enjoyed some success with Jack Biener. Wintering again in Havana, the trainer had run him half a dozen times at Oriental Park, winning twice. Returning to New York for the spring season, Jack Biener made a triumphant homecoming by winning three straight claiming races for Jacobs in the Mascia colors at Jamaica and Belmont. One of those marked Jacobs's first stakes win, although it seemed only fitting that it was also a claiming race called the Garden City Claiming Stakes. With the gelding on a bit of a hot streak, the sale would prove more costly than Bieber had hoped, but he gave Jacobs carte blanche to make the deal.

As it turned out, Bieber wanted more than Jack Biener—he wanted Hirsch Jacobs himself. Bieber had decided to get Jacobs to train all his horses and manage the B. B. Stable. Not only was Bieber tired of employing multiple trainers to saddle his charges, but he also believed he had finally found just the right up-and-coming horseman to team up with.

Bieber had suspected as much ever since he first met the red-headed lad in Cuba. Not long after that chance encounter the year before, Bieber had told an acquaintance, "When I looked into those baby blue eyes, I knew this was a man who could be trusted."

How badly did Bieber want his new recruit? For openers, he offered Jacobs a 50-50 partnership. More specifically, Bieber offered to provide the capital while Jacobs would contribute the horse sense and training savvy. To close the deal, Bieber offered to buy Mascia's whole string of fourteen horses that Jacobs was campaigning in New York, including Jack Biener. Jacobs was sold, and the deal was struck.

The two men shook hands, launching a partnership that would be far more successful than anyone could have imagined.

CHAPTER 5

STAKING HIS CLAIM

As luck would have it, Jack Biener's first time out for Hirsch Jacobs in the B. B. Stable colors was a disaster. Mere strides into a claiming race on an otherwise beautiful spring day at Belmont Park, the gelding inexplicably veered off course and crashed into a temporary fence, tumbling down a hollow in the infield. The jockey was thrown clear and escaped with minor bruising, but Jack Biener wasn't so lucky. He sustained a severe gash on his fetlock along with deep cuts all over his body and head.

Jacobs rushed into the infield, grabbed the reins, and helped Jack Biener to his feet. He led the gelding back to the barn, where he cleaned, disinfected, and dressed the wounds. Though the injuries weren't career-ending, they would sideline Jack Biener for weeks.

Always one to look on the bright side of things, Jacobs saw the layoff as a chance to deal with an ongoing issue: Jack's poor condition, which seemed to be due to lack of appetite. During the year he had been conditioning the lean gelding, Jacobs had often mused, "If only I could get him to eat more." After observing Jack for a while, Jacobs now concluded that a big part of the problem was nerves and loneliness. His solution was to move Irish Marine, a gelding who ate like a horse, next door to Jack. To make sure that Jack learned something from his new neighbor, Jacobs cut a two-and-a-half-foot square hole in the wall separating them and covered it with chicken wire.

When it was time to grain the horses, he put each one's feed bucket next to the hole so that Jack and Irish could see each other eating. The first time he did it, Irish tore into his grain as was his wont, while Jack just stood by watching. Within a few minutes, Jack started to poke around his feed bucket, picking at the grain. By the time Irish was done with his, Jack was wholeheartedly chowing down. When the groom came by to pick up the feed buckets, Jack's had been licked clean. Jacobs looked at it and smiled to himself.

From that day on, the two horses were stabled next to each other. During the day they would lean against the wall between them, their noses up against the chicken wire, snuffling and occasionally nickering to one another. Over time, Jack perked up and put on weight. He started whinnying for his feed like the rest of the horses in the barn.

The bond between the two geldings grew stronger with every passing day. When Jack and Irish were taken out to be hand grazed on the little grassy patches near the barns, they would tug on their lead ropes, eventually dragging their grooms to a spot where they could be nose to nose as they consumed the grass.

Once Jack's injuries had healed, Jacobs started to condition him again. In full flesh now, Jack showed far more vigor. It seemed like Jack had entered horse heaven. But it was not to last. Jacobs and Bieber had claimed a filly from a trainer named Fred Kraft, who retaliated by claiming Jack out of a race he won for $3,500. Racing for Kraft, the gelding started to drop weight again and his performances suffered. Kraft shipped him to Canada and, over time, entered him in a lower class of claiming races.

One day Jacobs got word that Jack had been entered in a $1,000 claimer with a low price tag at a Canadian track. He phoned his old friend Charlie Ferraro, who was running horses at the same track, and asked him to claim the gelding for B. B. Stable. Given Jack's poor recent performances, there were no other claims for the bony gelding. Ferraro haltered the horse and arranged to have him shipped back down to New York.

When the van arrived at the Jamaica barn, Jacobs grabbed a leather lead and walked up to collect his horse. Jack was barely recognizable. As Jacobs led the now bony and dull-eyed gelding down the ramp, tears glistened in the trainer's eyes.

As they walked toward the barn, Irish Marine, who had been taken out for some hand grazing, looked up. He spotted Jack, snorted, reared up, and bellowed a greeting. Soon he was dragging the groom toward his old friend. Jack instantly perked up and started prancing and jigging on the end of Jacobs's line. He let out a weak neigh and started dragging the trainer toward Irish.

With the two horses rapidly becoming fired up, Jacobs yelled, "Get Irish back in his stall before somebody gets killed!" By the time Jack was in his stall, he was beside himself. He whipped around several times until he spotted the familiar chicken-wire-covered opening and lunged for it, almost pushing his head through the wire. Irish was already waiting there, and within seconds the two had their noses up against each other, snuffling and nickering.

This time, it took longer for Jacobs to fatten up the skinny gelding. But when Jack looked ready, Jacobs entered him in a $2,500 claiming race at Empire City. Jack won it and was shipped for the fall season to Maryland, where he continued his winning ways. In the winter it was off to Cuba, where he won another $2,500 claimer—his twentieth victory for Jacobs—but was claimed by another trainer. The $1,000 purse and the $2,500 claiming price constituted small consolation for his erstwhile trainer.

* * *

The rehabilitation of Jack Biener was typical of the kind of magic Hirsch Jacobs brought to the backside. He seemed to have a sixth sense for figuring out what was holding a horse back, be it physical or psychological, and how to fix the problem, often with an ingenious and innovative solution. Hardened horsemen shook their heads, wondering how a poor city kid could have so quickly developed the ability to turn around horses that others had given up on.

Whenever anyone would ask him directly, Jacobs would simply shrug and say, "There's nothing to the training of horses but common sense. You just got to use common sense and know when a horse feels like running, that's all."

His underlying philosophy was to treat his horses as well as he treated the people around him and to recognize that they were all individuals with their own traits and habits, likes and dislikes. "They're like humans," he explained. "Like people, they're brave or cowardly, gentle or mean, willing or stubborn. You got to baby them and humor them, kid them along." He didn't expect his horses to function like machines, any more than he would his employees. "Horses, like humans, have their good and bad days," he said. "Overwork makes them track-sore, just like ballplayers and fighters go stale. As the saying goes among horsemen, I'd rather have him underdone than overdone. Some horses will stand more work than others. Many of them have to be treated like so much gingerbread, with care and attention, or they crumble in your hands."

With a bigger bankroll now, courtesy of Izzy Bieber, Jacobs was able to claim a higher class of horse. But that didn't change the day-to-day operation of what was still just a claiming stable. He was still acquiring underperformers, quickly diagnosing and fixing their problems, then returning them to the track to run in more claiming races.

It didn't take long for his methods to pay off for the new partnership. Jacobs, who was now handling all the B. B. Stable horses
along with those owned by a couple of individual clients he kept on
out of loyalty, saddled forty winners and earned $39,675 in purses
for 1929, the first year of the partnership. Despite the Black Friday
stock market crash that ushered in the Great Depression and stalled
the racing boom of the prosperous Roaring Twenties, Jacobs's good
fortune improved in 1930 as he won forty-seven races and $50,063
in purses.

That was the year he made a splash by claiming Sun Mission
from the society stable of future governor W. Averell Harriman for
$6,000 out of a race in which the well-bred colt finished last. Jacobs
ran Sun Mission in the colors not of the B. B. Stable but of his big
brother Irving, an eye surgeon who had the wherewithal to dabble
in the racing game by owning a few Thoroughbreds. Sun Mission
had reeled off four straight wins for the Jacobs brothers when the
trainer shipped all his charges up to Saratoga for its annual August
meeting.

Shortly before Sun Mission was scheduled to be led from his stall
to the Saratoga paddock for a $1,000 claiming race in which he
was the heavy morning-line favorite, Jacobs heard him make a pe-
culiar sound and walked over to investigate. Just as he got there,
he spotted a groom exiting the stall. Knowing that the groom had
been recently hired to take care of other Jacobs-trained horses and
had no business being in Sun Mission's stall, the trainer was instantly alarmed. He stepped into the stall to examine the horse and
immediately noticed a bit of sponge protruding from one of Sun
Mission's nostrils. He called the track veterinarian, who used a set
of forceps to extract the sponge that had been stuffed far up the
horse's nose. Though dismayed, Jacobs wasn't especially surprised.
He knew there had recently been an epidemic of "sponging," the

nefarious race-fixing practice in which a sponge was stuffed in a favorite's nostril to impede breathing and retard speed. The stewards, who already suspected the fix was in after a longer shot inexplicably displaced Sun Mission as the heavy favorite, promptly took both horses "Out" of the betting and authorized the track Pinkertons to arrest and prosecute the groom.

Sun Mission, following a disappointing third in that race, bounced back to keep winning for the Jacobses. In all, he would win eighteen races, including a couple of minor stakes, and $30,000 for them. That success went a long way toward the trainer's 1931 winnings of thirty-six races and $42,660. Although those numbers constituted a decline from the previous year, Jacobs couldn't be too discouraged given the Depression's deleterious impact on racing's purses and gate receipts. Bieber, on the other hand, went ballistic at the plunge in the profits he counted on to support his betting habit.

With the B. B. Stable horses mired in a slump during the summer of 1931, Beebee blamed his trainer. That September, when they were racing at Belmont Park, Beebee slipped into the backside barn housing Jacobs's horses late one night and walked four of them over to the barn of the trainer he was planning to replace Jacobs with. The problem was, none of the four actually belonged to Beebee. In fact, they were all owned by Dr. Irving Jacobs, including Sun Mission. When the Jacobs brothers got wind that the horses had been relocated to a new barn, they had Beebee arrested for horse theft.

Beebee insisted that he owned the horses in question and that he had the canceled checks to prove it, but the Jacobses countered that they had paperwork showing that Hirsch had indeed claimed all four in Irving's name. Beebee made bail and returned the four horses to the Jacobses. Not wanting to end up in the middle of an ugly spat, the Jockey Club, racing's governing body, refused to accept entries from either the B. B. Stable or the Jacobses until the matter was resolved. The ban was enough motivation for everyone to cool down and reach an amicable settlement that would allow them to resume racing a week and a half after the incident.

The partnership patched up, the B. B. Stable came back stronger than ever the following year. As for its trainer, Jacobs broke through in 1932 with seventy-three winners, placing him second nationally. His horses won $61,845 in purses that year—a remarkable haul considering they were mostly cheap claimers, but still less than a quarter of what Sunny Jim Fitzsimmons earned to top the annual money list. Despite saddling more winners than Fitzsimmons had, the rising young halterman dared not even dream of being mentioned in the same breath as a revered horseman who had confirmed himself racing's greatest trainer two years earlier by guiding Gallant Fox to history's second Triple Crown and was conditioning stakes horses for two society stables at the same time.

One typical spring afternoon at Jamaica racetrack, Jacobs was busy saddling the horses and Bieber was off betting them. All was fine until Bieber bet big on a couple of "sure things" that weren't and wound up owing the bookmakers $10,000. Once again, he had bet money he didn't have and would need to raise the cash fast so he could settle up in the betting ring as required before the next day's first race.

He was walking out of the track alongside his kid brother Phil, his mind preoccupied with possible schemes to scrounge the ten grand, when he spotted a famous face in the crowd. He nudged his brother and leaned over to whisper, "Look who's in front of us. Jolson. Now keep your mouth shut, and let me do the talking."

Izzy Bieber had known Al Jolson for years, since before the pioneering singer's star turn in the 1927 film *The Jazz Singer*,

Hollywood's first talkie, cemented his fame and fortune as "The World's Greatest Entertainer." Just a few weeks earlier, Bieber had given Jolson a tip on a filly named On Tap, who had been winning regularly for Jacobs and B. B. Stable, and the entertainer made a big bet at fair odds and then a killing when she came in. "I like her," Jolson had told Bieber after cashing in. "She's the kind I'd like to own."

Those words echoed in Bieber's mind now as he called out to Jolson and hurried to catch up. He told Jolson about his betting woes, his big debt, and his need for instant cash. Without waiting for a response, Bieber made his pitch: in exchange for a loan of ten grand, he would transfer On Tap's ownership to Jolson, who would then get to run her in his name until the debt was paid off. Jolson didn't even pause to mull it over. "Give me a pen," he said without missing a beat, "and I'll write you a check."

Bieber hastily dug out a pen, but when Jolson tried to write, it was dry. Bieber borrowed one from a passerby, but it was dry too. The next stranger he approached didn't even have a pen. "That's all!" Jolson blurted, throwing up his hands. "Three tries and no go means hard luck. Forget it." Bieber tried pleading with him, but couldn't budge Jolson from his superstition. "I'm not gonna tempt a three-time fate," Jolson declared, shaking his head as he took his leave.

Sighing at his own continuing run of hard luck, Bieber headed back into Manhattan with his brother for a scheduled appointment at Damon Runyon's Broadway penthouse. When they got there, Bieber regaled Runyon with a blow-by-blow account of his encounter with Jolson. Runyon nodded and offered a solution of his own. "This is Friday," he said, "and Al will surely go to Lindy's for the gefilte fish. He loves it. Let's go there to eat, and you leave him to me. But first I want to make sure my pen is loaded."

They headed down to Lindy's and settled in at Runyon's usual table facing the door. Sure enough, about half an hour later, Jolson made his customary grand entrance and began making the rounds. "Al!" Runyon called out, waving him over.

Jolson slid into the booth and started right in. "Now listen, Dame," he said to Runyon, cocking his head in the Biebers' direction, "these guys must've told you the story. Dame, even you wouldn't go up against a three no-go, so don't ask me to."

"You're absolutely right, Al," Runyon said. "But you had only a two no-go. Only two pens with no ink. The other guy don't count. He had no pen at all. Now listen, I'm going to give you a hell of a column about Al Jolson owning that good mare On Tap." He paused and reached into the inside breast pocket of his suit. "And by the way," he said as he drew his hand back out, "here, try my pen. This is the third try, and it counts."

The Biebers held their breath as Jolson slowly took the pen and began to write. Once again, no ink flowed. The Biebers were cursing the fates, and then, miraculously, the pen started to work. Jolson handed the $10,000 check to Izzy, who blew the ink dry and pocketed it.

Running now in the name of Al Jolson, On Tap won her next time out. As the filly's proud owner of record, Jolson rushed to the Belmont winner's circle and celebrated with Jacobs, his new trainer until Bieber could make good on his marker. "Dame," he told Runyon later, "you had it right. Boy oh boy, what could've happened to me if I'd stopped at two no-go. It would've been a disaster. But please don't tell the Beebs. They don't believe like we do." The Beebs may not have been as superstitious, but they were certainly as thrilled by On Tap's win, especially since Izzy Bieber had bet almost as heavily as Jolson. On Tap would have to run many more times in Jolson's name over the next year before Izzy won enough to pay off the $10,000 loan and reclaim ownership of the trusty filly he had put up as collateral.

Watching Jolson revel in his brief foray into ownership got Runyon thinking he might like having a couple of racehorses of his own. By now, horse racing had become Runyon's favorite sport to watch, to write about, and, of course, to bet on. As much as he had relished covering baseball and boxing through the Golden Age of Sports, he found himself thoroughly captivated by racetrack habitués, from the horses and horsemen to the horseplayers and hustlers. If Broadway was his self-described favorite spot on earth, then Jamaica now ran a close second. Every afternoon in the early spring and late fall, the same familiar crowd that frequented his Broadway stomping grounds migrated the fifteen miles east to Jamaica racetrack. Old Jamaica was a popular hangout for all his Runyonesque sources and subjects, from mobsters like Arnold Rothstein, who had been approached there in his clubhouse box between races to fix the 1919 World Series, to hustlers like Isidor Bieber, who based his B. B. Stable there and had the good sense to partner up with Hirsch Jacobs to put it on the map.

At the very time the Great Depression was bankrupting much of the nation, Runyon found himself rolling in more disposable income than ever, the better to support his burgeoning horse habit. Augmenting his Hearst newspaper salary, Runyon was now regularly publishing the short stories that introduced his indelible Broadway characters in popular magazines like *Collier's*, *Cosmopolitan*, and the *Saturday Evening Post*. He was churning out the magazine stories so prolifically that, just two years after they started appearing alongside those of Hemingway, Faulkner, and Fitzgerald, book publishers were already collecting them into anthologies, starting with 1931's famously titled *Guys and Dolls*.

As Runyon advised in one of those early short stories, "Always try to rub up against money, for if you rub up against money long enough, some of it may rub off on you." In the slang lexicon popularized as Runyonese, money was so important that his Broadway characters and narrators had a wealth of terms to refer to it: "scratch," "dough," "do-re-mi," "sassafras," and his personal favorite, "potatoes." The gamblers, gangsters, and grifters who populated his short stories were always scheming to scrounge up the potatoes that they would invariably squander on slow horses and fast women.

One of those seminal stories, published in the October 1929 issue of *Cosmopolitan*, was "Madame La Gimp," about a Spanish dancer who undergoes a Pygmalion-style makeover in order to pass as a Spanish countess. It was based on a young blonde by the stage name of Patrice Amati Del Grande, a Spanish dancer Runyon had taken up with a few years earlier, made over, and now passed off as a Spanish countess. In reality, Patrice Amati was just a poor eighteen-year-old showgirl from Mexico when the forty-five-year-old Runyon spotted her dancing at the Silver Slipper, a mob-run Times Square nightclub he frequented. Soon he was squiring the blond bombshell along Broadway, ultimately leaving his wife and two children to move into a penthouse apartment with this mistress half his age. In the summer of 1932, eight months after his estranged wife drank herself to death, he married Patrice in a civil ceremony performed by his friend Jimmy Walker, the New York City mayor who weeks later would resign in disgrace and flee the country to avoid prosecution for a corruption scandal.

By that time, Columbia Pictures had bought the screen rights to "Madame La Gimp," which Frank Capra made into *Lady for a Day*, the 1933 hit film that brought the acclaimed director his first Academy Award nomination. "Madame La Gimp" would be the first of many Damon Runyon short stories that Hollywood would adapt for the silver screen, providing him a lucrative new source of income.

Runyon could now afford to give his beloved Patrice whatever her heart desired. She wanted a winter retreat in the Florida sunshine, so he built her a big white house on Miami's Hibiscus Island overlooking Biscayne Bay in the state he branded "the land of sand in your shoes." She wanted to rub up against old money, so he escorted her almost every afternoon to his clubhouse box at Hialeah Park, the breathtaking new Miami racetrack that had displaced Havana's Oriental Park as the fashionable winter mecca for the horsey set. On top of all that, she wanted to have some racehorses of her own, so he promised to look into starting a racing stable in her name.

And he knew just the man to consult about starting a stable, a kindred spirit with years of experience both owning and playing the ponies: his old Broadway buddy Beeb. When Runyon broached the subject, Beeb proudly took him on a tour of the B. B. Stable setup and formally introduced him to the affable young trainer he had partnered up with. So positive was Runyon's first impression of Jacobs's ready smile and winning ways that there was never any question of hiring any other trainer for his prospective stable.

One morning when everyone was down in Florida as usual for the winter racing season, Runyon called Beeb with an invitation to spend the afternoon with him at his home on Hibiscus Island. Runyon wanted to discuss some matters with Beeb, including the logistics of getting a racing stable up and running. Beeb dispatched his kid brother Phil to Hialeah Park to place their bets on the horses Jacobs was racing in the B. B. Stable colors and then got a ride from a friend over to Hibiscus Island for his meeting with Runyon.

At the track that afternoon, Phil was telling a friend that he needed a lift to Runyon's house after the races so he could pick up his brother Izzy when, suddenly, he felt a tap on his shoulder. Phil wheeled around to see that the hand belonged to none other than Al Capone. At the sight of America's most notorious gangster, Phil's heart skipped a beat.

"Little Beeb," Capone said, "you need a lift to Runyon's? I'll take you. I live near there on Palm Island. I'd like to see Runyon. He writes a good story and I'd like to talk to him. OK?"

Little Beeb nodded and managed to stammer out a "Y-y-yes." Having second thoughts a moment later, he broke into a cold sweat and hustled over to the racing secretary's office so he could phone Runyon. Even though Runyon knew the mob boss well and had socialized with him often at the sprawling Palm Island estate, it occurred to Little Beeb that the writer might not welcome a surprise visit from the subject of a recent column wherein "your correspondent cheerfully yields the palm he has borne with distinction for lo these many years as the world's worst horseplayer to Mr. Alphonse Capone." Little Beeb was calling just to make sure that it would indeed be OK to bring the gangster over to Runyon's. "Phil," Runyon replied, "get him over here! I'd love to have a talk with him."

After the last race, a friend of Little Beeb's spotted him getting into Capone's bulletproof car with a chauffeur and bodyguard. "Hey, Beeb," the friend yelled, "where the hell you going?"

Just then, Capone leaned out the window and answered before Little Beeb could. "I'm taking this guy for a ride," Capone cracked, laughing loud and hard. "But don't worry. He'll be coming back."

Over a sumptuous dinner at Runyon's house, the brothers Bieber enjoyed the banter between the infamous gangster and the famous writer who had made his bones uncovering the under-world. Late that night, as Capone's chauffeur drove the Biebers back to their modest winter home in Miami Beach, Little Beeb told his brother the whole story of how the dinner with the mob boss had come about. "Well, Phil," Izzy replied nonchalantly, "what next?"

CHAPTER 6

KING OF THE CLAIMERS

Each year, Hirsch Jacobs would ship his stable up to Yonkers for Empire City Race Track's summer and fall meetings. After settling his horses into their stalls at Empire City, he would walk across the street from the track and rent his usual room in a nearby boardinghouse. It was in the family home of Joseph Dushock, a Czech immigrant who owned and operated a small Yonkers bottling company. The Dushocks—Joseph, his wife, Josephine, and their three children—lived on the lower floor of the two-family shotgun home on Clark Street and rented out the rooms on the upper floor to boarders during the racing seasons.

One summer evening not long after he first started boarding there, Hirsch knocked on the Dushocks' door and asked Josephine if he could use their telephone to call his mother. She invited him in, and as they walked to the kitchen so he could use the phone, he noticed the Dushocks' eldest daughter, Ethel, doing dishes at the sink. Hirsch took in her dark hair and fine features, and was immediately drawn to the brown-eyed beauty. Ethel, looking up from the dishes for a moment, noted the young man's bright red hair, baby face, and easy, inviting smile. As he spoke on the phone, she couldn't help but listen in. She quickly realized he was talking to his mother and thought he sounded like a sweet guy. When he hung up after making sure all was well with his family back home in Brooklyn, he introduced himself to Ethel and they started to chat.

Because he called his mom every evening, his kitchen chats with Ethel became just as regular an occurrence. In the two short weeks he roomed there that summer, Hirsch grew close to Ethel. They shared their life stories and talked about their dreams. This was 1930, when he was a twenty-six-year-old horse trainer on the rise and she a twenty-year-old bookkeeper at the Yonkers Trust bank.

Finally, he got up the nerve to ask her out. Although Ethel had grown up just a horseshoe's toss from Empire City, she had never been to the races until Hirsch asked her to join him at the track on a Saturday. She liked it enough to go back there with him a couple of times, but she was happier when Hirsch eventually asked her to see a movie with him.

At the end of his stay in Yonkers that summer, Hirsch asked Ethel if she would continue seeing him even after he went back to his family's home in Brooklyn. She said yes, a response that would have distressed her parents if they had overheard the conversation. They had always assumed that Ethel would meet and marry a nice Catholic boy, and this relationship with Hirsch was making that look less likely. They were relieved when he left, figuring Ethel would now have a chance to meet someone else.

That fall, when he was busy racing at Aqueduct, Belmont, and Jamaica, he started asking her to meet him for dates in Manhattan. They would catch dinner and a movie, after which he would give her a $20 bill for cab fare back to Yonkers. It would have been impossible for him to have escorted her up to Yonkers (north of New York City), taken the subway all the way down to Brooklyn, and gotten any sleep before having to rise by dawn to get to the track. Ethel understood, knowing how much his work and horses meant to him. She was also a very practical girl. Once he was out of sight, she would stuff the twenty in her purse and then walk to the nearest subway.

They had been dating for nearly three years when Hirsch decided it was time to propose. Ethel said yes, with one condition: any children the couple might have would be brought up Catholic. Hirsch had no problem with that. Although he was Jewish, he wasn't religious. Emboldened, Ethel made one more request: Would Hirsch be willing to convert to Catholicism? That was one step too far. He dismissed the suggestion by quipping, "If they go to the moon and a Catholic greets them, that's the day I'll become a convert."

When Ethel shared the news with her parents, they were horrified—even after she reassured them that any future grandchildren would be brought up as Catholics. They enlisted the help of their parish priest to convince her that marrying out of her faith would be a terrible mistake. Ethel wasn't convinced, and she was deeply in love with Hirsch. So she made a plan with her kid sister, Frances, to catch a train down to Florida, where Hirsch was racing for the winter.

On December 21, 1933, Ethel and Hirsch were married in a Miami civil ceremony by a county judge. There was no time for a honeymoon, though, because Hirsch had to get back to work. The very next morning, he was at the racetrack saddling his horses as usual.

The wedding put an exclamation point on the single most momentous year of Hirsch Jacobs's young life. It had begun auspiciously with the emergence of his first trophy-winning stakes horse. Character, a short, scrawny gelding he had claimed for $2,500 the previous fall at Empire City, reeled off seven straight wins to start his three-year-old campaign—including two stakes at Hialeah Park. So unaccustomed were the B. B. Stable partners to stakes racing that when the owner was presented with the gleaming silver cup in the Hialeah winner's circle after Character had captured the Bahamas Handicap by a head, Izzy Bieber dropped it. Not to worry, the magic touch Jacobs had shown with the coarse little claimer promised many more trips to the winner's circle for the butterfingered Bieber to get the hang of it.

Back at Empire City that October, Jacobs saddled his one hundredth winner of the year, thereby garnering his first blush of acclaim as only the third "century trainer" in the annals of Thoroughbred racing. The milestone elevated the young city slicker into the rarefied century company of two Western horsemen: H. Guy Bedwell, the aptly nicknamed "Hard Guy" who in 1919 forged Sir Barton from irascible loser into history's first Triple Crown winner, and Cowboy Charlie Irwin, the Wild West showman whose exploits riding alongside Teddy Roosevelt and Buffalo Bill Cody made him an American legend long before he saddled a record 147 winners in 1923. As if joining the century club were not enough for Hirsch Jacobs to make a name for himself and shock the racing establishment, he went on to close out his banner year by claiming the title of 1933's winningest trainer in America.

On the last racing day in December, right after posting his 116th and final win of the year, Jacobs ran into Damon Runyon at Tropical Park, the new Miami racetrack that the New York bootlegger Big Bill Dwyer had built as a no-frills answer to Hialeah for the proletariat of hardcore horseplayers. Jacobs was there training horses not only for the fast-growing B. B. Stable, but also for Runyon's fledgling string. Runyon warmly greeted Jacobs with congratulations on his week-old marriage. Then Runyon congratulated him on clinching the title of the nation's winningest trainer for 1933 and becoming "one of the all-time horse racing champs of the American turf."

Now that his trainer had risen to the top, the writer worried that Jacobs might drop some of his smaller clients like the Runyons. In fact, ever the hard-nosed reporter, Runyon knew for a fact that Jacobs had recently been approached by several "rich stables" with offers to pay top dollar for his exclusive training services.

"You ought to make a lot of money now," Runyon observed.

Jacobs smiled and shook his head. "That wouldn't interest me," he replied matter-of-factly. "I've never wanted to make a lot of money. I guess I'm pretty lucky that I was born that way. A lot of money wouldn't make me any happier than I am now. I want just enough to live on comfortably, and I've got that. And I've got my health. A lot of money wouldn't add a thing to my life as I live it."

Runyon listened, too dumbfounded to respond, as Jacobs continued to impart his philosophy of life and making a living. Given the crowd Runyon ran with, he had never heard anyone talk like this with a straight face. Then again, the Great Depression had just hit its nadir, America reeled under a record 25 percent unemployment rate, and Jacobs, having grown up poor, counted himself among the luckiest. His horses had earned $76,965 in 1933 prize money, from which he got to keep 50 percent of all the B. B. Stable purses as well as the standard 10 percent trainer's commission of his individual clients' winnings. Still, Jacobs harbored no illusions of being anything but a halterman training a stable full of claimers—including Character, whose two stakes wins earned barely $2,000 each. There would be no rich society stables in Jacobs's foreseeable future, no Kentucky Derby horses, no major stakes winners. He was happy simply training claimers for B. B. Stable and for a handful of individual clients including the Runyons.

"I'm perfectly content to go along with the way I am now," he assured Runyon. "To be with the horses, and to be more or less my own master, and to win a race now and then. I envy no man, and I ask nothing better than I've got now. I get lots of pleasure out of life. I've got many friends. The world is very pleasant. Why should I give up contentment for a lot of money?"

Runyon could think of no answer to this, offhand. That left Jacobs to break the silence by excusing himself so he could go saddle another claimer in the next race.

A few days later, in his first syndicated column of the New Year, Runyon introduced this different breed of trainer to the general public. "I have at last found a man who seems to have the ideal philosophy of life," Runyon began the column. "He is a trainer of racehorses, and his name is Hirsch Jacobs. We have never met another man who so sincerely loves a horse." After regaling his readers with The Pigeon Man's unlikely path from rooftop coops to backside barns, Runyon concluded: "The manly art of racing pigeons is unknown to those parts of the country that produced 'Doc' Bedwell and 'Cowboy Charlie,' but it is quite popular in Hirsch Jacobs's home country. They say he uses some of the same methods in training horses that he applied to the pigeons. I am inclined to doubt that story. I imagine Hirsch Jacobs's success with the gallopers is due to the fact that he has a genius for training horses, as the late Tod Sloan had a genius for riding 'em, and that sort of genius is born, not acquired."

Spending more and more time around Jacobs, Runyon got to witness that firsthand. Other newspapermen found Jacobs a tough interview—not because he was anything other than gracious, but rather because he was by nature reserved and modest. When he was approached by the turf writer from his hometown paper, the *Brooklyn Daily Eagle*, Jacobs at first politely declined an interview request by explaining, "It would seem as though I was trying to show off, to make capital out of a little bit of success that I've had here." While most reporters found Jacobs to be the polar opposite of his querulous and quotable partner, Bieber, Runyon was able to break through by employing the same fly-on-the-wall powers of observation that had gained him inside access to tight-lipped mobsters. Runyon had made a point of hanging out with Jacobs as much as he could—right from the day they had begun a partnership of their own the previous summer at Saratoga.

For anyone with plenty of money to drop on top racing prospects, the Saratoga Sale was *the* place to go shopping. In the cool of the evening every summer since 1917, Fasig-Tipton, the venerable Thoroughbred auction house, sold the most royally bred Kentucky yearlings to the most royally bred American aristocrats. "The world's biggest crapshoot," Fasig-Tipton called its annual Saratoga Sale. For Damon Runyon, a betting man known to drop $800 in an hour playing craps at the Saratoga casinos, that kind of gamble proved irresistible. Even though odds heavily favored crapping out, everyone dreamed of being the next Sam Riddle, who was a relative neophyte to Thoroughbred ownership in 1918 when he bid $5,000 for a strapping chestnut yearling he would name Man o' War.

In the summer of 1933, Patrice and Damon Runyon went shopping for their first horse at the Saratoga yearling sale. They came armed with their checkbook, their Derby dreams, and their newly hired trainer, Hirsch Jacobs. Seated among regular bidders like the Whitneys and the Vanderbilts, Runyon discovered what it felt like to rub up against old money. He sounded pleasantly surprised to report in his column, "They are nice people, these Whitneys. There is nothing snobbish about any of them." Nevertheless, for someone always more at ease in the company of Runyonesque characters like his old Broadway buddy Beeb, he couldn't help feeling out of place among the society stables' blue-blooded owners. Neither could Jacobs, who was used to shopping for all his horses not in the sales ring but rather in the claim box.

Prancing into the Saratoga sales ring that evening came a filly whose chestnut coat gleamed like gold under the arc lights. Glancing around as she was being led in, the yearling's bright eyes soon locked on to those of Jacobs and the Runyons. Jacobs was instantly struck by her laidback shoulder, her powerful hindquarters, her rippling thigh muscles. At the same time, Patrice Runyon was taken by her beauty and her graceful, almost dainty, prancing. Both Runyons looked toward Jacobs, who nodded his approval. Had this auction been held before the Depression had deflated bloodstock prices, the trainer figured his clients would have been lucky to get her for $5,000. When the hammer fell at the bargain-basement price of $700, Jacobs and the Runyons were as surprised as they were elated.

Approaching their new acquisition, the Runyons were immediately won over by her sweet disposition. "Angelic," Patrice described it. The name stuck. Whenever visitors would ask Jacobs how Angelic got her name, he'd lead them right into the docile filly's stall and say simply, "Just look at her."

Sweet disposition notwithstanding, Angelic would pose a novel challenge for a claiming trainer. Instead of claiming a racehorse that another trainer had already broken and developed, Jacobs would have to start Angelic himself. In the morning works, she was relaxed and would always trounce Jacobs's most promising colt. But in the afternoon races, running in the orchid and scarlet colors of the Runyon stable, she seemed unnerved. She lost her debut as a two-year-old in January 1934 at Hialeah and, after breaking her maiden her second time out, had to survive a harrowing scare before she could even start her third race.

After prancing around the Hialeah track in the post parade, Angelic was still fidgeting in the starting gate. As the rest of the field was being loaded into the gate, she suddenly lost her footing, fell in her starting stall, and became wedged with her feet in the air. Jacobs rushed over. After the three long minutes it took to get her back on her feet, Jacobs examined her and found nothing worse than a superficial cut near her hock. He glanced up at the clubhouse boxes and noticed Runyon going through "the agony of hell." Only when Jacobs loaded Angelic back into her starting stall did Runyon feel reassured enough to breathe a sigh of relief. Noticing that Patrice still looked distressed, Runyon took a moment to set her mind at ease. "He is a most humane man," Runyon told her. "He will not run a horse that has the slightest thing wrong with it."

When the race finally got under way, Angelic rewarded her trainer's faith, charging from behind to put her nose in front at the wire. She went on to capture the Kindergarten Stakes at Bowie and the Youthful Stakes at Jamaica that spring, defeating better-bred juveniles from society stables owned by the likes of the Whitneys. Jacobs praised Angelic as the best horse he had ever trained. She was his personal favorite, the only horse that made him nervous when she went to the post and that brought him up rooting during the race. He and the Runyons all figured they had something special when they shipped her to Saratoga that summer for its annual meeting.

Every day after supper that August, Runyon would stroll over to the Saratoga stables with Patrice on his arm to look admiringly at Angelic, to gaze with awe at all the other Thoroughbreds in the B. B. barn, and to "sit around in the cool of the evening gassing about horses." As parsimonious as Jacobs normally was with his words, this was the one topic Runyon could draw him out with. "Horses are his whole life," the writer observed. "He talks of little else."

When Jacobs wasn't talking about horses, he was talking *to* them. He did so in that soft, soothing voice of his, in a language that was foreign to Runyon.

"I am sure Hirsch Jacobs talks to horses," Runyon insisted in his column. "Hirsch is a very mild and gentlemanly chap and his approach to the horses in conversation is the sympathetic, especially when he is trying to find out what ails them. I have eavesdropped on him around the stables many a time and heard him soft-soaping those equine characters. He generally wins their confidence and learns all their troubles. I do not say that they up and tell him, understand. No, I do not say that, because it is something I cannot prove, inasmuch as Hirsch Jacobs himself denies there is any open banter between him and his horses. But if they do not tell him, who does?"

One sunny afternoon at Empire City, shortly before a race in which the B. B. Stable horse was the favorite, a pigeon fluttered down from the rafters of the grandstand and fell clumsily near a bench where Hirsch Jacobs was sitting. Observing that the bird appeared injured, exhausted, and terrified by the crowd, Jacobs rose and walked softly over to it, all the while making the same cooing sounds with which he used to soothe his own pigeons. When he leaned over and reached down, the frightened bird allowed him to pick it up. By the band on its leg, Jacobs could tell it was a racing pigeon. He could also tell it had suffered a broken leg. Forgetting for the moment the horse race that had just begun, Jacobs tore his handkerchief into strips for a bandage and, using matchsticks for splints, wrapped the bird's leg to set the fracture. Then he gently carried it back to his stable and fixed up a cage for it. He kept the pigeon around the stable and fed it for a few weeks as its leg healed. When it was strong enough to fly away, he released it.

This was the same kind of amateur doctoring that The Pigeon Man was known to perform with the racehorses in his charge.

It was said that Jacobs could take one look at a horse he was thinking of claiming and see things wrong with it that even a veterinarian couldn't find on examination. One time a client of his bought a colt for $5,000 in a private sale before Jacobs had a chance to examine him. Later, when the colt arrived at the barn, Jacobs took one look at him from six feet away and told the new owner, "You made a bad buy. That horse is going to go lame." When the colt did, as Jacobs predicted, the owner had to sell him off for a $3,000 loss.

Jacobs's perceptiveness made him a master diagnostician. Once he took possession of a horse after a claiming race, he would lead his acquisition to his barn and stand in its new stall, leaning against the wall and observing it silently. He was already trying to discern any issues that might have been holding the horse back. It wouldn't take long for Jacobs to diagnose the problem, be it lameness, neglect, emotional distress, or some other affliction.

Then the trainer would proceed to work his healing magic with a combination of home remedies and equine psychoanalysis that he would shrug off as simple "common sense." If a horse wasn't eating, Jacobs would move it next door to one that actually ate like a horse. If a horse seemed lonely, he would find another one to share the stall. If a horse appeared nervous around others, he would remove it to a remote stall for some peace and quiet. If a horse was lame, he would reach into his bag of home remedies for special mudpacks, compresses, salves, liniments, vinegar, even the white iodine he might have just used to cure a troublesome corn on his own foot.

Many of his therapies were ahead of their time. One winter in Florida, he carted some of his charges to the beach every day and made them swim in the surf for hours. His theory was that exercise in the salt water would strengthen their muscles without the damage that could come from galloping on hard ground. Beyond that, the change of scenery might improve the temperaments of the more fractious ones. After two weeks of this hydrotherapy, they returned to the racetrack refreshed and winning more than ever.

Skeptical veterinarians would shake their heads at Jacobs's unconventional treatments and wonder, "Why are you doing *that*?"

"Because," he'd reply matter-of-factly, "it works."

His magic touch spurred racetrackers to saddle Jacobs with a backhanded compliment of a moniker: "the voodoo veterinarian." Any time a horse in his barn got sick or injured, he personally attended to the doctoring. At a time when there were few actual vets working at the track, trainers needed a knowledge of basic medicine so they themselves could treat ailing horses. Jacobs was more studious than many of his counterparts, poring over every book he could find on veterinary science. He was proud of his ability to perform minor operations by himself. He had plenty of opportunities to practice what he'd learned, given the type of cheap, and often broken down, claimers that populated his stable.

Jacobs's confidence in his methods—both conventional and innovative—enabled him to turn around horses that everyone else had given up on.

When Octaroro, a son of Man o' War trained by Jacobs, came up lame, the owner tried to sell him before the stable shipped south to Florida for the winter, but could find no buyers. "Then give him away," a vet advised the owner. "That horse will never run again."

When the owner couldn't even find anyone to take Octaroro for free, Jacobs suggested, "We may as well take the horse to Florida."

"You're crazy," the vet snorted. "He won't be worth his keep."

"You're probably right," Jacobs admitted, "but you can't sell him;

you can't give him away. May as well bring him along with the string. We might be able to do something with him."

In Florida, Jacobs let Octaroro just laze around, taking him out for occasional hand walks and patiently waiting for the day that the horse might bloom again. One day, as Jacobs watched the chestnut gelding walk by, he said, "That horse looks pretty good to me. Let's enter him." When Jacobs started galloping him, it was clear that Octaroro's mini-vacation had paid off. Raring to race, Octaroro rewarded his trainer's patience and persistence with four wins inside a month, including a Hialeah track record for a mile and a sixteenth on turf.

What made Jacobs more successful is that he knew not only when to run a horse but also when to scratch one, when to sell one, when to retire one. When Angelic went lame late in her two-year-old season after winning half of her fourteen starts and $8,505, he gently let the Runyons know it was time to retire their pride and joy.

Jacobs would personally examine every one of his horses several times a day. In the evening after the day's races, he would make a final check, carefully looking over all his charges. If he found an ailing horse on that last check, it was not out of the ordinary to find him sitting up at night with the patient.

Each morning upon arriving at the track, he would check out the condition of the racing surface. He would take the penknife that he always carried in his pocket and stick the blade into the dirt to determine that day's track condition. If the knife didn't go very deep into the dirt, it meant the surface might be too hard; if it went in too far, it meant the track had been harrowed too deep. Either way, if he determined the conditions might risk his horses' safety, he would scratch them. Regardless of the track conditions, if any horse seemed off in any way, he would scratch it without hesitation—or at least he'd try to.

One fall morning in 1933, Jacobs arrived at Empire City planning to send The Heathen, a nine-year-old campaigner who had won several stakes in his prime, out for the second race. But when the trainer ran his hands down the horse's legs during his customary prerace examination, he discovered a hot and swollen tendon. He immediately went to the racing secretary's office and filled out the scratch slip required to formally withdraw an entrant. "The horse's tendon has filled," Jacobs told the track judge, "and if I run him, he's a sure thing for a breakdown." Because The Heathen was among the top two favorites in the betting, the judge had to dispatch the official track veterinarian to examine him.

When Jacobs returned to the racing secretary's office a while later, he found the judge consulting with the vet, Dr. Clarence Richards. "Is the horse excused?" the trainer asked.

"No," the judge replied. "Doctor Richards says there is nothing the matter with the horse."

"There is nothing the matter with the horse?!" Jacobs exclaimed incredulously. "Why, the horse's tendon is filled. If I run him, he'll break down. You excuse the horse, I will turn him out and will not race him anymore this year. Please, let that horse out."

Dr. Richards cut in. "Why, I was over at the barn," the vet said, "and the man, the groom of the horse, said there is nothing the matter with the horse, that he is no different than he has been."

"If that groom told you that," Jacobs retorted, "he is a darn liar and I am going back and fire him."

Jacobs stormed out and returned to his barn to query the groom. As it turned out, the vet had never even examined the horse's legs when he briefly stopped by the barn. Incensed, Jacobs continued pleading his case to the stewards. "Well, the horse has got to run," the head steward decreed with an air of finality.

Now that the time had come to lead The Heathen to the paddock for saddling, Jacobs had no choice but to follow the ruling. He held his breath while watching The Heathen thunder down the stretch in front only to be overtaken at the wire by a nose. His heart sank as he saw the horse come up lame a few jumps past the finish line. The Heathen gingerly limped back to the barn, where he would spend weeks confined to his stall. Finally, he had to be shipped down to the farm and turned out for rest and recovery.

As disturbed as Jacobs felt over the whole incident, his partner, the ever-belligerent Bieber, was incensed. Bieber dashed off a letter to the Jockey Club demanding that Dr. Richards, the governing body's veterinary adviser, be fired for incompetence and unfitness: "Dr. Richards, quack, Canadian draft dodger, liar and assassin of good men's character, may yet wind up as their official veterinarian in the Federal jail at Atlanta," Bieber wrote. For good measure, Bieber also called Richards "a drug fiend."

Nobody was shocked when Richards filed a $175,000 defamation lawsuit against Bieber. The jury found for the plaintiff, but awarded Richards damages of just six cents. For a plunger like Bieber who had once lost $120,000 on a single bet, that sounded like a win.

Of all the idiosyncrasies that distinguished The Pigeon Man from his fellow racetrackers, there was one that especially baffled them: he didn't bet.

It wasn't always that way. As a teen, Hirsch Jacobs placed small side bets on his racing pigeons; and as a young halterman breaking in to the business in his twenties, he occasionally wagered as much as $500 on his horses because that's how most Thoroughbred trainers supplemented their earnings in those days.

Then came the time he confidently bet $100 on one of his horses to win at Havana's Oriental Park. Not only did that horse proceed to lose, but it also didn't even finish in the money. Jacobs resolved, then and there, never to bet heavily again. "I can't beat the horses," he decided, muttering the same lament as countless horseplayers. "I don't see how anyone can."

Even though he had won more of those wagers than he'd lost, he came to realize that betting and training were not as compatible as his counterparts thought they were. "I wouldn't run half as many horses if I knew I was betting on them," he would explain. "I'd always be thinking that maybe something I hadn't figured on would come up and beat me, and I'd get scared and scratch out of the race. The way it is now, I got nothing to worry about if a horse fools me." Besides, the way he looked at it, he had already made the biggest gamble of them all before he even took possession of any of his horses: "I bet on them by claiming them," he would quip.

He resolved to derive a surer, if more modest, income from prize money won by the horses he conditioned. "It's the purse that pays the freight, not wagers," he liked to say.

On those rare occasions when he did wager on a race before he swore off betting altogether in the late '30s when the horse he picked to win and place came in third, it was never more than $2. That was only fitting, since Jacobs reigned as the favorite of the $2 bettors. Their axiom, heard around all the New York tracks, was to "get out with Jacobs"—that is, to save a losing day by betting one of his horses. Because he stood to make nothing from betting and instead relied on purses to make a living, horseplayers banked on the conviction that he would never send a horse to the post that wasn't fit, ready to race, and trying its best to win. The $2 horseplayers took to calling him "Always Trying Jacobs."

In a sport swarming with unsavory bookmakers, touts, fixers, mobsters, and the like, Jacobs stood out as incorruptible, his integrity beyond reproach. Never was that clearer than the time, a few years earlier, when the owner of a horse he was training approached him with a moneymaking proposition. Before a race that the horse was heavily favored to win, the owner asked Jacobs, "How is the mare?"

"She's got a chance," Jacobs replied matter-of-factly.

"She's got a chance?!" the owner snorted. "Why, she can't lose! The bookies have her at four-to-five." The owner glanced around furtively and then leaned in to whisper, "Hirsch, if that mare should lose, we could win a nice bet on the second choice."

Jacobs shot him a cold stare. "I'd rather win a race than a bet!" the trainer growled.

The mare won by five lengths, and word soon got around that Jacobs couldn't be bought. No owner ever again suggested that Jacobs throw a race. Whenever a horseplayer would try to pump him for inside information on a horse Jacobs was running that day, the trainer would respond with the same stock answer he had given that owner: "He's got a chance."

Jacobs's stance was all the more remarkable since his owners were such big bettors that they often stood to make more from wagers on their horses than from purses. That was especially true of Jacobs's own partner, who was the biggest plunger Damon Runyon had ever known at the racetrack. "Jacobs never bets a dime; Bieber bets all he can," the writer marveled. "Oddly enough, Bieber does not always bet on his own horses. He has very decided opinions on races, and often in a race in which he has a horse running, he will bet on something else, only to see his own horse win and at big odds. That always tickles Jacobs. No one but Bieber himself ever knows how much he is betting on a race, not even Jacobs. He never tells Jacobs how much he bets, and Jacobs never asks. He considers betting a waste of money, but he does not attempt to convert Bieber to his theory. He knows it wouldn't do any good."

Not that Bieber's stubbornness deterred Jacobs from bad-mouthing the habit. Jacobs considered gambling to be the worst vice a man could have. "You can only smoke so many cigarettes till you run out; you can only drink so much till you pass out; but with gambling, there's no limit," he would preach. "You can gamble everything you have and then you can gamble what you don't have. You can lose your house; you can lose your family; you can lose everything."

It wasn't unusual for Bieber to gamble what he didn't have. When he would get himself deep into debt, his first inclination was to bail himself out by raiding the B. B. Stable account. Every so often, Jacobs would catch his partner trying to take money out of the stable's coffers to pay off his gambling debts. That always led to heated arguments between the two partners. When those rows happened over the phone, Ethel would go around the Jacobs house shutting all the windows so the neighbors couldn't hear her husband screaming at his partner. No matter how loud Beeb protested, he always lost the argument.

Despite their differences, Bieber and Jacobs usually got along fine, and the stable kept running like clockwork and racking up the wins. In 1934, Jacobs led all trainers in number of wins for the second straight year, upping his total to 127 while earning $113,055 in purses. That made him the first trainer ever to reach the "century" mark in successive years, an assault on the record book that stunned the racing establishment. If anything could have shocked the establishment more that year, it was B. B. Stable leading the national owners' standings in wins for the first time.

Now that B. B. Stable had reached the top, Izzy Bieber, nearing fifty and balding, decided it was time to shed that hated Kid Beebee nickname once and for all. One sunny Miami afternoon, Bieber, Jacobs, and Runyon congregated in the winner's circle to celebrate a stakes victory. While the governor of Florida was making his way down to the winner's circle to present the trophy, Bieber got a sudden inspiration. He leaned over to Runyon and whispered, "Damon, ask the governor to make me a colonel on his staff. If I'm a colonel, maybe people won't call me Kid Beebee anymore." Runyon, knowing full well that Beebee had come out of the army after World War I as a buck private, smiled and nodded. Right after the presentation ceremony, Runyon put the question to Governor David Sholtz, who said he would be happy to oblige.

From that moment on, Beebee always insisted on being addressed as Colonel Bieber. While some people did stop calling him Kid Beebee, plenty did not, and he would curse whenever he saw the infernal old nickname crop up as it often did in the New York papers.

Of course, his name was so ubiquitous in the papers only because Jacobs kept on saddling winner after winner. In 1935, Jacobs saddled 114 of them, topping the national trainers' list for the third straight year while earning $95,155 in purses. Leave it to Damon Runyon to get the last word on the significance of that achievement in his year-end column: "They used to dismiss Hirsch Jacobs as an accident. Now racing men generally agree he is one of the greatest trainers that ever lived."

CHAPTER 7

THE WINNINGEST
TRAINER EVER

By the spring of 1936, Hirsch Jacobs was well on his way to having his best year—in fact, the best year any trainer had ever had. He was racking up wins at a clip reminiscent of the way Babe Ruth had swatted home runs a decade earlier to put the single-season record beyond the reach of mere mortals. Jacobs was on pace not only to break the all-time record of 147 annual winners, but also to smash it to smithereens. That May, the unassuming trainer confided to friends that he expected to saddle 180 winners by year's end, an uncharacteristically bold prediction that betrayed his cloaked ambition.

What made his assault on the record book all the more remarkable was the way he was doing it. Whereas Cowboy Irwin had set the mark mainly at bush tracks out West and south of the border in 1923, Jacobs was chasing it at the best tracks against the stiffest competition in the cauldron of the New York, Florida, and Maryland racing circuits. What's more, Jacobs was doing it with his usual assortment of worn-out and crippled-up claiming horses he had bought on the cheap and then rejuvenated.

Most notable among them was his greatest reclamation project yet. At an auction that May, Jacobs bought a seven-year-old steeplechaser with a damaged tendon and a rank temperament. Though he paid just $1,000 for Action, people wondered whether the trainer had taken leave of his senses bidding anything on an ornery has-been that had been sidelined the past ten months by a bowed tendon. He decided to convert the gimpy steeplechaser into a flat runner and, nine days after buying him, entered him in a $900 claiming race over a mile with no jumps. Action's eight-length romp surprised everyone, including his trainer, who expressed relief that the stallion's age and iffy legs had apparently scared off any potential claimants at the $1,500 price tag. Jacobs kept sending him into cheap claimers every few days, dissuading interested parties by stepping up the price tag from $1,500 to $2,500 to $4,000 to $5,000, and Action kept winning them easily.

After half a dozen claiming wins, Jacobs opted to step him up into the tough handicap division where the better performers must carry more weight. Once Action had won a couple of lower-level handicaps, Jacobs stepped him up again, this time into stakes company. Stunning everyone in the 1936 Aqueduct Handicap, Action charged from last place to overtake the leaders and hold off the heavily favored Rosemont, who in 1935 had beaten both Discovery, the Horse of the Year, and Omaha, the Triple Crown winner. Proving that the upset wasn't a fluke, Action captured two more prestigious New York handicaps in rapid succession. In all, he won eleven of his thirteen starts and more than $22,000 in purses for Jacobs that year. Newspaper headlines hailed Action as the "Wonder Horse" and Jacobs as the "Miracle Man."

The miracle man seemed to have a barnful of wonder horses. Amagansett, another geriatric jumper whose surliness and fractiousness had spurred his exasperated owner to dump him in a $1,000 claimer, stopped sulking in Jacobs's hands and proceeded to win eleven races and $11,000 that year. And there were dozens more success stories where those came from. For Jacobs, standard operating procedure was to claim a losing horse once it dropped down into the cheapest price range, rest it for a couple of days, then run it back to win a richer claiming race.

But it wasn't just that second- and third-rate horses turned into overnight sensations under his Midas touch; it was that horses consistently winning for Jacobs conversely fell apart virtually overnight when they were claimed by other trainers. Typical of this pattern was Shot and Shell, who won successive races for him that summer, including the one out of which he was claimed away. The gelding debuted for his new owner with a last-place finish four days later and failed to win again for months. His stablemate Night Raven, after being claimed away from Jacobs out of a victorious race, would never finish in the money again. Soon Jacobs's rivals were shying away from claiming his horses at cheap prices because they assumed he had already "squeezed all the juice out of the lemon."

By the opening of Jamaica's fall meeting, Jacobs was fast closing in on the all-time record for most wins in a single year. It was only fitting that he would get the record at Jamaica, the everyman's track where he based his stable, and that the horse who would get him there was a cheap claimer. Night Sprite, a five-year-old gelding everyone had dismissed as over the hill, was on a six-race losing streak when Jacobs picked him up at a bargain-basement price. After just two days in which Jacobs worked only on his starts, Night Sprite shot out of the gate like a cannon and upset classier handicap horses to bring his new trainer within one win of Cowboy Irwin's thirteen-year-old record. Three days later, on the final card of the Jamaica meeting, Jacobs notched his record-tying 147th victory with yet another cheap claimer and then sent Night Sprite out again in a low-level handicap to break the mark for annual winners with fully ten weeks to spare.

Not that he was about to pull up now. With an audaciousness that shocked newspapermen accustomed to his modesty and understatement, he revealed the private prediction he had made back in the spring and then revised it. "I'll do my one hundred and eighty," he told reporters upon his arrival in Florida for the winter season, "perhaps more."

By year's end, Jacobs had pushed the record to 177 winners. When the *Daily Racing Form* published the official trainer standings for 1936, Jacobs rummaged through his detailed memory of all things equine and corrected, "It was really one hundred and seventy-nine winners. The Racing Form people were wrong." By either count tantalizingly close to his goal of 180, he had put up a Ruthian record they were now saying would never be broken. Remarkably, he did it by winning one out of every three starts, maintaining the unheard-of 30 percent rate he had been averaging for three years running. Perhaps most remarkably, the $155,789 that his horses earned propelled him into the top five on the annual money list. It was mind-boggling that Jacobs and his claiming stable had come within $40,000 of Sunny Jim Fitzsimmons, who after training his second Triple Crown winner topped the 1936 money list by saddling well-bred stakes champions for the society stables of William Woodward and Gladys Mills Phipps.

The Pigeon Man was now a force that the racing establishment could no longer deny or ignore.

In the midst of all that unprecedented winning, the racing establishment had been growing increasingly suspicious. What had begun as whispers about presumed wrongdoing had become very public accusations of cheating.

At a loss to explain how a pigeon fancier was winning all those races, rivals were sure he had to be doing something nefarious. It couldn't be that Jacobs was that much better than everyone else. Every time he claimed a losing horse for $1,000 and then moved it up to win a $3,000 race three days later, his vanquished rivals would cry foul. It couldn't be his training that had transformed the horse, they contended, since Jacobs had had no time to condition it and had done nothing more than move it into a new stall. Ergo, he must have been doing something illegal to win all those races.

In response to all the grumbling and innuendo, the racing authorities and the federal government launched formal investigations into his operation. Track stewards hired private investigators to watch Jacobs and his stablehands, staking out his barn twenty-four hours a day. The Jockey Club sent grooms in as spies to get hired by Jacobs and then report back about the goings-on. Even the bookmakers, who felt burned by Jacobs's winning ways and the betting public's unconditional confidence in his horses, paid informants to snoop around and find out what he was doing, what he might be giving to these claimers that trudged slowly into his barn and came out running like hot favorites.

In the red-hot summer of 1936, the racing establishment sicced all manner of investigators on Jacobs and his stable. Agents of the Internal Revenue Service's narcotics division and the secret-service men of the New York State Racing Commission swarmed around Jacobs's barns, keeping his operation under constant surveillance day and night. They lurked behind hay bales and feed bins, scrutinizing the trainer's stable for any sign of impropriety. The Racing Commission's veterinarians examined all of his horses with a fine-tooth comb. After every race, the vets looked for indications that the animals had been injected with illicit substances and collected saliva specimens to be checked for traces of drugs, especially stimulants. The saliva samples were sent out daily to be analyzed at the laboratories of the IRS's narcotics division, the

Racing Commission, and the Rockefeller Institute for Medical Research.

At that time, the saliva test was a brand-new attempt to solve an age-old problem. Drugs had already been used to stimulate and sedate racehorses in England for almost three centuries before they started turning up at American tracks in the 1890s. Stimulants were soon such an open secret that they were advertised in American turf publications under the euphemistic name of "Speed Sustaining Elixir." During the Prohibition era, the doping of horses became so systematized and scientific that racing officials admitted that stamping it out would be as difficult as stopping people from drinking alcohol. By 1934, it had reached such epidemic proportions that the National Association of State Racing Commissioners sent a chemist and veterinarian to Europe to study the saliva tests being used in France to detect heroin, cocaine, caffeine, and other stimulants. That spring, the commission urged adoption of the saliva test, the mere existence of which would reduce trainer suspensions at U.S. racetracks from eighty-two in 1935 to twenty-three in 1936.

In the summer of '36, the racing and government investigators were sure Hirsch Jacobs would be one of those caught. While awaiting the test results from the labs, the investigators continued to surveil his stable round the clock. In the meantime, Jacobs, who like everybody else at the track knew what the New York State Racing Commission was up to, went right on winning races at a record-smashing clip. If he had changed anything that he was doing in the barn, there certainly was no evidence of it on the track.

Finally, after all the drug tests had come back negative, the investigators cleared Jacobs. They explained that if he was resorting to anything more stimulating than healthy food and insightful training, they had not been able to find it.

But that didn't stop the suspicion or the scrutiny. Racetrackers were sure there was something "funny" about Jacobs's unprecedented and unlikely success. "It was just unbelievable," one well-known racing figure later told the *Morning Telegraph*, the *Daily Racing Form*'s sister paper. "Here was a man who would claim a horse of no particular account at all. Seemingly, the animal had no future. His record would be dismal. Jacobs would lay money on the line and claim him out of a race. Then, right off the bat, next time out, the horse would go out there and run like crazy. He didn't do this once. He did it time after time. He did it so often that any man might get suspicious. It wasn't natural. After all, where did Jacobs come from? The heart of Manhattan. Nobody ever heard of learning how to train a horse like that while riding the subway. This fellow must have something strange going for him—or so I thought."

Even after he was cleared by the IRS and the Racing Commission, Jacobs was still under surveillance by everyone, day in and day out for weeks, months, and years on end. His horses continued to be closely examined when they won, as per standard practice, and the doping tests continued to come up negative. While every winning horse was tested, Jacobs's charges were scrutinized more closely than any. Time and again, investigators made surprise raids on his stable. They would drop by unannounced to examine the legs of his horses, often taking the opportunity to rummage through his tack and other equipment.

Sometimes the scrutiny was so surreptitious that Jacobs never even knew he was being surveilled. Sometimes he would find out only years after the fact.

One afternoon many years after the fact, Jacobs was grabbing lunch at Laurel Park with his son John when he spotted J. Edgar Hoover, then at the height of his power as director of the Federal Bureau of Investigation, seated in the clubhouse restaurant at his usual table. Over the years, Jacobs had often seen Hoover around the Laurel and Bowie racetracks and had gotten to know him well. Throughout the FBI chief's autocratic reign, Hoover had been known to slip out of his Washington headquarters around lunchtime to spend the afternoon watching and betting the races at the nearby Maryland tracks he frequented.

That day in the Laurel clubhouse restaurant, Hoover invited the Jacobses to sit down and join him for lunch. After exchanging some pleasantries, the FBI director turned to Hirsch and made a startling confession. "I had you investigated," Hoover revealed. "You have no idea over the years how many people I had working for you. I had FBI men working for you as grooms and exercise boys. Checking you out. I had to find out if you were using something." Jacobs's eyebrows rose, but he said nothing.

Jacobs knew Hoover to be an inveterate horseplayer who publicly insisted he never made more than a $2 bet but who secretly dispatched FBI special agents to place his real wagers at the $100 window. Unbeknownst to many, Hoover had a weakness for hot tips on sure things fed to him by the mob boss Frank Costello. Like everyone else back in the '30s, Jacobs assumed Hoover was too busy hunting the FBI's most-wanted "Public Enemy" gangsters to bother with policing the racetracks—and certainly too busy to bother with sending undercover G-men into the trainer's barn.

"Congratulations, you were clean," Hoover continued, breaking any suspense Jacobs had about the FBI snoops in his barn. "They came up with absolutely nothing. Not one could come up with a story of drugs or anything like that. You were one hundred percent clean."

If Hoover's FBI investigators couldn't find anything, it's hardly surprising that no one else would ever uncover even a hint of wrongdoing either. There were no drugs, no electrical stimulating devices, no race or betting fixes. Jacobs was on the level. In fact, it was a matter of record that Jacobs was, ironically enough, one of the few trainers who had never been punished for even a minor infraction of the official Rules of Racing.

All of which only intensified the carping and the sniping.

Jacobs was, his detractors liked to point out, still "just a claiming trainer" who wouldn't know what to do with a champion-caliber stakes winner if he ever got his hands on one. They scoffed at how he just kept buying cheap claimers and, as one racetrack veteran sneered, "ran them like a fleet of taxicabs." Jacobs simply dismissed it all as jealousy.

He was accused of giving his horses everything from mystery potions to "pigeon milk." The "pigeon milk" rap especially dogged The Pigeon Man, surely the only horseman who knew that it was in actuality a nutrient-rich secretion from the rock dove's throat produced by both parents to feed their newly hatched squabs. Jacobs laughed that one off as too ludicrous to dignify with a response.

His detractors even mocked him as the only trainer they knew who didn't get around the stables riding a horse. Setting the record straight, Jacobs explained that he had tried riding a stable pony early on but didn't like it. "I do all right on the ground," he quipped with his usual mastery of understatement.

Shrugging off all the envy and resentment swirling around him, Jacobs cheerfully went about his work, finding peace and serenity in the company of his horses. The first thing everyone noticed about him was his smile. It seemed to be ever present, whether he was greeting people around the racetrack or simply standing alone in the barn with his charges. "The Smiling Man from Brooklyn" was what Damon Runyon dubbed him.

Jacobs certainly had plenty of reasons to smile. Along with the hundreds of trips to the winner's circle, his stable had grown beyond anything he could have imagined. Since the day he and Izzy Bieber shook on their partnership agreement, the B. B. Stable had expanded steadily from a handful of horses to more than sixty at a time by the mid-1930s. Of those, about forty were always in active competition at the racetracks while the others were off resting or rehabbing.

Over the years since breaking into the business, Jacobs would look around at the other racing outfits and shake his head. "If these guys ran their businesses like they run their stables," he'd cracked to Bieber, nodding toward the captains of industry who treated their society stables as a hobby, "they'd never have enough money to buy a horse." The pair had resolved to run their stable like a real business, and they could boast one of the few racing operations to be self-sustaining.

By 1936, what had begun with a handshake seven years earlier had become profitable enough to require a formal partnership agreement. B. B. Stable was dissolved, and the two men incorporated their 50-50 partnership. Of Bieber's 50 percent stake, Izzy owned two-thirds and his nephew the remaining third; of Jacobs's 50 percent, Hirsch owned two-thirds and his wife, Ethel, the remaining third.

That year, most of the horses in the stable started running in the name and colors of Ethel D. Jacobs. The salmon-pink and emerald-green silks sported by her horses' jockeys became ubiquitous both on the track and in the winner's circle. When Hirsch shattered the single-year mark for winners by a trainer with 177, Ethel debuted as the owner of record for 149 of those. That not only placed her atop the 1936 owners' list for winners, but also broke the record for a single year.

Ethel may not have actually spent much time around the barns, but plenty of other Jacobses did. Hirsch ran it like a family business. To keep up with the stable's exponential growth, Jacobs hired more and more family members to help out around the backside. After his father lost his tailoring job early in the Depression, Hirsch brought him in as a hot walker to cool out the horses after races and gallops. He hired his big brother Harry as a night watchman and his younger brother Sidney as an assistant trainer.

When characterizing the relationship between owners and their trainers, it was generally said that so-and-so trains horses for such-and-such an owner (as in "Sunny Jim Fitzsimmons trains horses for William Woodward"). But with the incongruous partnership known as the Odd Couple of racing, it was said, by Damon Runyon among others, that "Isidor Bieber owns horses for Hirsch Jacobs."

Right from the start, the partners agreed that Jacobs would handle all training and racing decisions without any interference from Bieber. That was good, because Jacobs had his own idiosyncratic methods of training and running his horses. Many of his theories on training flew in the face of traditions that had been handed down for generations.

One of the most basic was his belief that it was often better to race a horse than to work it. While other trainers were working their horses hard between races with regular morning breezes, Jacobs would rest his charges for a day or so and then run them back in another race. Beyond that, Jacobs couldn't see the point in working the horses day in and day out. His philosophy could be summed up with one rhetorical question: Why run a horse five furlongs at 6 A.M. for laughs when you can run him six furlongs at 3 P.M. for an actual purse?

His competitors insisted he ran his horses too hard, raced them too often. In 1936, when he sent his horses to the post a whopping 632 times "like a fleet of taxicabs," the criticism reached a crescendo. "It's better to run a horse than to work him approximately the same distance," he countered. "And there's actually less chance of a horse getting hurt in a race than in a workout."

Whereas other trainers might exercise a one-size-fits-all regimen, Jacobs viewed his charges as individuals and tailored his training to fit each horse's quirks. He understood that horses couldn't all be brought along at the same rate. He also understood there was an art to choosing just the right race for each horse. He would pore over charts, learning the strengths and weaknesses of his own horses and those of their potential competitors. "The most important thing about training horses is to place them right," he explained. "I like to place a horse in its own company: put it with horses which are of its caliber, then hope that he'll win because you have him maybe in a little better shape than the other horses are in." Above all, Jacobs was always careful not to put his horses in over their heads. "The horse running against horses which have more natural speed may win and in winning kill himself," he said. "A horse will run his heart out for you if you ask him to."

Despite all his talents bringing along the rejects, there was only so far the ambitious trainer could go with his cheap claimers. For all the winners he had saddled, Jacobs still ran what was dismissed as a low-quality, high-quantity operation. He would still be saddled with the claiming trainer tag until he could get a stakes horse that could win at the highest levels. A fleet of taxicabs could take him only so far. What he coveted was a Cadillac.

Every Sunday, an off day from racing at the New York tracks, Jacobs and Bieber would head over to the Long Island farm where they usually sent their injured horses for turnout and rehab. One such Sunday in the spring of 1937, amid all the grazing laid-up horses that belonged to them and several other racing stables,

Jacobs was struck by two good-looking Thoroughbreds that were being galloped out behind the barns. Both were muscled up and appeared as fit and healthy as any racehorses winning at the track. Wondering what they were doing among the convalescing horses, Jacobs discovered the chestnut mare and bay stallion were at the farm taking it easy after their long voyage from Chile.

That rang a bell in Jacobs's mind. A while back, Jacobs had received a tip from a Madison Avenue adman he knew that a couple of fast Chilean racehorses were on their way north. The adman's brother had spotted the two horses in Panama on a layover en route to the United States. The brother told the horseplaying adman to watch for their U.S. debut, figuring they would be live longshots since there was no past-performance form charts on them. The adman then passed the tip along to Jacobs, assuming they might be bargain claims for the same reason. It didn't take long for Jacobs to figure these Chilean horses galloping in the farm's fields might be the very same ones his friend had told him about. Whether they were or not, the more Jacobs saw them galloping on his subsequent Sunday visits, the more he liked their conformation and movement.

The next time Jacobs encountered the Chilean horses was that June in the early dawn hours at Belmont. Like everyone else watching them gallop through the morning mist, he was struck by their odd attire: they were wearing white hoods that masked their heads and white sheets draped over their backs, a getup that spurred racetrackers to dub them the "Ku Klux Horses." All of that added to the mystery shrouding the alien arrivals at a time when South American horses were rarely seen on American tracks.

A couple of weeks later, early that summer of '37, Jacobs and Bieber were in the Aqueduct paddock watching the horses being saddled for the first race when they suddenly recognized one of the two Chilean horses from the farm and, checking the program, discovered this was a six-year-old mare named Sahri II making her North American debut. Bieber rushed to the racing secretary's office to put in a claim at the $2,000 price tag. Before he could finish writing out the claim slip, however, the deadline—exactly fifteen minutes before post time—passed and the claim box was closed. "Maybe it's for the best," he said with a shrug.

He consoled himself by hurrying over to the betting ring in the grandstand, where a hundred bookmakers perched on high stools were making their pitches. Each bookie ran what he called a "store" in which his two chief assistants flanked him on lower stools, one holding aloft a slate signboard with the odds offered on every horse in the next race and the other keeping spreadsheets to record the bets. Sahri, dismissed by all the touts as the longest of shots, had opened at 30-to-1 and drifted up to 50-to-1. But then Sahri's American owner and his coconspirators started betting as much and as fast as they could with as many "stores" as they could, locking in their wagers at those long odds before the bookies could get wise to their scheme and drop the price back down. By the time Bieber got to the betting ring, the best price he could find among the bookies was 20-to-1, which he grabbed for the $2,000 he had saved on the missed claim.

Sahri, whose odds had been driven down to 8-to-1 by post time, powered to the front deep in the stretch and flashed to a stunning one-length win. Her owner had burned the bookies for well over a quarter of a million dollars in what was instantly hailed as one of history's greatest betting coups. As a bonus, he got to keep the horse along with the $700 first-place purse—all because Bieber had been seconds late to the claim box and every other horseman had been scared away by the poor performances of past South American imports.

No sooner had Bieber collected his own $40,000 windfall from the bookies than he began thumbing through the program in search of horses to bet it back on. That's when he noticed that Sahri II's owner had another entrant running in the fourth race, a six-year-old stallion named Caballero II. This, Bieber realized, must be the other horse that Jacobs had admired galloping in the farm's field during those Sunday visits.

Tracking down Jacobs in the paddock as he saddled a cheap claimer for the third race, Bieber delivered the bad news about barely missing out on the Chilean mare for $2,000 and then the good news about her stablemate running in the fourth race for a $4,000 claiming tag. "I like Caballero the better of the two, anyway," Jacobs said, figuring that the claiming prices meant the stallion must be twice as good as the mare. "I hope we get him."

"Well," Bieber said, flashing his winnings from Sahri's race, "if we get Caballero, it will cost us nothing." Excusing himself to head over to the racing secretary's office, he assured Jacobs, "I won't be late for this one."

After putting in the claim, Bieber headed back to the betting ring to boost his investment. He waited as the 5-to-1 opening odds receded to 8-to-1 and then bet $1,500 on Caballero. In the six-furlong sprint, Caballero shot from the back of the pack to hook a horse named Isaiah in the stretch and then duel him head to head all the way to the wire in a stirring photo finish. After the photo showed it to be a dead heat and the bookies divided the payouts in half, Bieber had won another $6,000. More important, he and Jacobs had gotten Caballero for $4,000—a price that, considering what they had just witnessed, seemed a bigger bargain than they had expected.

Caballero II proved as much right away. Like his old stablemate Sahri II, he would never run another claiming race. Jacobs started stepping him up in the handicap division, where the stallion carried the salmon-pink and emerald-green colors to four wins his first five times out. When Caballero trounced a couple of top stakes winners in a midlevel handicap at Saratoga that August, Jacobs determined he was ready for a world-class race. The next day the trainer took him up to Boston for the Massachusetts Handicap, the nation's richest summer stake with a purse of more than $70,000. Waiting for them there was a deep field of elite handicap horses headed by America's darling, Seabiscuit.

Seabiscuit was just the kind of Cinderella horse that gave every claiming trainer like Jacobs hope. For Seabiscuit started out as a claimer, albeit far from a cheap one. Before he could break his maiden eighteen starts into his two-year-old season, the knobby-kneed little colt had run multiple claiming races without any takers—once for a $2,000 price tag, twice for $2,500, and once for $4,000. He would run two more, going unclaimed for $5,000 and $6,000, before being sold for $7,500 as a three-year-old and blossoming at four into an unlikely superstar. By the summer of 1937, "The Biscuit" reigned supreme as the nation's preeminent handicapper.

His connections had been pointing him toward the rich Massachusetts Handicap for his eagerly anticipated showdown with War Admiral, the Man o' War scion who had swept the Triple Crown that spring. Despite War Admiral's absence due to a foot injury suffered in his crowning Belmont Stakes triumph, the Mass-Cap still presented Seabiscuit with plenty of topflight competitors and weighty challenges. The clear favorite in every sense of the word, Seabiscuit was assigned the heaviest weight handicap of 130 pounds—a backbreaking impost for any horse, let alone an under-sized one with crooked legs. That couldn't dissuade the overflow crowd of 40,000 at Suffolk Downs from making Seabiscuit the even-money betting choice against a deep field that included both

Chilean invaders. Sahri, the second choice at 6-to-1, would shoulder 110 pounds, and Caballero, the third choice at 7-to-1, would carry 108 pounds.

With Seabiscuit conceding 22 pounds to Caballero, a handicap believed to be worth at least seven lengths, many thought the underdog had a real shot at pulling a major upset. Among them were Alfred Vanderbilt and Al Jolson, who liked Caballero's chances so much that they tried to buy him from Jacobs before the race. Jacobs turned them down flat, saying Caballero wasn't for sale, mainly because he thought the stallion was top class.

Right from the start, all eyes locked on Seabiscuit as he hooked up in a speed duel with a longshot filly, while Caballero hung back biding his time. As Seabiscuit pulled away from the filly in the stretch, Caballero suddenly came charging down the lane in hot pursuit, slicing into the lead with every stride until he simply ran out of track. Seabiscuit held on by a shrinking length, needing to break the track record for a mile and an eighth in order to secure the $51,780 winner's purse. Caballero's consolation prize of $10,000 for second place gave Jacobs his richest purse yet as well as his first taste of the big time.

In the wake of that surprising performance, everyone wondered how Jacobs knew that Caballero, who just four days earlier had raced hard in a $1,200 Saratoga handicap, was ready to give Seabiscuit a run for his high-stakes money. The secret, Jacobs explained, was simply being able to tell when a horse was primed to run. He summed it up with one of his favorite aphorisms: "When a horse looks good, he feels good; and when he's feeling good, he'll run good." That, of course, begged the question of how exactly he could look at a horse and divine how it felt.

One afternoon that summer, Damon Runyon was hanging around Jacobs's stable when, only half kiddingly, he ventured, "Why don't you try just asking a horse how he feels one day?"

"I did," Jacobs replied. "I went in the stall of Caballero the other morning and, just to make conversation, I said, 'Well, old boy, how do you feel?' He just took a kick at me."

"What did you do?" Runyon followed up.

"Why, I took a kick right back at him," Jacobs said, pausing for effect before delivering the punch line. "We both missed."

A month after taking on Seabiscuit, Caballero returned to New York as the headliner in a Labor Day feature, the Aqueduct Handicap. This time assigned the highest weight in the race, he seemed unburdened by the 122-pound impost as he made up five lengths in the stretch and won the $5,100 first prize going away. He raced Seabiscuit three more times that fall, but the closest he could manage was another runner-up finish. Riding Caballero's breakthrough 1937 season, Jacobs topped the national trainers' standings for the fifth straight year, this time with 134 victories to go along with his $142,474 in purses, while Ethel defended her title as the winningest owner.

The following year, they picked up right where they left off. That spring, just two days after winning the Fayette Handicap at Jamaica, Caballero faced his toughest challenge yet, in the prestigious Excelsior Handicap. To ride Caballero on the first Saturday in May, jockey Wayne Wright turned down an offer to pilot Lawrin, his regular mount, in the Kentucky Derby. At the same time as a budding star named Eddie Arcaro was winning his first Kentucky Derby aboard the longshot Lawrin before 60,000 at Churchill Downs, Wright was riding Caballero to an impressive victory in the Excelsior before 15,000 at Jamaica. If Wright's choice of mounts was a measure of the esteem with which horsemen held Caballero in the tough handicap division, the winner's purse of $6,650, a fraction of the Derby's $47,050 first prize, was a measure of how far removed Jacobs remained from the big time.

With 109 wins in 1938, Jacobs topped the national trainers' list for a record-tying sixth straight year, thanks to claiming horses that earned a grand total of $100,907. To put that amount in perspective, a horse could make almost as much in a single race just by winning the annual Santa Anita Handicap, whose rich purse earned it the nickname of the "Hundred-Grander" and whose 1938 edition earned Stagehand $91,450 for upsetting Seabiscuit. By contrast, Jacobs was thrilled that Caballero, his $4,000 bargain claimer, would wind up earning him $33,727 in purses.

The success of Caballero II, and to a slightly lesser extent his fellow traveler Sahri II, sparked a boom in the importation of South American horses. By making the only claim for either of the Chilean horses on the watershed day of their North American debuts, Jacobs and Bieber stood at the vanguard of that southern invasion. Once Jacobs discovered that Caballero was far from the best racehorse in Chile, he dispatched his partner to South America in search of the better Thoroughbreds he heard were for sale down there.

In the winter of 1937–1938, Bieber flew to Chile on a Clipper— a "flying boat," as it was called—with enough cash to buy several of them. Before boarding the prop plane for his shopping spree, he had tucked $15,000 in U.S. bills into a porous plaster in the small of his back for safekeeping. A popular pain reliever of the time, Allcock's Porous Plaster was a medicated bandage that adhered to the skin and was touted as a cure for everything from rheumatism to lumbago. If the Chilean authorities discovered it, Bieber was prepared to tell them it was a treatment for his bad back. When Bieber regaled Runyon with the scheme to smuggle $15,000 into Chile, the writer had to work hard to suppress a chuckle. "You could not buy one leg of War Admiral for fifteen thousand dollars," Runyon deadpanned. "About the best Mr. Sam Riddle, War Admiral's owner, would do for you for that sum would be a set of his steed's old racing plates."

To be sure, that might have been true in the United States, where such blue-blooded Thoroughbreds born and bred in the Kentucky Bluegrass fetched a small fortune; but Bieber and Jacobs figured they could get a lot more than some old racing plates in Chile, where the favorable exchange rate promised much more bang for their U.S. bucks. It would be the first of many shopping excursions Bieber would make to South America, mainly to Chile and Argentina, in search of foreign bargains. He was hardly alone, as evidenced by the veritable parade of South American imports that were debuting on North American racetracks.

With champions like War Admiral beyond his means and onetime claimers like Seabiscuit a million-to-one shot, South America offered an affordable path to glory. It was yet another measure of how far Bieber and Jacobs remained from the big time. They were still shopping in the bargain bin, still mining for gold in the dirt, still chasing the dream of anyone who's ever owned a racehorse.

Chapter 8

QUEST FOR A CHAMPION

By most measures, Hirsch Jacobs was living the American Dream.

Judging by the headlines in newspapers across the country and the glowing profiles in such popular magazines as *Time*, *Collier's*, and the *New Yorker*, Jacobs stood at the top of his profession. By the end of the 1930s, he had reigned as America's winningest trainer for a remarkable seven consecutive years—a streak that broke Doc Bedwell's longstanding record of six straight at a time when no other horseman had ever led the annual winners list more than three years in total, much less in succession. A self-made man who had climbed the ladder all the way from rank outsider to king of the haltermen, Jacobs had added 106 winners in 1939 to bring his career total to a mind-boggling 1,120—more than any other trainer in history. In the fourteen years since taking out his trainer's license, the horses he saddled had earned over a million dollars in purses. All of this before his thirty-sixth birthday.

In the process, Jacobs had built a tiny claiming stable into one of the few racing operations that was not only self-sustaining but also quite profitable. Among the countless small operators for whom racing was a business rather than a hobby, Jacobs was the most successful, so much so that he was continually declining offers to train for the big-time society stables. He definitely dressed the part, always conservatively clad in three-piece suits that made him look more like a businessman than a horseman. If he wasn't the only trainer nattily attired to saddle horses for the afternoon races, he certainly was easy to pick out in the mornings when none of his counterparts dressed up to work their charges. He managed his stable with an attention to detail that would put an accountant to shame. Whenever anyone would ask why he was always walking the track to inspect the recently harrowed dirt surface, he would succinctly explain, "That's my livelihood out there." To Jacobs, horse racing was more a business than a sport, and his was flourishing at a time when most Americans were still mired deep in the Great Depression.

Among the most tangible signs that he had achieved the American Dream was the large redbrick Georgian Colonial house he had recently bought in the upscale Queens neighborhood of Forest Hills. The ten-room, two-story home stood back from the road in a lush, leafy section of New York that seemed more suburb than city. The three racetracks where Jacobs spent most of his workdays—Jamaica, Aqueduct, and Belmont—were less than a twenty-minute drive in his big, green Cadillac.

By the time he purchased that Forest Hills house, Hirsch and Ethel Jacobs had started their family with a son, John, and a daughter, Patrice, who had been named after Damon Runyon's horse-loving wife. Hirsch had been raised by a mother who stressed the importance of family. True to that family-first value system, he stayed close to his nine siblings, eventually bringing four of his five brothers into horse racing. He made sure his mother never wanted for anything, especially after her husband had left her. It spoke to Hirsch's strong sense of family that he even gave his father a job despite the fact that Pops had walked out on Mom. Hirsch brought that ethos with him when he was starting his own nuclear family. He was a devoted family man, a homebody who spent all his free time with his wife and kids.

Of all the characteristics that made his business partnership with Izzy Bieber seem so incongruous, those family values ranked near the top. While Jacobs was the devoted family man, Bieber was the confirmed bachelor. Bieber seemed to have a revolving door of women and liked to be seen around town with a beauty hanging on his arm. But for the most part, he relished the bachelor life— hanging out at the track, gambling everywhere from the betting ring to the casinos, dropping in at the Broadway bar he owned and operated with his big brother Herman, spending quiet evenings reading the classics alone in his room at his sister Jennie's Far Rockaway house. Though he steered away from family life, Bieber did enjoy the company of the Jacobs children, taking them to the beach on occasion and demonstrating a fondness for them second only to his passion for betting.

Hirsch Jacobs's success on all fronts was all the more remarkable considering that he had realized the American Dream at a time when that Horatio Alger ideal was more elusive than ever. While millions of Americans were losing everything during the Depression—their jobs, their savings, their homes, and their very faith in a bright future—Jacobs seemed to ride through the financial crisis untouched. Right from the 1929 stock-market crash that triggered the Depression, Jacobs realized how fortunate he was to have stashed his savings in a Florida bank that survived unscathed while more than 10,000 others had failed by the time President Franklin D. Roosevelt took office in 1933. As the first order of his presidency, Roosevelt proclaimed a four-day "bank holiday," stemming nationwide panic and starting America on the long and arduous road to recovery.

Each day at the racetrack throughout that calamitous decade, Jacobs saw stark reminders of the less fortunate. From the parking lot to the clubhouse, the formerly rich and powerful could be found hawking their wives' jewelry and furs to buy the necessities of life. Every once in a while, a downtrodden acquaintance from the old neighborhood would recognize him and plead, "Hirsch, can you give me some money? I'm in bad shape." Jacobs would always reach into his pocket for the extra cash he kept just for such moments and discreetly slip the man enough to keep the wolf at bay.

By any measure, Hirsch Jacobs, the impoverished immigrant tailor's son, had achieved a level of financial success beyond anything he could have imagined. It looked like he had it all: fame, fortune, family—all the trappings of the American Dream and the Horatio Alger myth. And yet, he still felt something was missing. The one thing he didn't have, and coveted more than anything, was a champion racehorse and all the respect that would come with it.

Hirsch Jacobs and Izzy Bieber were hardly the only ones obsessed with the pursuit of a champion. So was their famous friend Damon Runyon. As much money as Runyon had gambled away betting on nags over the years, it was small potatoes compared with what he had sunk into the ones racing in the name and colors of his wife, Patrice. After the early success of their first horse, Angelic, Runyon's racing luck had run as cold as his betting fortunes.

His old lament about all horseplayers dying broke now extended to racehorse owners as well. He used to be amused by the old racing axiom: "If you want to make a small fortune with horses, start with a large fortune." Now that he had horses of his own, he didn't find the punch line so funny anymore.

It didn't matter that Runyon could afford to sink a large fortune into horses. Unlike Jacobs and Bieber, who still found themselves priced out of anything better than cheap claimers, Runyon had the wherewithal to shoot the works on high-quality racing stock. He was making more money than ever, his Hollywood income exceeding his newspaper salary and magazine payments combined. *Little Miss Marker*, the 1934 film based on his short story about a degenerate horseplayer who leaves his little daughter with a Broadway bookmaker as collateral—the IOU "marker" of the title—for a $2 bet, made a superstar of five-year-old Shirley Temple and a moonlighting scriptwriter of Damon Runyon. At a time when downtrodden Americans sought escapism at the movies, Runyon was providing comic relief by adapting his short stories for the silver screen at the rate of nearly one a year.

One night late in 1938, Runyon was holding court as usual in Lindy's deli when the talk got around to two of the most galvanizing sporting events in that or any other year. Four months after the American hero Joe Louis had knocked out the German villain Max Schmeling for the world heavyweight championship in the most socially transcendent sports event of all time, Seabiscuit outdueled War Admiral in the greatest match race ever run. The crowd around Runyon's customary table knew how much he dreamed of having a Seabiscuit of his own, but they also knew how much he had invested over the years in prizefighters in the hope of owning a "piece" of a heavyweight champ. That's why everyone at Lindy's that night was shocked when Runyon revealed that he would rather own a great racehorse than anything else in the world.

"Would you rather own Seabiscuit than Joe Louis?" a friend asked incredulously.

Runyon nodded emphatically. "You don't have to split the purse with a horse," he cracked.

Problem was, his horses weren't winning many purses, certainly not enough to cover what he was shelling out to buy, feed, and train them. He was sure he had the best trainer in the nation, but not even Jacobs's magic touch could turn Runyon's hayburners into champions. Throughout his string of disappointments, Runyon marveled at Jacobs's kindness and empathy even for the losing horses. He was touched by how Jacobs always came up with "some kindly excuse" for underperformers.

Over just the few years since Jacobs began training Runyon's horses, the two men had become fast friends. On the surface, Runyon seemed to have much more in common with the mutual friend who had brought them together, Beeb: a passion for Broadway, a proclivity for gambling, a love for the classics. But there was something about Jacobs that drew Runyon closer. Deep down, perhaps they were just kindred spirits: both quiet men, both ambitious strivers driven to the top of their respective professions, both keen observers of psychology whether it be human or equine.

Their relationship had blossomed while Runyon was hanging out at Jacobs's stable. Before long, they were socializing away from the track. On winter Sundays during the Florida racing season, Runyon would often invite the Jacobses to his Hibiscus Island mansion. While the Jacobs kids frolicked on the front lawn overlooking Biscayne Bay, Hirsch and Ethel would spend the day chatting with Damon and Patrice about everything from racehorses to politics.

Runyon was surprised to learn that he and Jacobs shared a passion for another sport, one that belied the horseman's mild-mannered, soft-spoken persona: boxing. Jacobs was only sixteen, the minimum age required to attend a prizefight in a state that had just legalized the sport, when he saw the great Benny Leonard knock out Richie Mitchell to retain the world lightweight championship at the old Madison Square Garden, back when the arena was still actually located down in Madison

Square. Hearing Jacobs relive the thrilling experience, Runyon revealed the inside story that Arnold Rothstein, based on his friend Leonard's boast, had gotten huge odds on his $25,000 bet that "The Ghetto Wizard" would deliver a first-round knockout and promised the reigning champ a piece of the proceeds. Charging out like a wild bull at the opening bell in a furious drive to win the bet, Leonard scored three quick knockdowns and survived one himself in an unforgettable first round but, much to Rothstein's chagrin, couldn't finish off his challenger until the sixth.

After learning that Jacobs had religiously followed the big fights on the radio and in the Movietone newsreels, Runyon began taking his friend to them. For the heavily hyped heavyweight title bouts, especially through Joe Louis's long reign, Runyon would invite both Hirsch and Ethel to join him at ringside. While Runyon pounded out his newspaper column from the front row, the Jacobses would sit close enough to feel the sweat and blood. Beeb, always able to scare up ringside seats from the Broadway ticket brokerage he still ran, would often be there as well, making bets not only between bouts but also between rounds.

Just as Runyon could give Jacobs the inside scoop on boxing, the trainer could return the favor, sharing his expertise on the racing game. Of particular interest to Runyon was Jacobs's knowledge of pedigrees. Over the years, Jacobs had read every book he could find on successful Thoroughbred bloodlines and had also been picking the brain of the master of all the Kentucky breeders, E. R. Bradley. Jacobs may have been limited to training claimers, but he dreamed of someday not only owning a champion but also breeding one. Runyon would often query him about this sire or that dam, about pedigrees of horses that raced when Jacobs was still training pigeons. Sometimes Jacobs needed a few moments to search his memory bank, but he always managed to come up with the pedigree and reel off the lineage with remarkable facility and accuracy.

Runyon had become interested in pedigrees because he was starting to think he might have a better shot at owning a champion if he bred one himself. When Angelic went lame late in her two-year-old season, he retired her to the breeding shed at the Maryland farm where Jacobs and Bieber sent their own horses when they were done with racing or needed a long layup. The farm belonged to Henry Salisbury, a New York–based Paramount Pictures executive who had worked with the writer on *Little Miss Marker* and another 1934 movie adopted from a Runyon short story, *The Lemon Drop Kid*, about a hapless racetrack tout. At Runyon's recommendation, Salisbury had joined the handful of outside clients whose horses Jacobs took on. Runyon often visited Angelic at Salisbury's suburban Baltimore farm and, in 1936, bred her to Sting, a stakes-winning stallion owned by James Butler, the grocery magnate whose racetrack holdings included nearby Laurel Park as well as Empire City.

The following spring, Angelic delivered her first foal, a handsome bay colt. The Runyons named him Tight Shoes, after a short story Damon had recently published in *Collier's* about a horseplayer who, distracted by his pinched feet, places losing bets that exacerbate his physical as well as psychic pain. The story had been inspired by Beeb, whose gingerly strides across the Saratoga lawns after a losing afternoon at the track had taught Runyon about the "definite association between a horseplayer's puppies and his betting operations." Years afterward, Bieber would ask Runyon, "Do you remember the time you wrote about me walking on the grass?" Runyon remembered that decade-old column well enough to turn it into a quirky short story, a screwball Hollywood comedy, and an oddly named racehorse.

In the spring of 1940, Tight Shoes burst onto the racing scene seemingly out of nowhere. Unraced as a two-year-old and unimpressive in his Florida debut late that winter, he made a splash in his second career race by romping to victory over six furlongs of Jamaica mud as a 7-to-1 longshot and earning a *New York Times* headline as a Kentucky Derby hopeful to watch. Just four days later, in another six-furlong sprint at Jamaica, Tight Shoes again easily wired the field to score an even bigger upset over the prohibitive favorite, the Whitney-owned Calory. So carried away were the Runyons with the stunning four-length win that they practically beat Tight Shoes and Jacobs to the winner's circle.

When the Runyons got there, Jacobs sidled up to Patrice and quietly quipped, "How does it feel to finish ahead of a Whitney?"

They shared a laugh. Then, turning serious, Jacobs said, "I believe you ought to take a chance with this horse in Louisville. Send a wire to Louisville right now and tell them the horse is coming."

A big smile spread across Patrice's face at the suggestion that the Runyons should run Tight Shoes in the Kentucky Derby against the best three-year-old Thoroughbreds in the nation. She wheeled around to her husband and asked imploringly, "Oh, Damon, the horse runs in the Kentucky Derby?"

Damon simply smiled and said, "Carissima mía, whatever you want." He then took off his wire-rimmed glasses and began to wipe them. Any number of poker players who had cleaned him out would have recognized that gesture as a Runyon "tell": he would always wipe his glasses when he didn't want anyone to see that he was excited or emotional.

The next morning, six days before the Derby, the Runyons shipped their colt to Louisville on the Cincinnati Limited in a specially designed horse car. If all went as planned, Tight Shoes would have plenty of time to adjust to the Southern climate and the Churchill Downs track. No sooner had he stepped into his stall at Churchill Downs, however, than colic set in. The Runyons and Jacobs immediately scratched him, and then commenced a tense vigil praying for the colt to recover. The next day, Runyon was relieved to report that Tight Shoes was eating again and would soon be able to travel home. Dan Parker, the New York *Daily Mirror* sports editor, offered consoling words to his good friend and Hearst newspaper-chain stablemate, positing that Runyon might well have won the Derby if Tight Shoes hadn't fallen ill.

The tale of Tight Shoes, the most promising of all the horses Runyon had ever owned, turned out to be an omen for the year itself. He wound up winning just four races and $4,290 for the Runyons through his short career. His trainer's luck was a bit better. Jacobs rode the stakes-winning coattails of a couple of Beeb's South American imports to earn $115,160 in 1940 purses: Conde Rico dead-heating in the Bowie Handicap and Confiado giving Jacobs his richest victory yet in the $10,000 Rhode Island Handicap. For the most part, Jacobs was still relying on his string of claimers to pay the bills. For the first time since 1932, though, Jacobs failed to reach the "century" mark that year, snapping his record seven-year streak. With just ninety-eight official victories for 1940, another seven-year streak came to an end when Jacobs was dethroned as the nation's winningest trainer. Jacobs graciously sent a congratulatory telegram to Red Womeldorff, who had saddled 108 winners for Emil Denemark, the Chicago car dealer who custom-built the classic bulletproof Cadillac that Al Capone used to motor around in. Jacobs would have retained his title if the sixteen winners that his brother Sidney had saddled for him could have been included, but the official statistics only counted the ones a trainer personally girthed up in the paddock.

For New Year's, Runyon invited Jacobs to the Hibiscus Island mansion to toast the bittersweet luck they had had in 1940. Neither man was inclined to raise a glass of bubbly—and only partly because Runyon had long since sworn off booze in favor of about forty cups of coffee a day while Jacobs never touched alcohol or caffeine.

Shortly after Jacobs left, Runyon sat down at his white typewriter and started to compose his first column of the New Year. "Hirsch Jacobs, one of the greatest thoroughbreds of the human race it has been our pleasure to encounter, an American sportsman and gentleman, dropped in to see us the other day, and we remarked that for a king knocked from under his crown he seemed mighty cheerful," Runyon began, noting that the reason Hirsch was beaming like a proud papa was because he was one, as Ethel had just delivered a bouncing baby boy named Thomas. "Although the Jacobses already have two children, Johnny and Patrice, it was obvious that the new baby compensated for any disappointment that Hirsch might have felt over finally losing his championship title. He spoke so enthusiastically of Tommy's vitality that we would not have been surprised to see the infant come walking in the door. It took us 15 minutes to divert Hirsch's thoughts to a discussion of the end of his long reign as top man of one of the most difficult of professions."

When Runyon had finally gotten Hirsch to talk some horse that day, the trainer was characteristically philosophical. "Oh, I knew I couldn't stay up there always," Jacobs told Runyon. "I was surprised that I lasted as long as I did. I had a world of luck. I'll just go on doing the best I can with my horses, and if I can win even fifty percent of the number of races I have in each of the past seven years, I'll consider myself lucky. You have to have a lot of luck in training horses."

To hear Jacobs tell it, Runyon might have thought that luck was the key to the trainer's success. In fact, in a fit of modesty and superstition, Jacobs often attributed his unlikely success not only to "common sense," but also to good old racing luck and fate. As superstitious as anyone Runyon knew, Jacobs had a closet full of lucky suits, hats, and ties to prove it.

"I once noticed that Hirsch Jacobs was wearing a necktie that struck me as pretty much on the seedy side for the champion trainer of racehorses," reported Runyon, a dapper dresser known to spend an hour most days choosing a tie from his prodigious wardrobe. "The necktie was really a most depressing object. It was crumpled and frayed and stained in a manner that suggested it was a veteran of many a hasty meal. I saw this tie around Hirsch's neck day in and day out during a Miami winter meeting and it became such an eyesore to me that finally I sent him a $6.50 tie. But the following day he was still wearing that beaten up old-timer, and, noting my reproachful glance at it, Hirsch blushed and confessed that when he is on a winning streak he never changes the tie he is wearing at the time the streak begins until it is over, and he was then on one of the longest streaks."

The more obvious telltale sign would be the rumpled suit the natty trainer might wear week after week during a winning streak. While plungers like Beeb scoffed at the very idea of superstition as being a sign of weakness and a concession to fate, Jacobs had enough superstitions for the both of them. He worried about jinxes, hexes, curses, bad luck in general. He would drive nothing but green Cadillacs. He would habitually avoid the press, partly because he was the retiring type but mainly because he believed stories and photos in the papers could ruin his luck. "Every time someone writes a story about me, I have a losing streak," he complained to a reporter from *Collier's*. "It's never failed yet." That rule apparently didn't apply to Runyon, who despite taking few notes during their conversations was the only reporter Jacobs trusted to quote him accurately.

For a guy who wrote so much about gangsters, ne'er-do-wells, and the seamy underworld they inhabited, it turned out that Damon Runyon was a sucker for fairytales, for Cinderella stories, for Horatio Alger myths.

During the darkest depths of the Depression, Runyon was sure he had found all three of those rolled into the perfect rags-to-riches Cinderella fairytale in the person of James J. Braddock. A down-on-his-luck pug with busted hands and six cents to his name, Braddock desperately scrounged for work on the Hudson River docks and had to go on the public welfare relief rolls to feed his wife and three kids. His incredible comeback inspired Runyon to famously nickname him "The Cinderella Man." Battling back from skid row to earn a shot at the world heavyweight title, the 10-to-1 underdog pulled off boxing's greatest upset to unseat Max Baer and uplift a downtrodden nation. "This fistic fairytale comes true," Runyon led off his column on that 1935 title bout from Madison Square Garden Bowl in Queens. "James J. Braddock, 'The Cinderella Man' of pugilism, is the new heavyweight champion of the world. And you cannot match his story anywhere in the realm of the most fantastic fiction."

By 1937, when Joe Louis's knockout punch ended The Cinderella Man's fairytale reign, Seabiscuit had raced into America's consciousness as a new Algeresque underdog folk hero to inspire the downtrodden. Seabiscuit's rise buoyed Hirsch Jacobs's dreams of someday spotting a future champion in the claiming ranks—an heir to Seabiscuit's throne—and pick him up for a song.

Now that Hirsch Jacobs had already stamped himself the Cinderella trainer, Damon Runyon certainly had a rooting interest in his good friend finding an underdog claimer worthy of being dubbed "The Cinderella Horse."

CHAPTER 9

A KINGDOM FOR A HORSE

Just as Hirsch Jacobs got his start in racing with pigeons, so did Robert Kleberg Jr. get his start in breeding with cattle.

At the dawn of the Depression, when Kleberg took the reins of the King Ranch, it was already the largest spread in America, sprawling over a million acres of Texas prairie and home to a hundred thousand head of cattle. The ranch was the creation of his grandfather, Captain Richard King, an entrepreneurial steamboat pilot with no previous livestock experience. General Robert E. Lee, a good friend of King's, once offered him a piece of advice that became the riverboat rancher's motto: "Buy land, and never sell." King started by snapping up 15,500 acres for $300 in 1853, then kept amassing more and more of South Texas until, at his death in 1885, he passed down 614,000 acres and a legacy as "the cradle of American cattle ranching." His successor, son-in-law Robert Kleberg Sr., modernized the operation and continued the expansion until the King Ranch covered twice as much land as the entire state of Rhode Island.

When Robert Kleberg Jr. took over upon his father's death in 1932, his main focus became improving the quality of the livestock bred on the world's biggest beef-producing ranch. Tall and ruggedly handsome in his mid-thirties, Bob Kleberg was a hard-riding, hard-drinking Texas cowboy with a scientist's eye when it came to breeding. Having studied genetics for two years before dropping out of college to help his ailing father run the ranch, Kleberg endeavored to create a new breed of cattle—something that had never been done in America before and had not been done anywhere in the world for over a century. Seeking to create a breed more suited to the blazing South Texas sun than the native Longhorn, he crossed the English Shorthorn with the Indian Brahman and ended up with the Santa Gertrudis, which he formally named for the creek feeding the Wild Horse Desert oasis known as the King Ranch.

The cattleman's true breeding passion, however, was horses. Legend has it that Jesse James had given his fastest iron-gray stallion to Captain King in gratitude for a night's board and that Kleberg began riding the descendants they called "the Jesse James horses" on roundups at the age of four. Kleberg's ardor for breeding was ignited when at nineteen he happened upon a striking Quarter Horse suckling at a nearby farm. That sorrel colt, which he purchased for $125, would grow up to be the foundation stallion for the King Ranch's Quarter Horses, a string of cow ponies that would become as renowned as the cherry-red Santa Gertrudis cattle they herded. From experimentation breeding Old Sorrel and his other Quarter Horses, Kleberg learned that he had to modify the crossing patterns he developed with the cattle. Whereas close inbreeding worked with cows, it didn't produce good results in horses. Kleberg still kept crossing back to his favorite bloodline, but he began breeding more-distant relatives than he had initially. The point of this linebreeding was to intensify desired traits. The result was a consistent herd of 3,000 Quarter Horses that possessed the versatile blend of agility and blazing speed ideal for working cattle.

In the mid-1930s, Kleberg had set his sights on a certain Quarter Horse mare at a neighboring ranch. Knowing that the owner would never sell his favorite broodmare if he knew the degree of Kleberg's desire, the cattleman cum horse trader decided to feign interest in the neighbor's Thoroughbreds. To Kleberg's surprise, when he took a tour of those Thoroughbreds, one of them caught his eye: a big bay stallion with the bulky muscling of a Quarter Horse. Kleberg forgot all about the Quarter Horse mare he had come for and instead left with the Thoroughbred stallion, an ex-racehorse named Chicaro.

Not long after the Whitney-bred stallion had settled in at the King Ranch, Kleberg decided he had to journey to the heart of the Kentucky Bluegrass country—"to see how a horse like that was produced." He spent several days in the summer of 1935 traveling around Lexington, the self-proclaimed "Horse Capital of the World" and the acknowledged center of the Thoroughbred industry, dropping by farms, chatting up breeders, checking out bloodstock.

As his car pulled into another farm one day, Kleberg glanced out at the pasture and his eyes widened. "Stop the car!" he shouted at his driver. "I see the mare I want!" Kleberg told his driver to proceed to the farmhouse, where the owner, the veteran breeder Morton Schwartz, told him that that mare, Corn Silk, was a daughter of Chicaro's sire. An excited Kleberg offered to buy the mare on the spot, but Schwartz told him that Corn Silk had already been consigned, along with most of his other horses, to that year's Saratoga Sale.

With his trademark white Stetson upswept to reveal his craggy face and piercing eyes, Bob Kleberg strode into staid Saratoga that August and shook up the racing aristocracy by bidding like the Texas oilman and cattleman he was. He ponied up $23,400 and came away with seven of Schwartz's mares and fillies, including Corn Silk and, more important to his budding racehorse breeding aspirations, Sunset Gun, a Man o' War daughter who was bid up to $8,600. For good measure, Kleberg successfully bid another $16,000 for ten yearlings. By the time the Saratoga Sale was over, Bob Kleberg had signaled the King Ranch's intentions to put its brand—the registered "Running W" that had famously marked its cattle since 1869—on Thoroughbred racing.

Although he had initially sought Thoroughbred bloodstock as a means of improving his Quarter Horses, Kleberg now wanted to breed a better racehorse as an end in itself. He was convinced that if he approached Thoroughbred breeding as a science, he could improve on the results of all those Kentucky hardboots who lived by the old maxim: "Breed the best to the best and hope for the best." For Kleberg, that meant studying horses' pedigrees up to ten generations back. He believed he could use the same process that had worked with his Quarter Horses, finding a superior ancestor and choosing breeding combinations that repeated that ancestor multiple times.

His study of Chicaro's pedigree had sparked an interest in one particular sire line: Domino, America's fastest, gamest, and richest racehorse of the nineteenth century whose bloodline Kleberg deemed "one of the greatest in the world." That discovery sent him on a quest to find the best Domino descendants available, those imbued with the heart that had made the stallion such a tough competitor. The best of those by far was Equipoise, the aptly nicknamed "Chocolate Soldier," whose gritty dominance on the track inspired America during the depths of the Depression. The problem was, Equipoise wasn't for sale. But his owner, Cornelius Vanderbilt Whitney, did have a good-looking colt from Equipoise's first foal crop: Equestrian, a chestnut ex-racehorse whose dam was a stakes-winning Man o' War daughter named Frillette.

As soon as Kleberg bought and shipped Equestrian to Texas in 1939, his focus turned to finding Domino-bred mares to cross with his new acquisition, hoping to intensify the influence of his favorite bloodline. He mentioned what he was looking for to the veteran trainer he had hired to run the King Ranch racing stable, Max Hirsch. The trainer told Kleberg about a mare he happened to own, Stop Watch, a black ex-racehorse who, like Equestrian, also was by a Domino-bred sire and out of a Man o' War daughter. Kleberg jumped at the idea of matching Stop Watch with Equestrian. They agreed on a price, and Stop Watch was shipped to the King Ranch.

Stop Watch offered Kleberg an enticing possibility: three more crosses to Domino to be added to the one coming from Equestrian. What's more, her dam, Sunset Gun, was also a Man o' War daughter, just like Equestrian's dam. In addition to the four crosses with his beloved Domino, he would get a doubling of Man o' War close up in the foal's pedigree.

In the spring of 1940, Kleberg sent Stop Watch to the ranch's bustling breeding barn for an assignation with Equestrian. Kleberg may have been eagerly anticipating the results of his inventive breeding program, but the racing world wasn't exactly holding its breath. Breeders dismissed the mating as hardly the cloth from which champion racehorses are cut, hardly the stuff of which Thoroughbred dreams are made.

On the track, Equestrian had been a great disappointment, the ultimate underachiever considering that his father was the great Equipoise and his dam was a stakes-winning Man o' War daughter who had already produced major stakes winners herself. In his brief career, Equestrian won two very minor races in eight starts and earned a total of just $1,580 in purses before being retired to stud at three. For her part, Stop Watch had shown even less promise on

Newlyweds Ethel and Hirsch Jacobs enjoying a day at the Hialeah Park races shortly after their 1933 wedding, capping a banner year in which the trainer led the nation in winners saddled for the first of a record seven straight years.

Proud parents Ethel and Hirsch posed with their firstborn, John, in this 1935 family portrait. John would grow up to be Hirsch's assistant trainer and heir apparent, saddling the Preakness and Belmont winners just a few months after his father's death in 1970.

Hirsch, shown here strolling at Hialeah with Ethel in the mid-1930s, reigned as the king of the claimers by smashing records for number of winners saddled—many of them in his wife's name and racing colors.

Hirsch took this snapshot during one of the Jacobs family's regular Sunday outings at the Runyons' Miami Beach winter home. Clockwise from left: wife Ethel, Damon and Patrice Runyon, and the Jacobs children John and Patrice, who was named after Mrs. Runyon.

Jacobs, America's winningest trainer, chatting with America's winningest jockey, Ted Atkinson, at Tropical Park in December 1944 on the eve of the wartime racing ban. Jacobs had by then tapped his fellow Hall of Famer to ride a youthful Stymie in eight races ranging from uninspiring early claimers to a 1944 Kentucky Derby prep stakes.

Stymie, with Bobby Permane up, made a sudden postwar transformation from cheap claimer to emerge, swanlike, as the Champion Handicap Horse of 1945. A "wonder jockey" whose light touch let Stymie make his patented come-from-the-clouds burst, Permane rode him to his first-ever stakes win and six more that breakthrough year.

Unleashing his rousing stretch run, Stymie thrilled the Saratoga crowd by running off with the 1946 Whitney Stakes under Hall of Fame jockey Basil James. Thus bringing his career winnings to $360,710, Stymie—the $1,500 claimer called "the Cinderella horse" by newspapermen—officially supplanted Alsab as the biggest bargain in racing history.

In the epic 1947 race that defined his legend, Stymie came from 22 lengths back with his furious finishing drive and outdueled Natchez deep in the Belmont stretch to win the $100,000 International Gold Cup by a neck and reclaim the crown of history's money-winning king.

For the gardenia-blanketed Stymie, as well as Ethel and Hirsch, the Gold Cup celebration in the crowded Belmont winner's circle represented the crowning glory of their rags-to-riches saga. For Hall of Fame jockey Conn McCreary, it was "the second greatest thrill of my life"—behind only his first Kentucky Derby win.

After the thrilling Gold Cup triumph, the Jacobses had to push their way through the frenzied Belmont crowd to the track so Hirsch could grab the bridle and personally lead Stymie to the winner's circle. The smiles on their faces betray how much more this triumph was worth to them than the $73,000 purse that raised their bargain baby's career earnings to $678,510—passing third-place finisher Assault as the all-time leading money winner.

Jacobs welcoming Stymie back to New York and their Jamaica racetrack barn in April 1948 for the start of a career-capping campaign in which the stout old warhorse would defend his title as the world's all-time money winner. This AP wire photo ran in newspapers nationwide on the eve of Stymie's bid to become the first equine millionaire.

Hirsch Jacobs and Isidor Bieber, taking in the races from their Saratoga clubhouse box in 1955, were the ultimate underdog outsiders back in the late 1920s when they forged an unlikely partnership that would turn the aristocratic racing establishment upside down by building America's leading Thoroughbred empire from the bottom up.

In a caricature drawn for the *Daily Racing Form*'s 1994 centennial celebration, the renowned cartoonist Peb captured the incongruous partnership of the sport's "Odd Couple": Jacobs, the buttoned-down trainer whose claim to fame was discovering Stymie, and Bieber, the Runyonesque high-stakes horseplayer whose claim to fame was discovering Jacobs.

Stymie's popularity as a working-class hero was never clearer than in 1949 when 30,000 adoring fans feted "The People's Horse" with an emotional farewell ceremony. TOP: Stymie's jog past the Jamaica grandstand elicited a crescendoing roar as if this were another of his majestic stretch runs. BOTTOM: Just before groom Joe Jones led him off the track he had graced for years, Stymie paused, his head held regally high as ever, to bask in the resounding cheers for one last time.

the track, failing to finish in the money in any of her four career starts.

As far as everyone was concerned, Kleberg had taken the old adage of "breed the best to the best" and flipped it on its head. As *Sports Illustrated* would put it years later, he "came as close as possible to breeding the worst to the worst." It was hardly the most auspicious beginning for the Equestrian–Stop Watch foal that was expected the following spring.

In the wee hours of April 9, 1941, the ranch hand who had been assigned to foal watch that night heard a rush of fluid coming from Stop Watch's stall. He knew it meant that her water had broken and that she would soon be delivering her foal. Within minutes, a tiny brownish muzzle appeared under the mare's tail, followed by two little front hooves, one slightly in front of the other. Stop Watch dropped to the floor of the stall, and as she started to push, the foal's shoulders appeared.

About fifteen minutes later, a bright chestnut colt with a white streak running down his face, big soulful eyes, and an unusually long neck lay at the mare's side. Stop Watch started to lick her foal dry, then stood up and watched him struggle to rise. It didn't take long for him to make an attempt at standing, though he quickly lost his balance and crashed back down to the soft bedding. After a few more tries, he got the hang of it and then wobbled over to his dam. Once there, he started running his nose along her side, instinctively searching for her udder. Soon, suckling sounds began to emanate from the stall as the colt vigorously slurped down his mother's milk. When he'd had enough, he began trying to figure out how to get back down on the floor to take a nap. It took a few attempts, but eventually he plopped down in the thick straw bedding and quickly dropped off to sleep.

Within a day, Stop Watch and her perky little colt were turned out in a grassy enclosure so he could start learning how to handle his body. As his dam grazed, he started to trot and then to canter around her, running back to her periodically to nurse. When he was full, he would drop down to nap for a bit, and then was up and running again, his blond tail flagging. At dusk, mother and son were brought back into the foaling barn, where they could rest and relax for the night. In a couple of weeks, they would be turned out in the pastures with all the other King Ranch mares and foals.

The birth of this colt was met with none of the fanfare that might have welcomed some Bluegrass country foal born to a champion mare and sired by a champion stallion. He could be lost in the anonymity of the vast Texas prairie, far removed from the limelight of the vaunted Kentucky Bluegrass. Born of obscure breeding, he would have to make his way from a state known for producing cattle and cow ponies rather than blue-chip Thoroughbreds.

It was indeed the humblest of beginnings for the little colt that would eventually be named Stymie.

While Bob Kleberg was busy trying to build the perfect racehorse deep in the Texas prairie, Hirsch Jacobs was wondering how he was going to get his own magical prospect. Until he figured that out, Jacobs would continue buying up cheap claiming horses and turning them into winners. In 1941, he did that well enough to reclaim the crown he had ceded the previous year as the nation's winningest trainer, saddling 123 winners to go along with a career-high $165,964 in purse earnings. But he was not content simply to go on as he had been, making a living one cheap claimer at a time.

Like Kleberg, Jacobs had Texas-sized dreams of creating a champion. And so, like Kleberg, Jacobs immersed himself in the study of pedigrees.

Most claiming trainers had been schooled to ignore pedigree in favor of past performance, since the idea was to run the horse back as soon as possible for a slightly higher purse in a race from which it might be claimed away. But Jacobs, the king of the haltermen, was not like most claiming trainers. Pedigree may not have been foremost in his decision to put in a claim—he maintained he went strictly by the horse's looks and his own gut—but he deemed good bloodlines a bonus. And pedigree certainly figured in his dreams of finding a future champion in the claiming ranks. What's more, he was starting to develop an interest in breeding. If he couldn't afford to buy a well-bred champion anytime soon, maybe he could make one.

For years, when he wasn't busy running his claimers, Jacobs was studying everything he could on champion bloodlines, poring over pedigree charts and the breeding books that lined his home library. While Kleberg was journeying to Bluegrass country in search of bluebloods and knowledge, Jacobs was going to the source himself: the master of all Kentucky breeders, Colonel E. R. Bradley. If a young horseman were going to handpick a mentor, he couldn't do better than Edward Riley Bradley.

Pushing forty by the time he claimed his first Thoroughbred, Bradley had already led a swashbuckling existence as a Wild West cowboy, a scout in the Indian Wars, a friend of gunslingers ranging from Wyatt Earp to Billy the Kid, a gold miner, a bookmaker, a casino operator, and, in what he always deemed his primary occupation, a high-stakes gambler. If buying a Lexington breeding farm after the turn of the century constituted his biggest gamble yet, Bradley resolved to remove some element of chance through the careful study of pedigrees. He soon emerged as the nation's preeminent breeder, earning the honorary commission of "Kentucky Colonel" for his pioneering role forging the Bluegrass State into America's Thoroughbred capital and the Kentucky Derby into its marquee race. By the time Jacobs started picking his brain in the 1930s, Colonel Bradley had rewritten history as the first owner ever to win the Kentucky Derby four times as well as the first to do so twice in a row.

Every chance he got, Jacobs would sit next to Bradley and talk pedigrees with him as they watched the races. Sharing a bench at the track, they made for an incongruous pairing: the short, stocky young trainer with the boyish face gazing up in rapt attention at the tall, thin, erect octogenarian with the high-band hard collar that had been all the rage in the Victorian era.

Jacobs would become so absorbed in their conversations that he'd lose all track of the time. One evening he got so distracted that he forgot he had made a date with his wife to do dinner and a movie. As the hours ticked by, Ethel started pacing back and forth in the living room, becoming more and more exasperated with him. When Hirsch finally arrived home, he apologetically explained that he had been with Colonel Bradley discussing pedigrees. That explanation was the only excuse Ethel would have accepted. It would not be the last time she would have to forgive her husband's tardiness when he was entranced by Bradley's words of wisdom.

Jacobs came away from those talks believing in bloodline nicks, in the dominance of the sire lines of Man o' War and Teddy, and in the importance of tail-female lines. Bradley was so convinced of the value of the tail-female families that he purchased and imported the mare La Troienne, a failed French racehorse whose pedigree traced back to the distaff progenitor of the family with the most winners of classic races. Another reason he was so taken by La Troienne was her sire: Teddy, the French distance runner whose dominance on the racecourse was exceeded by his brilliance in the breeding shed.

Although Jacobs had come to racing too late to see Man o' War run, he was well aware of the stallion's supremacy on the track and, following War Admiral's 1937 Triple Crown win, influence as a sire. Of the champions Jacobs had seen race, he was most enamored of Equipoise, the gallant and gritty Chocolate Soldier whose brittle, cracked hooves couldn't diminish his fiery determination to win. Because Equipoise had sired only four foal crops before his untimely death in 1938, Jacobs was always on the lookout for progeny that might have inherited the stallion's stout heart.

Bob Kleberg was looking for something similar as he watched Stymie and the five other products of Equestrian's first foal crop—Equipoise's grandchildren—romping through the King Ranch's pastures.

On January 1, 1942—only three weeks after the attack on Pearl Harbor provoked America's entrance into World War II—Stymie, like all foals born in 1941, officially turned one year old, per the Jockey Club's rules.

All of the King Ranch 1941 foals had been turned out together after weaning, but now they were separated by gender to prevent any unplanned breedings. The energetic youngsters would spend the day racing and play-fighting, kicking, rearing, and biting one another. Except for Stymie. The little chestnut was content to lope slowly along behind the others when they were racing around the pasture, with no ambition to rush to the front of the pack.

As a yearling, there was nothing about Stymie that caught the eye of visitors to the ranch aside from the way he carried his head: held high, in a manner that made him look almost as big as the other yearlings and reminded Kleberg of the colt's double great-grandsire Man o' War. Perhaps part of the reason Stymie didn't stand out was that he was a very balanced individual, with all parts fitting together harmoniously.

When fall came, Kleberg chose three dozen yearlings to begin race training and moved them to the big barn he had built next to the ranch headquarters. The barn overlooked the training track, a one-mile oval that reproduced the sandy turf of Belmont Park, where the King Ranch based its racing stable from late winter through the fall.

Once the yearlings had settled into their new digs, their initial training began. The early work was done in the youngsters' stalls. There they would be taught to accept bridle, saddle, and rider. They were fitted with a bit and bridle, then left alone with the tack on until they were used to wearing it. The following day, a saddle was placed on their backs and the girth tightened. If they offered no resistance, the next step was to let them feel the weight of a person on their backs. A groom would grab the rider by the shin, giving him a boost up so that he could lie, belly down, across the yearling's back. After a few minutes, he would quietly slide off the young horse.

When the youngsters seemed comfortable with carrying weight, they were led around the stall with the rider lying across their backs. The next day, the procedure would be repeated, except that the rider would now try swinging his leg over the youngster's back. Sometimes a yearling would become nervous at this point and hump up his back as if to buck or start wriggling around as if hoping to shake the rider off like a fly.

As soon as the yearlings were used to carrying an upright rider around in their stalls, they were led out to the training track. If the youngsters remained calm, the grooms would let go of the bridle and the riders would experiment with steering their mounts, pulling on the left rein to turn left and the right rein to turn right. When steering seemed dependable, the youngsters were sent out on the track in groups of two or three to slowly jog and get adjusted to the new sights and sounds. When the riders felt their mounts were ready, they would ask for an easy gallop.

Once they were galloping calmly around the track, the yearlings began their formal education under the supervision of the ranch's trainer, Bill Egan, and its longtime veterinarian, Dr. J. K. Northway. On the mornings when Kleberg wasn't needed out in the cattle pastures, he could be found at the training track, checking on the progress of his yearlings, watching them go out for their easy gallops and, later, timed breezes over an eighth of a mile—in track parlance, a furlong. Leaning on the rail with a stopwatch in hand, he anxiously awaited this first demonstration of what all his study, planning, and money had wrought.

Stymie's times betrayed an alarming sluggishness. Just like when he was out with the yearlings racing around the pasture, Stymie seemed to lack ambition when he was breezing on the training track. There was hardly a colt on the King Ranch that couldn't outrun him. Even with the long, powerful stride he seemed to have inherited from his famous ancestor Man o' War, Stymie would never win a race without drive and determination. That didn't prevent Kleberg from putting the Equestrian–Stop Watch yearling on his fall list of King Ranch prospects.

That November, Max Hirsch, the racing stable's hard-bitten trainer, made his annual pilgrimage to the King Ranch to look over the yearlings, compare notes with Kleberg, and determine their individual futures. Hirsch would choose the best of the crop for shipping to his winter training base in South Carolina and then on to his racing stable at Belmont Park for the spring season. Kleberg would always argue for giving every horse that had made it this far a shot on the racetrack, but Hirsch was stubbornly and coldly pragmatic, selecting only the most promising prospects and culling the rest.

When it came to Stymie, the trainer had to weigh the little colt's sluggish breezes against his big stride, good legs, and balanced conformation. That near-perfect structure meant Stymie had a better chance of holding up under Hirsch's infamously tough training regimen. In the end, it was enough for Hirsch to add the colt to the manifest of youngsters shipping east. Somewhat improbably, Stymie had made the cut.

Just before New Year's, the chosen colts and fillies were taken to a railroad siding outside of Kingsville, the city named after Captain King and located on the outskirts of the King Ranch. They were loaded onto specially equipped Pullman cars, first-class traveling stables with accommodations for horses and grooms making the journey to South Carolina. Stymie was on his way to a competitive cauldron where he would be in the iron hands of racing's toughest trainer.

Chapter 10

SLOW STARTER

Max Hirsch and Hirsch Jacobs were often mistaken for one another. Considering the similarity of their names and of their professional standing among racing's top trainers, even their fellow racetrackers could be forgiven for occasional mix-ups.

When *Time* magazine first profiled Hirsch Jacobs in 1936, the newsweekly's editors felt compelled to introduce him with an asterisk: as in "a 32-year-old pigeon fancier named Hirsch Jacobs.'" Readers consulting the fine print at the bottom of the page learned the meaning of the asterisk: "'Not to be confused with Trainer Max Hirsch and his sad-faced daughter, Trainer Mary Hirsch."

Despite all the confusion, the two Hirsches couldn't have been more different. For one thing, they had reached the pinnacle of their profession via very different paths from very different starting points. If Hirsch Jacobs was the New York city slicker, Max Hirsch was one tough Texas cowboy.

By the time he was ten years old, Maximilian Justice Hirsch was already riding Thoroughbreds in wildcat races at county fairs in the Texas Hill Country and working as a live-in exercise boy at a breeding ranch owned by the venerable Morris racing family. One hot spring day, twelve-year-old Max was helping load the ranch's yearlings onto a freight train bound for the Morrises' East Coast racing stable when suddenly he was seized by the impulse to hop aboard the boxcar with them. Four days later when the train rolled into Baltimore during a snowstorm, the young stowaway, still barefoot and clad only in his jeans, was found huddled, shivering and starving, in a corner of the freight car. The Morrises wrapped him in blankets, thawed him out with hot soup, and let him stay on as an exercise rider with their racing stable.

At fourteen, still two years shy of the minimum required for a jockey's license, Hirsch lied about his age so he could start riding races in the Morrises' familiar solid scarlet silks. A self-described "whoop-dee-doo rider" whose only strategy was to "go to the front as fast as I could and stay there as long as I could," the sixty-pounder booted home 123 winners before a growth spurt and weight gain forced him out of the saddle. Still a teenager when he segued into training at the turn of the century, he scraped by more on bets than purses for well over a decade before finally building a self-sustaining public stable. By the 1920s, he was conditioning well-bred champions like Grey Lag and Sarazen for well-heeled clients like the Vanderbilts and the Pulitzers.

Max Hirsch had already made a good name for himself as a trainer when he began saddling Arnold Rothstein's horses under a pseudonym. To hide an unsavory association with the notorious mob boss and World Series fixer, Hirsch put down "Willie Booth" as the trainer of record for Rothstein's horses. On a steamy Fourth of July in 1921, Rothstein took one look at all the bookmakers jamming the betting ring on the Aqueduct lawn and greeted his trainer, "What a great day for an old-time killing!" The pair proceeded to plot the greatest betting coup in the annals of horse racing. Spurred by Hirsch's tip that Sidereal, a young colt he owned and trained, was primed to finally break his maiden after three out-of-the-money finishes on bad feet, Rothstein arrayed a dozen hired guns around the betting ring just before the last race. At the sight of Hirsch leading the colt into the paddock long after the other entrants had all been saddled, Rothstein and his beards simultaneously bet Sidereal to win with multiple bookmakers, locking in 30-to-1 odds before his wagers drove the longshot price down to even money. In the fifty-eight seconds it took Sidereal to run away with the cheap maiden race, Rothstein made an $850,000 killing—the biggest bet ever won on a single horse. That night Hirsch arrived home lugging a trunk and announced to his wife, "Mama, here's the bet I win today," as he dumped his cut of the killing onto the table: a heap of bills totaling $200,000.

Hirsch, under the *nom de course* of Willie Booth, continued training for Rothstein's Redstone Stable another few months until the authorities ordered the serial race fixer to sell off his horses and stay away from the tracks. Losing one filthy-rich client couldn't make a dent in Hirsch's sprawling public stable. The same sportswriters who crowned Hirsch Jacobs "the king of the haltermen" had dubbed Max Hirsch "the millionaires' trainer." While Jacobs was buying up cheap claimers and running them like a fleet of taxicabs, Hirsch was catering to wealthy patrons who stocked his barns with high-priced Thoroughbreds. Hirsch's large public stable boasted a client list that featured fifteen millionaires at the same time, many of whom would often rendezvous there for lunch before the races and cocktails afterward. A *Saturday Evening Post* headline made Hirsch's stature clear: HE TRAINS HORSES AND MILLIONAIRES.

One of those millionaires was Morton Schwartz, a New York banker whose family's Wall Street stock speculation during the Roaring Twenties had earned them the nickname of the "Golden Boys." In 1935, when Schwartz was selling off most of the horses he had bred at his Kentucky farm, Hirsch tried to buy an untried two-year-old named Bold Venture at a Belmont Park auction. Before the hammer could drop on Hirsch's high bid, Izzy Bieber suddenly jumped in. Schwartz had enlisted his friend Bieber to surreptitiously buy the colt on the owner's behalf if the bidding didn't go high enough. Bieber bid $7,100 to win the auction, then promptly sold Bold Venture back to Schwartz for the same price.

Hirsch may have been irked by the ruse, but he continued to train Bold Venture for Schwartz, entering the unproven chestnut in the 1936 Kentucky Derby as a 21-to-1 longshot with an eighteen-year-old apprentice jockey on his back. After surviving a bumper-horse rodeo start involving the top contenders, Babe Hanford rode Bold Venture to a rousing upset, staving off the even-money favorite by a head, to become the first apprentice ever to win the Derby. As if to prove Hirsch's first Derby win wasn't a total fluke, Bold Venture unleashed a furious stretch drive to capture the Preakness by a nose, only to miss out on a Triple Crown bid when he bowed a tendon prepping for the Belmont Stakes and had to be retired to stud.

That same year, Bob Kleberg, who had stocked his King Ranch broodmare band with the seven Schwartz horses snapped up at the 1935 Saratoga Sale, hired Schwartz's trainer as well. He didn't have to wait long for Max Hirsch to forge the King Ranch's first champion with a big Schwartz filly that Kleberg had bought for a bargain bid of $4,100. Dawn Play dominated three major stakes, whipping the colts in one offering a richer purse than the Kentucky Derby, to earn the honor of champion filly of 1937.

Despite the wins that had put King Ranch on the racing map, Kleberg coveted a homebred champion, one that would prove his unconventional breeding theories correct. Although he greatly increased his chances of producing such a homebred when he bought Bold Venture from Schwartz in 1939 for $40,000 to reign as the

King Ranch's foundation stallion, Kleberg never gave up on his breeding experiment with his Equipoise son, Equestrian. That's why Kleberg had consulted Hirsch on finding the right mare to breed to the stallion, and why he purchased Stop Watch from the trainer.

Because the King Ranch had been late in informing the Jockey Club of the purchase, Max Hirsch was still officially listed as Stop Watch's owner when she foaled out in the spring of 1941. Which meant that Max Hirsch was listed as the breeder of record for the 1941 Equestrian–Stop Watch foal. Despite his vain efforts lobbying the Jockey Club to retroactively transfer the registration of the dam to Kleberg, Max Hirsch would forever remain Stymie's breeder. That gave Hirsch something of a vested interest, albeit not an ownership stake, in Stymie's future on the racetrack.

Right from the start, Stymie and Max Hirsch clashed.

Stymie's handlers at the King Ranch had not thought highly of him, and once the colt arrived at Hirsch's winter training base in South Carolina, it didn't take long for the trainer to discover why. If Hirsch thought poorly of Stymie, the feeling was mutual. What developed was a standoff between a most demanding old trainer and a most stubborn young horse.

As much as any trainer of his time, Hirsch treated all his charges like workhorses. It was not unusual for him to breeze his horses every other day, sending them out for hard works at fast clips. That kind of regimen was anathema to trainers like Hirsch Jacobs, who preferred to give his charges lots of rest, walks, and slow gallops between races to keep them fresh and eager to run when it counted. Max Hirsch believed in training all his horses hard, and he was quick to cull those that couldn't, or wouldn't, take it.

Stymie, an opinionated sort, wasn't willing to go along with the program. He bridled under Hirsch's iron hand. Born with an independent disposition and a strong will, Stymie did whatever he wanted to do, no matter what his handlers wanted. Nowhere was that more obvious than on mornings when the colt would put on the brakes without warning in the middle of a work. His trainer and his exercise rider would be left muttering about how difficult, headstrong, and disagreeable the colt was. Young Stymie's philosophy was translated by the breeder and turf writer Abram Hewitt: "Why be difficult when with a little more effort you can be impossible?"

The trainer had mixed feelings about even shipping Stymie north to Belmont Park with all his other racehorses for New York's spring season. On the one hand, Hirsch conceded that Stymie was "a good-looking colt" who would probably improve on the track, and he knew Kleberg had a vested interest in racing him. On the other hand, Hirsch didn't suffer hayburners that had shown no promise and were taking up valuable stall space in his Belmont barns that were crammed with real runners.

Hirsch settled on a compromise: he would run Stymie, but only in a claiming race. There was always the chance that the colt would surprise everyone and run as good as he looked. Of course, there was also the chance that someone would claim him for the $2,500 price tag, but Hirsch wasn't very worried about that.

On May 7, 1943, Stymie would make his debut in the first race of the day at Jamaica, a claimer for two-year-olds with a purse of only $1,500. He went off at 31-to-1 odds, the longest shot in the field of nine, and he ran true to form. Breaking slow from the gate, he was never a factor over the five furlongs, hanging around the middle of the pack for a bit before fading badly in the stretch. He finished a disappointing seventh, eight lengths off the pace. Not surprisingly, no one had put in a claim for him.

Hirsch could only shake his head. The trainer put Stymie back to work, sending him out for a series of three-furlong breezes over the next couple of weeks before determining the colt might be ready for another race. This time, Hirsch entered him in a maiden race for green two-year-olds who, like Stymie, had yet to win anything. It was the first race at Belmont on the Saturday of what promised to be an eventful Memorial Day weekend.

As the nation headed into Memorial Day weekend, World War II seemed to pervade every facet and fiber of daily life. Americans were heartened by the recent news that the Allies had taken North Africa from the Germans, paving the way for the imminent invasion of Italy as the first step in wresting back occupied Europe. Racegoers passing newsstands on their way to the track that Saturday, May 29, 1943, saw front-page banner headlines announcing President Roosevelt's creation of the Office of War Mobilization to oversee efforts stateside. Even more striking was the cover of the *Saturday Evening Post* featuring one of Norman Rockwell's most classic paintings: "Rosie the Riveter" flexing her muscles on behalf of all the American women toiling in factories and shipyards on the home front to produce the munitions that enabled their countrymen to fight overseas.

Like all spheres of U.S. society, the sport and industry of horse racing had been profoundly impacted by the war ever since the Japanese bombing of Pearl Harbor. In California, racing had been shut down in the immediate wake of Pearl Harbor so the tracks could be pressed into military service. Santa Anita Park had been converted into the nation's largest assembly center for Japanese Americans being forcibly relocated from their homes to internment camps, housing 19,000 at a time in converted barns and makeshift barracks. Everywhere else across the country, the rationing of gas and tire rubber, coupled with the curtailment of public transportation, was driving down track attendance; and a federal directive was forcing cancellation of entire race meetings at all venues reachable only by car.

On the eve of the 1943 Memorial Day weekend, it was announced that Saratoga could not host its time-honored summer meeting due to wartime rationing of gas and rubber as well as recently mandated travel restrictions banning pleasure driving. Saratoga's summer meeting, for the duration of the war, would be moved somewhere more accessible to fans and horses: Belmont Park.

In the face of all that, horse racing needed to prove it was part of the fabric of the American way of life that the nation was fighting to preserve. Roosevelt had famously given major league baseball the green light to continue without interruption, proclaiming "it would be best for the country" to have some distraction to cheer about and pronouncing the national pastime a force in boosting the morale of all Americans from the front lines to the home front. Racing officials saw their chance to make the case that America's oldest sport also provided an essential boost to national morale and to the war effort itself. The best way to accomplish that, they concluded, was to make a tangible contribution to the war effort.

As chairman of the powerful New York State Racing Commission, Herbert Bayard Swope forged war-relief drives aimed at raising and donating millions. Swope, the storied old *New York World* editor with the influence to spearhead a national coalition, devised a "Racing War Relief Fund" in which tracks across the country would donate profits on specified fund-raising days. Each track would set aside a "War Relief Day" on which all or part of its profits would be donated to the USO, the Red Cross, and similar organizations. Through its War Relief Fund, the racing industry had contributed over $3 million in 1942—more than any other sport—and was well on its way to nearly doubling that figure in 1943.

This Memorial Day was designated Belmont Park's latest War Relief Day, on which track officials expected a big holiday crowd and a record-smashing betting handle to raise funds. The first such War Relief Day had been made possible in 1940 when New York State finally adopted pari-mutuel wagering, the system whereby all bets were placed in a centralized pool from which odds would be calculated and payouts shared among the winning ticket holders after the track's commission was deducted. The advent of the betting windows and pari-mutuel machines at New York's tracks marked the end of an era—that of the old-time bookmakers patronized in the betting ring by high-stakes horseplayers like Bieber, Rothstein, and their friend Swope himself. It ushered in an era of mass wagering for the last state to adopt pari-mutuel windows, making the sport more profitable and facilitating the big betting handles from which the war-relief contributions came.

By the end of the war, well over $16 million would be raised from those War Relief Days. Tracks contributed in other ways too, bringing racing's total fund-raising contribution to $25 million. Many tracks sponsored war-bond drives, including one in which Kentucky's Keeneland Park auctioned off breedings to stallions donated by Bluegrass horse owners. In addition, high-society owners contributed all or part of their horses' purse winnings, while jockeys donated a percentage of their earnings as well as their racing silks to be auctioned off for war bonds. Even the racehorses did their patriotic part for the war effort.

None did more for the cause than Whirlaway. In the golden spring of 1941, the flaming chestnut had captured both the Triple Crown and America's heart, thrilling fans with come-from-behind stretch bursts, his long blond tail billowing in the wind. In the wake of America's entry into World War II that December, the champion nicknamed "Mr. Longtail" emerged as a true national hero. He spent 1942—the year he supplanted Seabiscuit as history's richest racehorse with half a million dollars in career winnings—crisscrossing the country as one of America's leading fund-raisers. To support the war-relief effort, Whirlaway went to the post a staggering twenty-two times in 1942, more races than any all-time great other than Seabiscuit had ever run in a single year. Every time he raced that year, the host track would pledge the day's receipts toward war relief. At the end of a year in which he had helped raise $5 million, it was no surprise that Whirlaway topped every poll as the single most popular athlete in America.

On the Saturday of Memorial Day weekend in 1943, everyone was speculating how Count Fleet, fresh off his runaway wins in the Kentucky Derby and Preakness, would dominate the Belmont Stakes as the 1-to-20 favorite seven days hence to complete his Triple Crown sweep just two years after Whirlaway's. Racetrackers who arrived early on this Saturday morning were treated to the sight of Count Fleet prepping for his Belmont Stakes coronation by breezing a speedy three furlongs. Anyone who witnessed that breeze would not be surprised the following Saturday when he se-cured his Triple Crown by an unprecedented twenty-five lengths.

Most of the crowd would be much later in arriving for this Saturday's races, though. With cars precluded by the pleasure-driving ban as well as gas rationing and with the special racetrack trains dis-continued, the 26,041 racegoers had to walk over a mile from the nearest railroad station. They were still streaming into Belmont Park a little after 1:00 P.M. Eastern War Time when the horses began trick-ling into the paddock for the first race of the day—the one in which Stymie was scheduled to make the second start of his young career.

* * *

As Max Hirsch watched Stymie and his groom enter the Belmont paddock area for the first race, the trainer could barely contain his irritation. The colt was on his toes and jigging, occasionally brushing up so close to the groom that the man would have to move over to avoid getting his feet stepped on. In the saddling stall, the colt continued to be fractious, making it difficult to get the saddle set properly on his back and the girth tightened enough to keep it in place during the race. When Stymie was finally tacked up, the groom led him out of the stall to where the jockey, a young Texan named Israel Garza, was waiting. Hirsch made sure he got the jockey boosted up in a quick, smooth motion. He didn't want any mishaps. Once Garza was settled in the saddle, he urged Stymie on to the walking ring that rimmed the paddock.

Leaning against the paddock fence, Hirsch Jacobs had been observing the scene, on the lookout as always for potential prospects to add to his stable. As the twelve two-year-olds made their way around the walking ring, Jacobs's gaze lighted on the bright chestnut colt that was jigging and tossing his head. Jacobs wasn't the least bit perturbed that the youngster seemed a little rambunctious. The only thing he saw was a superbly conformed colt with some spirit. He rather liked the colt's high head carriage, since it brought to mind photos of the great Man o' War, who happened to be Stymie's double great-grandsire.

"My, that's a grand-looking horse," he thought. "Any horse that looks that good has gotta run great."

As the jockeys turned their mounts to leave the paddock area, Jacobs took one parting look at the chestnut with the Number 1 on his saddlecloth whose rider sported the King Ranch's distinctive cream-white and light-brown silks with the "Running W" brand.

He turned to Izzy Bieber, who had been standing next to him the whole time, and said, "I got a feeling about that colt. I like the way he walks. He's a proud little thing."

Bieber knew what that meant: his partner was going to keep a sharp eye out for that colt, and if Max Hirsch dropped him into another claiming race, they should have their checkbook ready.

As the twelve horses disappeared into the tunnel leading under the grandstand to the track for the post parade, Jacobs turned back to the paddock, where he could await the arrival of the colt he would be saddling for the second race of the day—a cheap claimer, of course. That meant he would not get to see Stymie run in the first race, a maiden sprint with a paltry purse of $1,500.

Jacobs certainly didn't miss anything. In this uninspiring field of two-year-old maidens who were all, as they say, "green as grass," Stymie went to the post as a prohibitive 78-to-1 longshot. And he proceeded to once again run to his long odds rather than to his good looks. He broke dead last out of the gate and stayed there for most of the five-furlong dash down the straightaway course that cut diagonally through the infield, trailing lengths behind everyone else. The only reason he didn't finish dead last was because the horse in front of him abruptly broke stride, allowing Stymie to lope home eleventh, a galling sixteen lengths off the pace.

As far as Max Hirsch was concerned, that was the last straw. He resolved to sell off the darned hayburner, one way or another.

A couple of days later, he lucked out when an interested buyer stopped by the Belmont barn asking if Stymie might be for sale. They agreed on the price of $500, which Hirsch now considered something of a steal. The buyer, a small-time local claiming trainer who introduced himself as Falcone, handed over a $50 deposit, shook Hirsch's hand, and promised he would be back later with the rest of the cash and a halter to take possession of his new colt.

It was hard to tell which one appeared happier: the buyer, who couldn't otherwise have afforded even the cheapest claiming price for Stymie at the time, or the seller, who couldn't believe his good fortune in being able to unload this worthless nag he feared nobody would ever claim.

When Falcone got home to pick up the outstanding $450 so he could complete the purchase, however, he found his draft notice waiting in the mailbox. He turned around and headed back to Belmont. Finding Hirsch at his stable, Falcone explained his predicament and showed the draft notice to the trainer. Hirsch let out a sigh and reached into his pocket to dig out the deposit. Nodding solemnly, he handed the $50 to Falcone and wished him good luck.

If Hirsch couldn't sell Stymie privately, he decided to do the next-best thing: stick him in the cheapest claiming race he could find.

CHAPTER 11

CLAIM TO FAME

As he did every day around noon, Hirsch Jacobs came home from the racetrack and settled down for lunch. After a full morning supervising his stable and sending his horses out for gallops, he looked forward to eating a leisurely meal and then grabbing a shower and maybe a catnap before heading back to Belmont Park for the afternoon races. Seated on a bench in the breakfast nook just off the kitchen of his Forest Hills home, Jacobs took a bite of the sandwich Ethel had brought out for him and unfolded the *Daily Racing Form* on the table next to his plate.

He thumbed straight to the spread that listed the Belmont Park entries and form charts for this Wednesday, June 2, 1943, on the lookout as usual for any horses he might be interested in claiming. As soon as his eyes lit on the page with the entries for the first race, one name jumped out at him: "Stymie." The next line on the chart clinched it: "Owner, King Ranch. Trainer, M. Hirsch. Claiming price, $1,500."

This was the good-looking chestnut he had spotted in the Belmont paddock four days earlier and had made a mental note to claim the next chance he got. Not only was Stymie now entered in a claiming race, but it was also a cheap one to boot. Jacobs immediately put down the sandwich and glanced at his watch. Post time for Stymie's race, the first on the card, was 1:30 P.M. That meant Jacobs needed to get to the racing secretary's office at Belmont and fill out a claim slip by the deadline exactly fifteen minutes before post time.

Rising from the table, he called out to Ethel in the kitchen, "Hon, call the barn and tell them to get a shank ready."

He hastily pulled on his shoes and suit jacket, pausing only long enough to explain to his wife why he was in such a rush. "I'll finish lunch later," he said. "I've got to run out and claim a horse in the first race."

He hurried outside to the driveway, hopped into his green Cadillac, and headed toward the track. At the first light on Queens Boulevard, he checked his watch and realized he would be cutting it close. The drive to Belmont usually took almost half an hour, so he couldn't afford to hit any traffic. Fortunately for Jacobs, there were few cars on the road that day because of the wartime pleasure-driving restrictions. With the small weekday crowd of 11,902 having to walk the mile from the nearest train station to the track, the parking lot was all but empty. He pulled right in and made a beeline for the racing secretary's office.

He got to the office with only a couple of minutes to spare. That was just enough time for him to fill out the claim slip, which, as usual, he put in the name of Mrs. Ethel D. Jacobs. He didn't have to spend any time coming up with the $1,500 cash since the money was already in his track account, which was flush with his purse winnings from the previous three weeks of Belmont's spring meeting. He slid the claim slip into the machine timer to get it stamped and then stuffed it in the claim box. The wall clock in the racing secretary's office said it was exactly fifteen minutes to post time.

At the same time as Jacobs was spotting Stymie's name in the entries, the colt was still back at Max Hirsch's barn waiting for the groom who would walk him over to the paddock. Hirsch was hanging out at the barn when a little girl stopped by with her parents in tow. She walked up to the wizened trainer and said she wanted to buy a horse.

"How much money do you have?" Hirsch asked her in his slow Texas twang.

The little girl glanced at her parents beseechingly and then replied sheepishly, "Two hundred dollars."

Hirsch stroked his chin. "All right," he said, nodding toward Stymie's stall, "you can have this horse for two hundred dollars."

There was, however, one caveat that Hirsch had to explain to the little girl and her parents: Stymie was about to run a claiming race; if somebody claimed him for $1,500, the deal was off; but if nobody claimed him out of the race, the horse would be hers for $200. Little did he know that somebody, namely his rival Hirsch Jacobs, would indeed be putting in a claim.

Jacobs, having concluded his business in the racing secretary's office, made his way up to his clubhouse box to watch Stymie's race, another five-furlong sprint down the straightaway through the massive infield. As he watched the field of fourteen two-year-old maidens being loaded into the starting gate way out on the chute leading into the backstretch, Jacobs had no trouble picking out Stymie even without binoculars. He recognized the coppery chestnut by his distinctively high head carriage.

The instant the gate snapped open, Stymie officially became Jacobs's horse. Stymie's new owner watched his colt break slow, run evenly in the middle of the pack, and finish an uninspired seventh, four and a half lengths off the pace, splattered with all the mud that had been ignominiously kicked in his face from the rain-drenched track. Jacobs stayed only long enough to make sure Stymie looked sound as he galloped past the finish line, then headed back downstairs to the racing secretary's office for confirmation that he was the only claimant. No one was surprised, given Stymie's poor past performances, that there were no other claims made on him. In fact, many expressed surprise that Hirsch Jacobs had claimed this loser in the first place and wondered aloud whether the king of the haltermen had taken leave of his senses.

Out on the muddy track, the jockey dismounted, unsaddled his mount, and handed the reins to the King Ranch groom. Moments later, a steward's assistant informed the groom that Stymie had been claimed and instructed him to take the horse directly to the receiving barn. After each race, the receiving barn served as a way station for any claimed horse to be transferred to its new stable and as a urine collection site for the winner and one of the other purse earners to be tested for drugs. Upon arrival at the barn, the groom put Stymie in a stall and removed his bridle. Jacobs's groom, who had been waiting there since shortly after Ethel's phone call alerting the stable foreman to the claim, slipped a halter on Stymie and led him to his new home.

It wasn't until all of the day's races had been run that Jacobs finally had a chance to greet his new acquisition. Shortly after the last race, at about five o'clock, the trainer headed back to his barn for his customary last check on his charges, especially those that had run on the day's card. Typically he would spend most of the evening visit observing and inspecting any horses he had claimed out of the day's races. On any given racing day, that might include as many as five newcomers that were moving into stalls of horses that had been claimed away from him at the same time. On this day, the sole newcomer was Stymie.

As he did with each and every one of his new charges, Jacobs slowly entered Stymie's stall and quietly stood in the corner leaning against the wall. Stymie continued to munch his hay, ignoring the human sharing space with him. After a while, he stopped chewing and started to stare at Jacobs. Slowly, the colt made his way over to the trainer and started to sniff his chest. Jacobs reached into his jacket pocket to dig out one of the sugar cubes he always carried with him and offered it to Stymie. It was clear that the colt had never had a sugar cube before, and he sniffed it suspiciously. Then he put his lips around the cube and cautiously sucked it back into his mouth, letting it sit on his tongue for a moment before he started to crunch away. After a few seconds, he bumped Jacobs's arm, looking for another cube. The trainer dug back into his pocket and pulled out another treat for the colt. Then he scratched him on the withers and stepped out of the stall.

The colt walked over to the stall door and hung his head over it. Jacobs looked at his expressive face with the big soulful eyes and, between them, a big white star that flowed into a narrow strip and then widened near the nostrils. "He looks like an intelligent one," Jacobs thought. Just then, the colt snaked his long neck out and nipped at the trainer's arm. Jacobs chuckled to himself. "So you want to play, do you?" he said to Stymie, reaching up to rub the colt's forehead. "See ya tomorrow, little man."

That night at home after dinner, Jacobs went into his library and pulled down some stud books to research Stymie's pedigree. He discovered that the little colt he had claimed based on looks happened to have a pedigree that explained the superb conformation he had noted in the Belmont paddock, even if it was a few generations back. His sire's sire was the great Equipoise, one of Jacobs's personal favorites. What was more, both his parents' dams were daughters of the great Man o' War, which explained why Stymie had reminded Jacobs of all the photos he'd seen of that incomparable racehorse. Stymie gave Jacobs a chance to indulge his keen interest in Man o' War blood, albeit a poor man's approach with the stallion three generations removed.

The following day, watching as a groom hand-walked Stymie, Jacobs marveled anew at the little chestnut's conformation. "Any horse that looks as good as that has got to be running better than he is," he mused.

Jacobs suspected that Stymie had not thrived under Max Hirsch's intense work regimen. Which was fine because Jacobs's training philosophy tended toward the opposite extreme. He would put Stymie on the same kind of training schedule as the rest of his horses, rarely breezing them in between races, choosing instead to send them out on slow gallops or simply having them hand-walked around the barns. For the first six days since the claim, Stymie essentially rested. And on the seventh day, he raced.

For Stymie's debut in the pink and green Jacobs colors, the trainer picked a familiar spot: running him right back in another cheap claiming race for two-year-old maidens. Jacobs put a $2,000 price tag on the colt, figuring that was high enough to discourage any possible claimants. It was the first race at Aqueduct, and Jacobs made a point of arriving early. Stymie pranced into the paddock area, on his toes but reasonably well behaved. From the moment Jacobs stepped up to the colt, he started talking to him in a quiet, soothing voice. The comforting chatter went on the whole time he was tacking Stymie up. As Jacobs lifted the saddle onto the colt's back, he softly hummed one of his favorite songs. The sounds seemed to distract and calm the high-strung colt, and when he was brought out to be mounted, he stood quietly as Jacobs boosted the jockey up.

The trainer was entrusting the young colt to an apprentice jockey, a fellow Brooklynite named Joseph Rienzi. Known for his pithy prerace instructions, Jacobs simply looked up at the teenaged rider and said, "Do the best you can, kid."

By the time the field of twelve was loading into the backstretch starting gate for the five-and-a-half-furlong sprint, the bettors had made Stymie the surprising third choice at 8-to-1. The marked improvement from the previous race's 78-to-1 odds was more a reflection of the betting public's supreme confidence in Jacobs's knack for turning around claiming horses than in anything Stymie had yet shown on the track.

Once again, Stymie broke slowly out of the gate, but then he rocketed up to challenge for the lead heading into the turn. It looked as if he was on his way to breaking his maiden when, instead of rounding the stretch turn, he suddenly bore out, veering almost to the outside rail. By the time his jockey got him back on course, Stymie had lost so much ground that he'd dropped back to sixth place. Just when all seemed hopeless, he turned on the jets once again and drove to within a length and a half of the winner when he ran out of track. His second-place piece of the purse was merely $300, but Jacobs took much more than that away from the race: the trainer saw some mettle that he could build upon.

Jacobs's strategy was to race Stymie often, an on-the-job-training approach designed to condition him, season him, and settle him. Just four days after Stymie's first race for Jacobs, the trainer sent him into another maiden claimer, only this time raising the price tag to $3,500. The betting favorite for the first time, Stymie once again drove furiously down the lane, closing within a neck of the lead before again running out of track. The next day's *Daily Racing Form* suggested the only reason Stymie had to settle for second again was the inexperience of his jockey.

While realizing that such short sprints played against Stymie's long stride, sluggish starts, and penchant for stretch running, Jacobs knew that the colt needed more seasoning before stepping up to longer distances. In the meantime, it was also clear that the high-strung horse needed a more experienced hand on the reins than an apprentice jockey could provide. For Stymie's next race, another claiming sprint five days later, Jacobs enlisted Ted Atkinson, a leading jockey on the cusp of becoming the first ever to win a million dollars in purses in a single year. When Atkinson rode Stymie to yet another hard-driving, come-from-behind finish that left him just short of the winner, the bridesmaid pattern had become clear: Stymie's first five races in the Jacobs colors were all exasperating second-place finishes, spurring the *Daily Racing Form* to characterize him as "a throatlatcher."

When the New York racing season shifted from Aqueduct to Jamaica in late June, Jacobs was hoping the change of scenery might spark Stymie. This midsummer meeting had always been held up in Yonkers at Empire City, the smallest and least pretentious of the New York State racetracks, but wartime travel restrictions necessitated the relocation to a more accessible city track. It was only fitting that the meeting at Empire City, which was dubbed "the poor man's racecourse," would now be hosted at Jamaica, which was "the people's track" and the home base of Jacobs's stable. Alas, Stymie did not make himself at home when he was sent to post as a 2-to-1 cofavorite in another maiden race. Stymie seemed content hanging around the middle of the pack into the stretch, but at the time when he normally shifted gears, he came up empty, finishing a sluggish fourth, nearly five lengths off the pace.

The regression puzzled Jacobs enough that he decided to change things up. Over the first three weeks in Jacobs's hands, Stymie had run six races, one every three to five days, most of them five-and-a-half-furlong sprints against maiden claimers. Four of those were claiming races in which Jacobs risked someone taking him for prices that ranged from $2,000 to $5,000. Stymie had no takers and no wins. Because horses naturally love to run, Jacobs knew his job was to figure out why this one wasn't racing with enthusiasm. The trainer opted to give the colt a rest and see if that would freshen him up. After a three-week vacation, Stymie returned rested and refreshed, but no readier to run. He closed out the Jamaica meeting a well-beaten fifth as the 2-to-1 favorite in a $1,700 maiden race.

When racing moved from Jamaica to Belmont, which was hosting the Saratoga meeting that had been forced to the metropolitan area by the wartime transportation restrictions, Jacobs was still trying to figure out a good spot for Stymie. The trainer entered him in another maiden race, this time a claimer.

Max Hirsch noticed Stymie's name in the entries on July 28—with a claiming price of $4,000. Stymie's former trainer had been entertaining thoughts of claiming him back. Word was that Bob Kleberg, Stymie's original owner, was upset the colt had been claimed away and was urging Hirsch to get him back. Until now, Hirsch and Kleberg had been prevented from doing so by a rule that precluded previous owners from reclaiming a horse for thirty days. This was the first time since the deadline passed that Jacobs was exposing Stymie to a claim. Hirsch decided to claim the colt back on behalf of Kleberg and the King Ranch. The trainer had already filled out the claim slip in advance and was on his way to the racing secretary's office when he stopped to chat with a friend. By the time he excused himself and made it to the office, the deadline had passed and he found the claim box closed.

Shrugging, he went out to watch Stymie, once again the betting favorite, turn in another mediocre effort, finishing seventh. A week later, the slow starter got stuck in traffic and trudged home a galling nineteenth out of twenty-two in a $1,700 maiden race for which the betting public betrayed its loss of faith by making him an 11-to-1 longshot.

Six days after that, Jacobs stepped him up in distance to six furlongs but down in class, entering him in a cheap claimer for two-year-olds. Max Hirsch was all set to claim Stymie back at the $3,500 price tag. But at the last moment, he stopped himself because, as he would later admit, he "hated to give Jacobs that profit." What Hirsch really meant, to be precise, was that he hated the thought of helping Jacobs's business partner, Isidor Bieber, make a profit on Stymie.

That bad blood traced back at least to the Belmont auction eight years earlier when Bieber outbid Hirsch for Bold Venture as part of a scheme to win the colt back for the consigning owner. By the spring of 1943, the feuding pair had a complete falling out over Bieber's penchant for pumping Hirsch for inside information on whether a horse the trainer was saddling might be a good bet. "Bieber had a habit of snooping around in the paddock, coming right into the stall when you're saddling a horse and trying to find out if you're going with him," an anonymous trainer later told the *Saturday Evening Post*. "Max ran him out and Bieber got sore. He and Max stopped speaking, and Bieber took every horse Max ran in a claiming race that summer. He must have taken ten horses off Max."

Max Hirsch had mixed feelings about forgoing the claim as he watched Stymie take third that afternoon, suggesting that the colt might be finding his groove again. Jacobs had mixed feelings of his own, deciding to run Stymie back in a maiden claimer a week later and drop the price tag down to $3,300.

Right from the start, the favored Stymie seemed in rare form. He broke uncharacteristically well and quickly charged up to challenge the frontrunner, with only his jockey's restraint keeping him from grabbing the lead. As soon as he was allowed to run in midstretch, Stymie blasted to a five-length lead that he never relinquished. In his fourteenth career start and eleventh in the Jacobs colors, Stymie had, at long last, broken his maiden.

That didn't stop Jacobs from continuing to run him back in claiming races. Now that Stymie was done with maiden company, Jacobs raised the claiming price back up to $5,000 and put him in races with increasingly higher purses. Three times over the next couple of weeks, Jacobs ran him in claimers for that $5,000 tag. After Stymie grabbed a piece of the purse in each of those three with a second, a third, and a fourth, Jacobs decided the time had come to graduate Stymie from the claiming ranks. The trainer had rolled the dice ten times in claiming races at prices ranging from $2,000 to $5,000 without any takers. But he was done pressing his luck and, more than that, he deemed Stymie ready for a step up to allowance company.

Over the next month and a half, Stymie ran six allowance races, each succeeding one against tougher competition for increasing purses, and won two of them. Both triumphs came in the same rousing style that would become his trademark: breaking next to last in six-furlong sprints, working his way up through the field, then unleashing a powerful stretch drive past the frontrunners. Those wins, one by a length and a half and the other by a nose, earned Jacobs a total of nearly $5,000.

The last of the six allowance races, Stymie's runner-up placing at a mile and seventy yards, persuaded Jacobs that the colt was ready for a big step up in both distance and class. Trying stakes company for the first time just three days later, Stymie placed a driving second in a handicap at Jamaica over the same distance. Two weeks after that, tackling the distance again in a Pimlico handicap, he ran out of track while closing on the frontrunners and had to settle for third in a blanket finish.

For Stymie's last race of the year that November, Jacobs picked a featured handicap, a step up to a mile and one-sixteenth, in the middle of Jamaica's nine-day "Victory Meeting" for the benefit of war relief. Dead last going into the stretch turn, Stymie started muscling his way between horses and, within a hundred yards, he was on the lead. Pouring it on down the stretch, he kept widening the gap until he passed under the wire five lengths clear. A strong 2-to-1 betting favorite, he had thrilled the weekday crowd of 15,806—no one more than his owner.

Watching Stymie put an exclamation point on his roller-coaster two-year-old season with a rousing finish that showed some drive and determination, Jacobs realized he had a nice colt that liked some distance. If nothing else, Stymie had certainly proved himself a tough little colt. He had run a whopping twenty-eight races, a remarkably heavy workload for a two-year-old. Of those twenty-eight starts, he had finished "in the money" sixteen times: four wins, eight places, four shows. Moreover, he had grabbed a piece of the purse nineteen times, earning a total of $15,935—all of those winnings for Jacobs.

Of course, Stymie's contribution added up to only a small fraction of the numbers put up by a bustling stable that featured the stakes-winning Haile. The horses Jacobs saddled earned $210,775 in 1943 purses, bettering his career high of $186,371 from the previous year and bringing him within $60,000 of Plain Ben Jones, the rough-and-tumble cowboy who trained the likes of Whirlaway for the mighty Calumet Farm.

More to the point, Jacobs once again easily topped the annual trainers' list for most winners. The year before, he had saddled 133 of them, nearly double that of runner-up Jones. For 1943, his total of 128 made him the nation's winningest trainer for the ninth time in ten years.

That prompted the *Blood-Horse*, the venerable weekly turf magazine, to characterize Jacobs as the surest thing on the track. "About the easiest prediction for any given year of American racing was that

Hirsch Jacobs would be leading trainer, judged by the number of winners saddled," the article began, ticking off his record-smashing number of years topping the list. "As with Whirlaway, everything he wins now is a record." The headline on the *Blood-Horse* piece about the sure-thing trainer: DEATH AND TAXES AND JACOBS.

Damon Runyon couldn't have said it any better. Runyon, who knew a sure thing when he saw one, didn't even wait until season's end to send his long annual "Dear Hirsch" congratulatory letter from Hollywood, where he was producing movies based on his short stories. "Glad to hear of your success," he wrote in a December 3, 1943, letter on 20th Century Fox stationery, alluding to how slowly and sporadically news of East Coast racing traveled west. "I have followed you as much as possible and congratulations on coming out on top once more. I am delighted over your success the past season. I guess the boys will be shooting at your record for many a year to come." The postscript: "Also glad to hear you have that nice horse Stymie. Did you buy him or claim him?"

CHAPTER 12

WARHORSE

For more than five millenniums, horses had valiantly carried mankind's soldiers into battle. And for well over a century, U.S. Cavalry mounts had courageously charged headlong, as Tennyson poetically put it, "Into the jaws of death, / Into the mouth of hell." During the twentieth century, however, the role of the charger changed dramatically as the cavalry yielded to the mechanized reality of modern warfare, its mounted horses giving way to armored tanks. By the end of 1942, the U.S. Army, completing an evolution begun with World War I, had deactivated the last of its mounted cavalry regiments to become the first nation to fully mechanize its army.

Still, right from the moment the United States entered World War II as the most mechanized fighting force, horses continued to play an important role. After the Japanese invaded the Philippines in the immediate wake of Pearl Harbor, Americans on horseback led a cavalry charge against armored infantry regiments, improbably holding them off and later screening the retreat to Bataan for the savage and ill-fated battle to come. From the jungles of the Philippines to the mountains of Italy, horses could conquer terrain that stymied mechanized units. In both the European and Pacific theaters of operation, all the combatant nations relied on draft horses for transporting troops, supplies, and artillery. The Germans and the Soviets, in particular, would use a total of more than 6 million horses during the war. The Americans, in contrast, would use barely 52,000, their need dropping in inverse proportion to the accelerating mass production of tanks and jeeps.

Mirroring that evolution to military mechanization, the compound term "war horse" or "war-horse" eventually contracted into the single word "warhorse" and, at the same time, expanded to incorporate a modernistic dictionary definition: generally, a veteran of many struggles and conflicts, and, specifically by extension into the sports lexicon, a veteran Thoroughbred that indefatigably ran many races through gritty, grueling campaigns.

It was only fitting that one iconic warhorse would emerge from the racetrack as a home-front hero during each of the two great global conflicts. During World War I, Exterminator inspired a battle-weary nation by capturing the 1918 Kentucky Derby as a 30-to-1 longshot and then celebrated the armistice with twenty-one rousing races the following year. During World War II, Whirlaway followed up his 1941 Triple Crown sweep by running twenty-two uplifting races the next year to benefit war relief. The timing of their careers combined with the frequency of their races to expand the meaning of the word "warhorse." Exterminator would run a remarkable one hundred races in his eight-year career, Whirlaway sixty only because injury forced his early retirement two races into his five-year-old season in 1943. Warhorses like Exterminator and Whirlaway were exceptional even by the standards of that bygone era when Thoroughbreds would tune up for the Kentucky Derby with a hard race just four days beforehand and then go on to routinely make many times more career starts than their modern-day descendants.

Theirs was the golden age of the iron horse. The term "iron horse" had been coined to describe the newfangled steam locomotives that were transforming Victorian America. Coming full circle, it eventually became a term of endearment and respect for indestructible warhorses with the iron constitution and steely determination to soldier on furlong after furlong, race after race, year after year. The true iron horses were those durable older campaigners that ruggedly pounded out the miles against tough competition under backbreaking weight handicaps.

None of these iron warhorses, it turned out, would have anything on Stymie. The twenty-eight races Stymie had run in 1943 represented a staggering workload for a two-year-old still growing into an immature body—only seven fewer than Seabiscuit's 1935 benchmark by which all juvenile campaigns would be measured for quantity if not quality. If nothing else, Stymie had proven himself to be as tough and durable as any juvenile ever. He had run more times in a single season than Man o' War and many other all-time greats did over the course of their entire careers. Considering the strain racing puts on any Thoroughbred, let alone such a young one, it was remarkable that Stymie had emerged from his rugged and rigorous rookie season perfectly sound. While other trainers might have been tempted to give the youngster a long winter's rest to fill out and freshen up, Hirsch Jacobs shipped him to Florida early for a year in which the iron colt would race far more often than Seabiscuit, Whirlaway, Exterminator, or any other classy warhorse ever had as a three-year-old.

On January 1, 1944, the day he officially turned three, Stymie went right back to work, placing second in a cheap allowance sprint at Miami's Tropical Park. True to form, Jacobs was using Florida's winter season to tune up his colt, racing him into condition. After four more losses in sprints, Jacobs stepped him up to a distance better suited to Stymie's long stride and come-from-behind style. A third-place finish in Stymie's first mile-and-an-eighth race convinced Jacobs to take a chance in the Flamingo Stakes, Hialeah Park's Kentucky Derby prep. Stymie acquitted himself surprisingly well by closing strong to take third, five lengths behind Stir Up, the Whitneys' early Derby favorite. He capped his two-month Florida stint with a narrow allowance win, then shipped home to New York.

Back at Jamaica, after placing second in a handicap and romping in another allowance race, he was ready to try some of the nation's top three-year-olds again in New York's premier Derby prep, the Wood Memorial. Before a Saturday throng of 41,412 that would bet a record $3 million, the slow-starting Stymie again worked his way around the entire field to set up his stretch run and then closed gamely to take second three lengths behind Stir Up, whose triumph cemented his status as the prohibitive Kentucky Derby favorite. The surprisingly strong runner-up effort convinced Jacobs that maybe, just maybe, he might have a Derby horse for the first time in his career.

Stymie's Derby prospects, Jacobs told reporters, would depend on his performance the following Saturday in Pimlico's premier prep, the Chesapeake Stakes. The *Daily Racing Form* was so sure Stymie had already punched his Derby ticket that it reported he would be shipped down to Louisville right after the Chesapeake, listing him among the top half-dozen prospects in "The Run for the Roses" at potential odds of 12-to-1. Looking over the mediocre three-year-old crop that lacked a star like the 1943 Triple Crown winner Count Fleet, Charles Hatton, the eminent turf writer who had coined the term "Triple Crown," cautioned his *Racing Form* readers, "It might be unwise to take an upstage attitude toward

Stymie. That Texas-bred has exhibited a propensity for route racing."

The Chesapeake turned out to be a bitter disappointment. After getting stuck in traffic early, Stymie failed to fire up his usual kick, losing ground down the stretch and finishing seven and a half lengths off the pace in fourth place. His propensity for route racing, the very attribute that had made him a prospect for the mile-and-a-quarter Derby, had failed him in the stretch of the mile-and-an-eighth Chesapeake.

His Derby dreams dashed, Stymie stayed at Pimlico while the three horses that had beaten him shipped to Louisville. The Chesapeake runner-up, Pensive, went on to give mighty Calumet another Kentucky Derby win as a 7-to-1 shot, flying past the favorites in the final furlong and romping to the roses.

Jacobs wasn't ready to give up his dreams of saddling a runner in one of the Triple Crown classics, and he still thought Stymie could be that horse. To get the colt into the following Saturday's Preakness, Jacobs would have to make a supplementary nomination, a procedure permitting an owner who had missed the original entry deadline to sign a horse up at the eleventh hour for a stiff fee. Believing Stymie had a reasonable chance of earning it back in a small Preakness field that lacked star power, Jacobs ponied up the supplementary fee of $1,500. The superstitious trainer deemed it a good omen that the supplementary fee was the exact same amount he had paid to claim Stymie a year earlier.

Jacobs would have to scrounge up a jockey in a hurry. Because he ran a public stable of mostly claiming horses, Jacobs didn't hire contract riders like the private society stables did. That meant he had to recruit whichever jockey wasn't already spoken for by another trainer with a horse in the race. Stymie had been ridden by fourteen different jockeys in his forty races. The one who had piloted him to his maiden win, Conn McCreary, was the favored Pensive's regular rider. Nick Jemas, who had ridden Stymie in the Chesapeake, took the Preakness assignment, but at the last minute Jacobs had to substitute in Porter Roberts, a freelance journeyman unaccustomed to the opinionated colt.

Right from the fractious antics that made him difficult to load into the Pimlico starting gate, Stymie's first foray in the big time was a disaster. A 23-to-1 longshot, he ran like it in the Preakness. He loped along in dead last the entire mile and three-sixteenths, trudging home more than twelve lengths behind Pensive, whose driving win set up the third Triple Crown bid in four years.

It wasn't clear to anyone why Stymie seemed to have lost the will to run. Jacobs went back to the drawing board. His first inclination was to assume that the heavily raced colt had gotten worn out— or "stale," as horsemen put it—so he gave him a full month off. It would be an eventful month. On the track, Pensive's Triple Crown bid was dashed in the Belmont Stakes by a 16-to-1 longshot fittingly named Bounding Home, who overtook the odds-on favorite off the stretch turn to deny him by half a length.

Three days later, the world stopped and turned its unblinking attention to the war. D-Day had arrived. On the morning of June 6, 1944, America awoke to the electrifying news that the long-awaited invasion of Western Europe had just begun with 160,000 Allied troops storming the German-held beaches of Normandy. With racing at Aqueduct canceled in observance of D-Day, Jacobs joined the hundred million Americans hovering over radios for every scrap of news from the French coastline about the most massive and daring invasion in history. That's how it would be for days afterward, as the American GIs bitterly battled the Germans for every inch of ground through the hedgerows of northern France.

On June 12, Stymie finally returned to the track, placing third in an Aqueduct handicap. It was the start of a four-month stretch in which he lost nine in a row, managing to get a piece of the purse in several lower-level races but showing that he was not yet up to beating the top three-year-olds. When he broke the losing streak in a cheap handicap, Jacobs decided to try him again in stakes company. Stymie showed something in placing third in the Gallant Fox Handicap at Jamaica, but then he demonstrated just how opinionated and stubborn he could be if he couldn't run the race his way. In the Washington Handicap at Laurel Park, under yet another new jockey, Stymie was hustled up to the front early in the backstretch. He didn't like to be pushed so early in the race, much preferring to hang back and then run the frontrunners down in the stretch. He retaliated by suddenly dropping his famously high head to the level of his withers—"flattening out," in racetrack parlance for when a horse loses all oomph—and finishing dead last, a widening ten lengths off the pace.

If Jacobs gleaned some insight from Stymie's tantrum, the trainer learned much more from the next race. Back home at Jamaica for the Westchester Handicap, Stymie got wedged in the gate, and by the time he broke, he was half a furlong behind everyone. Faced with that much ground to make up, most jockeys would have let their mount gallop along easily in the back for the remaining mile and an eighth of the race. Instead, Bobby Permane, an apprentice jockey who had ridden Stymie four times before, let the colt run his race. From twenty lengths back of the pack, Stymie began making up ground on the backstretch and unleashed a furious stretch drive to grab third place, within a shrinking four lengths of the winner. After quitting in one race where he had been hustled to the front against his will, he had now shown real grit in fighting his way back into a race that other horses would have abandoned right after the starting-gate mishap.

Just when Jacobs was heartened by the highlight of an otherwise poor sophomore season, Stymie quit again in his next race, the Victory Handicap at Belmont. He then returned to Pimlico, scene of his Preakness disappointment, for two straight third-place finishes, the last one fully eleven lengths off the pace.

It seemed a fitting end to an uninspiring three-year-old season. A campaign that had begun with some longshot Derby dreams was ending with little promise. Stymie had run a staggering twenty-nine races, and won only three of them. He couldn't win any stakes races, though he did manage to place second or third in seven of them. By finishing in the money eighteen times, he won $36,325 in 1944 purses. That brought his total earnings to $56,260—not a bad return on a $1,500 claim, but not quite what Jacobs thought it could have been. Stymie had earned it the hard way like all claimers do: one small purse at a time. Through two seasons, he had made fifty-seven starts and won only seven, none of them stakes. If this colt was going to make the step forward into the tougher handicap division against more-mature iron horses, something had to change.

His iron constitution and sound legs notwithstanding, Stymie was in desperate need of a break. The colt had been in training for two entire seasons without a real letup, his fifty-seven-race workload just one shy of Seabiscuit's record total at the same stage of development.

At season's end on November 25, Jacobs decided against shipping Stymie down to Florida along with the rest of his racing stable as he had a year earlier. Instead, the tired colt was vanned directly to a Virginia farm where he could be turned out for the winter in the rolling countryside at the foot of the Blue Ridge Mountains. Jacobs trusted the farm's manager, Jack Skinner, one of the nation's leading steeplechase trainers and owners, to handle his racetrack layups with the tender loving care they needed.

As soon as Stymie was led off the van, Skinner pulled his shoes and turned him loose in a paddock. Stymie felt the sun on his back and looked around for a moment before finding a soft, muddy spot to roll in. He got up, shook himself out, cantered over to a nice patch of grass, and started to eat. At night and in bad weather, he would be put in a stall, but otherwise he spent his days wandering the grassy paddock that was his new home. For the first time in over two years, Stymie was out of training—and he thrived.

Then came the bombshell that would extend Stymie's vacation even longer than Jacobs could have anticipated: indefinitely.

Two days before Christmas, James F. Byrnes, the director of President Roosevelt's Office of War Mobilization, issued an edict that rocked the racing industry and stunned the sports world: "The operation of race tracks not only requires the employment of manpower needed for more essential operations, but also manpower, railroad transportation, as well as tires and gasoline in the movement of patrons to and from the track and in the movement of horses and their attendants. The existing war situation demands the utmost effort that the people of the United States can give to the support of its armed forces in production of needed war materials. The operation of race tracks is not conducive to this all-out effort. Therefore, with the approval of the President, I urge that management of these tracks take immediate measures to bring the present race meetings to a close by January 3, 1945, and to refrain from resuming at all tracks until war conditions permit. I am confident that the management of these tracks can be depended upon to take prompt action without the necessity of recourse to other measures."

Byrnes, the former U.S. Supreme Court justice whose sweeping powers in the Roosevelt administration earned him the nickname

"Assistant President," insisted that it was more a request than an order—"but," as he would later crack, "I am some requester." While the War Mobilization czar also called for closer scrutiny of the draft status for professional ballplayers, horse racing was the only sport singled out for a wholesale shutdown during the war.

Ironically, the edict came during a racing renaissance when the sport's popularity was soaring to new heights. In 1944, horse racing had shattered annual records with more than 18 million spectators, $1.2 billion in betting handles, $29 million in purses. Moreover, it had yielded $56 million in tax revenue to the seventeen race-sanctioning states and raised nearly $16 million for war-relief charities. All of that was considered a quantifiable measure of the intangible morale boost and diversion that the sport provided war-weary spectators and horseplayers. Racing had already resumed in England and other Allied nations closer to the theaters of combat, not to mention the U.S. winter hotspots of Florida and California. On Christmas Day, Tropical Park, returning after wartime restrictions had forced a one-year hiatus, opened to a near-record turnout for what would be an abbreviated eight-day meeting.

On January 2, 1945, U.S. horse racing came to a complete halt for the first time since the seventeenth century as Tropical Park and the two other tracks hosting meetings went dark. Racetrack operators, to a man, pledged their unconditional full cooperation. True to his political nature, Izzy Bieber was among the most vociferous of the patriotic cheerleaders at the track. "I'm surprised it didn't come sooner," he told reporters at Gulfstream Park on the day of Byrnes's directive. "I'll be tickled to death to go to work in a war plant." To make it easier for the war plants to find him, he asked the local papers to print his Miami Beach address.

One reason racing executives publicly embraced Byrnes's controversial "request" was that the war news coming out of Europe had turned unexpectedly dire. A week to the day earlier, the Germans had mounted a stunning blitzkrieg that forged a bulge within the Allied front lines in the Ardennes and triggered the bloodiest battle of the war. The dizzying news headlines that followed would become immortalized in U.S. military lore: the encircled 101st Airborne's gallant stand at the key Belgian bastion of Bastogne; the German surrender demand followed by the American commander's one-word typewritten reply of "NUTS!"; General George Patton's brilliant maneuver to relieve the besieged troops and turn the tide against Hitler's last major offensive of the war in the Battle of the Bulge. It was in the midst of all this that Byrnes had issued his racing edict. Nobody would breathe a sigh of relief until the bitter Battle of the Bulge was finally won a month later, breaking Hitler's last-ditch counteroffensive and poising the Allies to advance into Nazi Germany.

Jacobs followed the news from the Ardennes with his heart in his throat. His kid brother Sidney, who had worked as his assistant trainer before enlisting in December 1943, was wounded in the Battle of the Bulge. Their big brother Irving, a navy commander, was also wounded in combat. Both Jacobs war veterans would eventually return home to resume successful careers, Irving as a Brooklyn eye doctor and Sidney as a trainer striking out on his own at Hirsch's urging.

As a forty-year-old father with a wife and three young children as dependents, Hirsch had received a draft deferment. His racing stable supported not only his wife and kids, but also his mother, father, and several other family members. When the ban hit, many small-time owners had to deal with travel restrictions that stranded their racing stables and economic hardship that forced them to unload horses at fire-sale prices. That was not an issue for Jacobs, who ran a successful large stable and deemed Miami a home away from home where his family shared Bieber's beach house every winter.

Around Thanksgiving, just as Stymie was getting acclimated in Virginia, Jacobs had shipped the rest of his forty-horse racing stable to South Florida for the winter meetings at Gulfstream, Tropical, and Hialeah. When racing was shut down, the horses were stabled at Hialeah and the humans were staying at the Miami Beach house where blackout curtains were drawn tight every night against the threat of German submarine attacks.

All Jacobs and everyone else in the billion-dollar racing industry could do was watch and wait as the war—and the ban—stretched from fall into spring. On Easter Sunday, Byrnes recommended to Roosevelt that the racing ban be lifted on V-E Day.

Following Roosevelt's sudden death twelve days later, President Harry S. Truman, in his first press conference as FDR's successor, maintained he had no intention of lifting the ban. But with the war in Europe clearly winding down, the racehorses had to get back to work in preparation for what was assumed to be an imminent return to the track.

For Stymie, that meant it was time to wade back into training in Virginia. At the Middleburg farm, where the draft and the racing ban had depleted the workforce, Skinner found himself facing a scarcity of exercise boys to ride the few dozen horses wintering there. To fill the void that spring, he engaged a few local girls who had honed their riding ability foxhunting around Middleburg, which billed itself as "the nation's horse and hunt capital." One of them, Nathalie Hazzard, was assigned to ride Stymie.

"Good!" Jacobs said when informed of the girl's hiring. "It'll give him manners and make him easier to handle."

The girl's hands were considerably lighter than those of any exercise boy who had ridden the unruly and opinionated colt. Stymie, who had been known to bolt under the heavy hands of certain jock-eys and exercise boys, responded like a sports car under the girl's gentle touch. When Jacobs heard about the miraculous transfor-mation, he realized he needed to find the right jockey to handle the sensitive colt.

Stymie's training was coming along at the same time as earthshak-ing headlines, from Hitler's suicide to the fall of Berlin, signaled that the end of the war in Europe was imminent. On May 7, Germany surrendered unconditionally to the Allies. On May 8, America eu-phorically celebrated V-E Day. And on May 9, Fred M. Vinson, the Kentucky horse lover who had succeeded Byrnes as War Mobiliza-tion director a month earlier, officially lifted the racing ban.

Three days later, racing resumed in the United States, with the horses off and running at Narragansett Park in Rhode Island. In a little over a week, racing would return to its American birthplace of New York. At long last, Stymie was homeward bound—ready, will-ing, and champing at the bit.

Chapter 13

COMING FROM
OUT OF THE CLOUDS

On the warm weekday afternoon of May 21, 1945, horse racing returned to New York with a flourish that commenced with a flyover by a bomber during "The Star-Spangled Banner." The bomber was a stark reminder to the overflow Jamaica crowd that the bloodiest battle of the war in the Pacific was still raging on the Japanese island of Okinawa. The seven-race card that followed was a cheering reminder of the diverting excitement fans had been longing for the past six months.

The next afternoon, Stymie returned to the track with none of that fanfare to welcome his homecoming. Those among the smaller crowd of 28,211 who noticed him in the post parade for the sixth race would have been struck by the changes in the coppery chestnut's appearance. Since his last race in New York, Stymie had grown a little taller, gained some substance, and muscled up. At four, he still wasn't big by Thoroughbred standards, measuring just 15.2 hands, but he was stouter now.

In this debut tune-up of the season, a lower-level allowance race at a mile and a sixteenth, Stymie characteristically charged down the stretch overtaking the favored frontrunners but got caught by a longshot near the wire and lost by a head. He avenged that loss a week later with an easy three-and-a-half-length win in a lower-level handicap at the same distance. That was enough to convince Hirsch Jacobs that his rested and refreshed colt was ready for big-time stakes company.

Jacobs chose one of Jamaica's featured stakes races, the Grey Lag Handicap four days later over a mile and an eighth. Seeking a jockey with as much feel and sensitivity as the exercise girl who had ridden Stymie at the Virginia farm, Jacobs tapped Bobby Permane.

As a leading apprentice the year before, Bobby Permane had been anointed by the press as the latest "wonder jockey." With a boyish face framed by wavy blond hair, he appeared younger than his twenty years. With all of ninety-six pounds on his slight five-foot frame, he may have been too light for military service but just right for Stymie's back. The five times Permane had ridden him as an apprentice, Stymie had won twice and failed to finish in the money only once, suggesting that the particular colt appreciated the young jockey's exquisite balance in the saddle and soft touch on the reins. More than that, Stymie seemed happy that the jockey was willing to let him relax and run his own race. Permane had been aboard the previous fall when Stymie charged from twenty lengths back to make up all but three of them in his most promising race yet. That race had convinced Jacobs that the same colt who did little if pushed early on would instead run his heart out if allowed to go along easily for at least half a mile before settling into a long stretch drive.

Now, as he hoisted Permane into Stymie's saddle in the Jamaica paddock before the Grey Lag, Jacobs gave jockey instructions that were more specific than usual. Typically he gave few instructions, believing that the good jockeys didn't need them, the bad ones couldn't follow them, and the young ones would get them mixed up anyway. Sometimes his final directive amounted to little more than "just keep turning left." This time, Jacobs was more pointed.

"Let him run his race," the trainer told Permane. "He likes to come from way behind. So let him drop out of it, then let him make his one big run and come from out of the clouds."

Following those prerace instructions to the letter, Permane let Stymie lope out of the gate and then drop back as a sudden thunderstorm deluged the track. The colt seemed content to plod along for nearly a mile as the favorites drew farther and farther away. He was a full eleven lengths back when he finally started to make his move coming off the stretch turn. As if shot out of a cannon, he powered toward the pack and then started picking them off, one by one, as if they were standing still. Approaching the final furlong, he set his sights on the leader. Stymie came alongside the odds-on favorite, and the two colts dueled stride for stride toward the fast-approaching finish line. With seventy yards to go, Stymie surged ahead to win by a neck.

In the sixtieth start of his career, the little claimer had finally captured a stakes race, not to mention its $10,640 first prize. For Jacobs, it was proof that he had read his colt right. From now on, he would do his best to make sure that Stymie got to run races his way: dropping far back in the early going and then making his one big run to come from out of the clouds.

No racetrack vernacular better suited a horse than "out of the clouds" fit Stymie. In racing parlance, the phrase describes a horse that suddenly comes from way back off the pace. Whatever its etymology—whether it is some variation on "out of nowhere," "out of the clear blue sky," or "out of the clouds of dust" kicked up by the frontrunners—it described a special kind of closer whose thrilling from-the-clouds stretch drives yanked fans right out of their seats. The high-headed Stymie added his own unique twist. As he gathered himself to unleash his kick, Stymie would lift his regal head even higher at the very time that most racehorses tend to drop theirs down. His from-the-clouds racing style became the perfect metaphor for his overnight transformation from cheap claimer into stakes winner.

Two weeks after coming out of the clouds for his first stakes triumph, Stymie took on Devil Diver, the iron horse of his wartime generation, in the rich Suburban Handicap at Belmont. Devil Diver, the six-year-old pride of the Whitneys' stable, was the long-reigning champion of the tough handicap division, in which seasoned horses carry different weights assigned in an effort to level the playing field. For each of the previous two years, Devil Diver had earned the title of America's Champion Handicap Horse the hard way: taking on all comers under backbreaking weight handicaps. While the sturdy bay was often assigned the highest weights in his races, hauling up to 140 pounds, Stymie's lackluster past performances still qualified him for the lowest imposts from the handicappers.

For the Suburban's mile and a quarter, the heavily favored Devil Diver would have to lug 132 pounds, spotting Stymie 13 pounds. Right from the start, Stymie settled in at the back as Devil Diver led the field down the backstretch at a leisurely clip. Rounding the far turn, Devil Diver turned on the speed and began drawing away while Stymie still plodded along in dead last. Stymie was seven lengths back when he finally made his move, rocketing forward and passing all but Devil Diver, who was being urged on with the whip. At the wire, the favorite was still two lengths ahead of Stymie. The victory gave Devil Diver two legs of the so-called Handicap Triple Crown, setting him up for a potential sweep and a rematch with Stymie in the Brooklyn Handicap.

With Devil Diver resting and pointing toward that race a month away, his regular rider, the incomparable Eddie Arcaro, was open to new mounts. Arcaro was fresh off his third win in the Kentucky

Derby, which this year had been postponed five weeks to June from its traditional May date because of the wartime ban. When Jacobs offered him the mount on Stymie for the featured Queens County Handicap on Aqueduct's opening day, Arcaro jumped at the chance to check out the competition from the catbird seat.

From the first time Arcaro had laid eyes on the coppery chestnut, the jockey had dismissed Stymie as "a runty, awkward little clown that couldn't walk right, let alone run." Arcaro had secured his stature as "The Master" by taming the willful Whirlaway while artfully piloting him to the Triple Crown four years earlier. If he could instantly fix Whirlaway's zany habit of veering to the outside rail off the stretch turn, surely he could deal with another stubborn colt who insisted on running a race only one way—*his* way.

With Arcaro on Stymie's back, the big opening-day crowd at Aqueduct sent the colt to the post as the even-money betting choice. No sooner had they loaded in the starting gate than Stymie reared up, forcing Arcaro to step off his mount. Stymie proceeded to sit down and then bounce back up. Arcaro nonchalantly settled back onto the colt's back. The incident clearly had an impact since Stymie dropped back farther than usual, fully twenty-one lengths off the pace. The hole he had dug for himself was too deep to climb out of in a short race of a mile and a sixteenth, and his usual stretch drive left him two lengths short at the wire.

Jacobs could shrug off that runner-up finish as a glorified prep for the toughest test Stymie had yet to face: a rematch with Devil Diver in the prestigious Brooklyn Handicap, a historic $50,000 stakes race that had been won by the likes of Exterminator, Seabiscuit, and Whirlaway. So great was the hype for the Brooklyn Handicap that racing executives moved the Fourth of July card from Aqueduct to Belmont in order to accommodate the 52,169-strong holiday crowd that would bet a record $3.8 million.

Once again, Devil Diver, the even-money favorite to complete his sweep of the Handicap Triple Crown, was assigned the highest weight at 132 pounds. Stymie, a 6-to-1 shot, got 116. Based on the rule of thumb that a horse is slowed a length for every 2 to 3 pounds of lead added to his saddle pad, Stymie's 16-pound advantage could have been worth at least five lengths over the race's mile-and-a-quarter distance.

Jacobs, though, was more concerned with the bigger disadvantage that Stymie's come-from-behind style posed in a higher quality stakes race than he had ever run. A plodding come-from-the-clouds closer like Stymie needed an honest pace up front to run the finishing speed out of all the faster horses, tiring them out so he could pick them off down the stretch. To ensure that kind of early speed to set up the one big run, Jacobs decided to also enter Stymie's stablemate Haile, a stakes-winning sprinter, to serve as a pacesetting rabbit.

As the field moved down the backstretch, Stymie was loping along thirteen lengths behind the leaders while Haile was doing his job up front, dragging the favorites through a blistering opening three quarters. At the top of the stretch, Devil Diver shot to the front. Alert now, Stymie pricked his ears forward and raised his head. With no urging from Permane, the colt fired up his big engine and lengthened his stride. Coming wide off the turn, he gained more speed and started to pick off horses one by one, cutting Devil Diver's lead with every stride. Arcaro glanced back to see the onrushing chestnut and started slashing his mount with the whip. But Stymie kept coming. He passed Devil Diver midstretch and then surged ahead of the Whitney colt. By the time he hit the wire, Stymie was a length and a quarter in front.

The $1,500 claiming horse had just earned a $39,120 first prize for two minutes and two seconds of work, pushing his career winnings over the $100,000 mark. It was, as the Associated Press pronounced the next day in newspapers across the country, the climax of "a Horatio Alger story of the turf."

Things were about to change big-time for the equine Horatio Alger. In every sense, Stymie was stepping up in class. Upsetting the two-time reigning Champion Handicap Horse meant that his weight advantage would start shrinking. From now on, he would be shouldering a heavy load.

Still, there were some perks that came along with being a top handicap horse. He got the best stall in Jacobs's backside barn at the far end of the Jamaica property, where the only disturbances to break the peace and quiet were the trains that rattled past the nearby rail station. He had a regular jockey in Bobby Permane. And he rated the services of Jacobs's favorite groom, Joe Jones, who had a reputation for being able to calm even the most twitchy of horses. All of which would help Stymie prepare for the grueling stretch of tough stakes handicaps to come.

As the summer heated up, the war in the Pacific continued to cast a pall over the American psyche. Ever since Okinawa had finally fallen in June, the terrifying prospect loomed of an invasion of mainland Japan and an unthinkable cost in American casualties. That all changed on August 6 when a U.S. B-29, armed with a weapon scientists had been developing in secret, dropped the atomic bomb on Hiroshima. Three days later, the second atomic bomb rained ruin on Nagasaki. Finally, on the evening of August 14, President Truman announced Japan's unconditional surrender, ending the most massive and destructive war the world had ever known and sparking spontaneous V-J Day celebrations all across America.

The following day, still basking in the afterglow of mass euphoria, 45,576 revelers jammed Belmont Park to continue celebrating the peace in style. Many of them came to cheer and bet on Stymie,

New York's newest fan favorite, in the featured Whitney Stakes. Lugging 126 pounds, Stymie disappointed all his backers as he struggled to close a thirteen-length deficit and trudged home a distant third, seven lengths behind a three-year-old carrying only 103 pounds.

Three days later, Stymie again had to shoulder top weight of 126, in the Saratoga Handicap at Belmont. Once again, the burden proved too much over the same mile and a quarter. The gutsy closer, who a month earlier had made up twenty-two lengths to win a rich stakes race, this time fell woefully short. As gamely as he tried to make up twenty-five lengths, he lugged home in sixth place, a good six lengths off the pace. It was the first time all year, through ten races, that he had failed to finish in the money. Shaking his head, Jacobs lamented to reporters, "I don't think he can win under a hundred and twenty-six pounds. He's earned it all right—I don't mean he shouldn't have had it—but I don't think he can carry it."

As if responding to his trainer's doubts, Stymie carried the same 126-pound impost like it was a feather for a mile and three-quarters in his very next race, the Saratoga Cup at Belmont. By cruising home three lengths in front, Stymie showed himself to be a true stayer who got better every stride he gobbled up beyond the classic distance of a mile and a quarter.

Which is why the two-mile Jockey Club Gold Cup a month later should have played right into his strength and stamina. In a bizarre twist, the early pace was so snail-like that Stymie, the confirmed slow starter, suddenly found himself on the lead barely half a mile into the marathon. As he cruised past the grandstand with a full mile-and-a-half lap of the big Belmont oval still to run, Stymie was a length in front of the pack. Having never led this early in a race, the colt seemed slightly confused. Permane, mistakenly thinking his mount must be going too fast, started tugging on the bit to rate him. Stymie wasn't happy, sulkily dropping all the way to fifth. When it was time to summon his trademark drive, he refused, passing only a couple of tired horses to take third. He finished six lengths behind the winner, Pot o' Luck, whose eleven-pound weight advantage had helped make him the odds-on favorite over Stymie. Much as Jacobs would have preferred to forget the whole fluky affair, he did come away with one new bit of wisdom: given the colt's aversion to being by himself, make sure he always has someone to chase.

After bouncing back to win two of three handicaps during Jamaica's fall meeting, Stymie shipped to Baltimore in mid-November to close out his season with a trio of Pimlico stakes. Waiting for him there was the fellow four-year-old deemed the hottest handicap sensation of the year: Armed.

Born at Kentucky's Calumet Farm just three weeks after Stymie had been foaled in Texas, Armed was a little brown colt so ornery that he regularly bit anyone who got too close and kicked hay off his groom's pitchfork. As a yearling, he proved so stubborn and studdish that Plain Ben Jones, the no-nonsense trainer busy building Calumet into the nation's racing dynasty, declared him un-trainable and sent him back to be gelded, turned out to grow up, and put to work on the farm as a lowly stable pony. Armed didn't make it back to the racetrack until he was three, when he showed little promise in seven starts. It wasn't until the spring of 1945 that he seemingly came out of nowhere, winning nine of fourteen starts to put him on a collision course with Stymie.

If Armed and Stymie took measure of each other as they paraded onto the Pimlico track for the first of what promised to be many meetings, they might have noticed their shared lack of stature as the two smallest horses in the field. Once the gate snapped open for the Pimlico Special, though, there was no mixing them up. Armed settled into cruise control on the rail, stalking the leaders and waiting for his jockey to turn him loose. Stymie got out last and hung back, seven lengths off the pace. When Stymie finally made his move, Armed was already exploding into the lead and opening up five lengths of daylight. Stymie could close no better than third, six lengths behind Armed. Since both carried the same 126 pounds, there were no excuses. The only rationalization Jacobs could make was that the short distance of a mile and an eighth played right into Armed's strength and Stymie's weakness.

After Stymie redeemed himself by winning the Riggs Handicap a week later, Jacobs could focus on the race he had been pointing the colt toward all along: the Pimlico Cup Handicap, a two-and-a-half-mile marathon that would play to Stymie's advantage in his highly anticipated rematch with Armed. When Armed was assigned top weight in the loaded field, Jones decided to hold him out and let him rest on his laurels for the remainder of the season. That left Stymie, a slight favorite in a field that included two three-year-olds who had already whipped him, to carry the heaviest burden in the race—and in his career—at 128 pounds.

A couple of days before the race, Joe Palmer, the respected turf writer for the *New York Herald Tribune*, chanced by the Jacobs barn as Stymie was being walked. The colt was all puffed up, his neck curling and his nostrils flaring. He was so bursting with excitement that his feet barely touched the ground as he made his way back and forth under the shedrow. "The horse almost radiated energy—you expected to hear it crackle," Palmer wrote. "His coat had the sheen that a horse gets only when he is in the hardest condition. Moreover he was looking for trouble."

The newspaperman was careful not to get too close for fear of getting bitten or kicked. Jacobs saw this and said, "That's the way he is—when he's good, that is. When he's no good, you can lead him on a string. But when he's good, you've got to watch him. He isn't mean or anything like that. He just feels so good he can't stand it. Sometimes after a turn or two, he gets so we can't manage him and we have to put him back in the stall."

Stymie was so primed that Palmer half expected him to explode out of the starting gate like a rocket. But Stymie being Stymie, he broke slow, though not last. For the nation's longest race, Permane was perfectly content for Stymie to hang back in fourth place, half a dozen lengths off the pace, watching the frontrunners trade the lead for two laps around the mile track. As they headed up the backstretch the last time approaching the half-mile pole, Stymie was still settled in fourth but with Pot o' Luck now drafting at his hip. As soon as Stymie reached the pole, exactly half a mile from the finish line, Permane turned him loose unexpectedly early. The jockey ducked down and crouched over Stymie's neck, and the colt surged forward, leaving Pot o' Luck behind and passing all three frontrunners in half a dozen ground-eating strides. Rounding the turn, he kept opening his lead farther and farther. As he hit the stretch, a gust of wind lifted Permane's silk cap and blew it back over his mount's tail. Stymie was already a dozen lengths away by the time the salmon-pink cap landed on the muddy track. He was so far in the front of the field that Permane opted to ease him as they approached the wire. When Stymie cruised under it, he was still a full eight lengths ahead of runner-up Pot o' Luck.

Joe Palmer wasn't the only sportswriter in the Pimlico press box to be left speechless by Stymie's exhilarating performance. But he was the one who would later tap out words that have echoed through the decades: "This tourist, who doesn't scare easily in print, will long remember the way Stymie came around the turn in the Pimlico Cup Handicap with his copper mane flying in the wind, making pretty good horses look as if they had a pressing engagement with the quarter pole."

Stymie had closed out his four-year-old season the same way he ran his races: with a rousing rally and a forceful finish.

At year's end, against all odds, Stymie was crowned the Champion Handicap Horse of 1945. In the race for the honor, he didn't merely nose out the rest of the field—he got twice as many votes as the runner-up, Armed, from the *Daily Racing Form*'s panel of thirty staff experts.

The numbers on the form chart spoke volumes: Stymie had won nine of his nineteen starts, placing second on four occasions and third another four times while failing to come in the money only twice. He earned $225,375 in purses—second only to 1945's Horse of the Year, Busher, and the most ever won by a four-year-old. That was all the more remarkable considering that it was achieved in barely seven months, the first five months of the season having been lost to the wartime racing ban.

More than any numbers, it was the style with which Stymie had achieved them that made sportswriters gush. They expressed their awe at his thrilling performances with a thesaurus full of superlatives to describe what drove him down the stretch: "heart," "courage," "grit," "will," "determination."

Explaining Stymie's selection as a 1945 champion in the annual *American Racing Manual*, Charles Hatton suggested that just one look at the colt's conformation would reveal why he was the perfect handicap horse. "When he stands in the winner's enclosure after one of his sensational finishes, his appearance matches his achievement," Hatton wrote. "His head is of striking beauty, rather small for a horse of his size, very lean and clean and blood-like. His neck is long and equally clean and blood-like, his shoulder magnificent, breast both broad and deep, barrel rather long and slim, but very round. Over the hips he is Equipoise over again; his quarters are not particularly powerful, but his stifles immensely so. His limbs are slender, their extremities even daintily chiseled and their investiture of muscle and tendon slim and light. He is, in short, as one studies him with critical appreciation, the very beau-ideal of the Cup horse."

Stymie's Algeresque climb from cheap claimer to handicap champion paralleled the rags-to-riches rise of the man who had found him in the discard heap and transformed him into a prince in The Sport of Kings, Hirsch Jacobs. After reigning as the nation's winningest trainer eleven of the previous twelve years, Jacobs had slipped to fourth on the annual list with ninety-five victories. Nevertheless, he had just enjoyed his best year by the measurement that matters more to the racing cognoscenti: money. The horses he saddled had earned $499,985 in purses, just $10,670 shy of the top spot on the trainers' money list. And Stymie could be personally thanked for nearly half of those earnings.

With the emergence of his first national champion, Jacobs would finally be accorded the respect he had always been denied. No longer could he be dismissed as "just a claiming trainer" who wouldn't know what to do with a stakes horse if he ever got his hands on one. Now he had proven not only that he could transform a cheap claimer into a stakes horse, but also that he could then take that stakes horse and make him into a champion. That wasn't lost on rich owners who wanted to think they had the very best trainer for their stables full of the very best horses. In fact, they were lining up for Jacobs's services.

One of them was the movie mogul Louis B. Mayer, who had parlayed the fortune he had made running Hollywood's biggest film studio into one of the nation's finest racing stables and breeding operations. In just a few short years, he had assembled a Thorough-bred empire the same way he had built Metro-Goldwyn-Mayer: around A-list stars. In the afterglow of his prized filly Busher's Horse of the Year triumph, Mayer now coveted the best A-list trainer his money could buy. He asked if Jacobs would be inter-ested. Though Jacobs had always demurred whenever a society stable offered him a job because he preferred being his own boss, Mayer's offer was too tempting not to consider. Jacobs asked if his partner, Izzy Bieber, could come along in a package deal. When Mayer refused, Jacobs walked away.

Jacobs's loyalty to his partner was unwavering. Sportswriters and racetrackers could never understand the tie that bound Jacobs and Bieber into what the *Daily Racing Form* called their "Odd Couple" partnership. No one seemed to know what exactly Bieber brought to the table, though it was always assumed that he had something to do with managing the stable's finances. It certainly wasn't horse-manship. While Jacobs could famously identify individual horses from furlongs away without the aid of binoculars, Bieber couldn't even recognize his own horses. Or, as Jacobs once cracked, "He couldn't pick Whirlaway out of a herd of buffalo."

Bieber owned a Times Square bar and grill named The Paddock, the walls of which he covered with photos of the racehorses that he couldn't pick out of a herd of buffalo. The joint on Broadway near 50th Street was once a popular hangout where horseplayers drowned their sorrows while gazing at the racing photos. Though he had stopped dropping by every evening because "too many peo-ple began touching me for fives and tens," Bieber always made sure the gallery of gallopers was up to date. The walls served as a pictorial history of all the cheap claimers that had carried the Bieber-Jacobs partnership to this pinnacle: Character, Jack Biener, On Tap, Action, Caballero II. Now, for the first time, Bieber could hang the pretty picture of a cheap claimer who had blossomed into a classy champion: Stymie.

How exactly they had gotten to this point was a mystery to even the trainer who had engineered the metamorphosis. Was it the maturity that one more year brought Stymie? Was it the six-month rest mandated by the wartime racing ban? Whatever it was, all Jacobs knew was that he wasn't about change things up anytime soon.

His grueling four-year-old season behind him, Stymie would be sent back to the Virginia farm where he had spent the previous winter and spring. Before the shipping van arrived, Jacobs took both sides of the colt's halter in his hands and looked Stymie in the eye. "Do just what you did last year," Jacobs told the colt with a smile. The next day, a barefoot Stymie was picking out an especially muddy spot for a nice, relaxing roll.

CHAPTER 14

"THE PEOPLE'S HORSE"

The golden age of horse racing was hitting its stride just as post-war America was starting to boom. Scaling new peaks of popularity, The Sport of Kings was captivating the masses of common folk like never before. During the seven months of the war-shortened 1945 season, nearly 20 million Americans had flocked to the racetracks and bet nearly $1.5 billion at the windows—shattering records for attendance and handle set over the course of a full year. Now that more than a decade of turmoil and chaos had given way to a spirit of optimism, 1946 promised to be racing's biggest year yet.

Center stage in New York, where the tracks took turns boasting the nation's largest daily crowds, was the high-headed little chestnut colt who had seduced racegoers with his spellbinding charges from way behind. Before their very eyes, Stymie had metamorphosed in 1945 from ultimate underdog into fan favorite and hometown hero. With every stride, his local following grew wherever he raced—at Belmont, at Aqueduct, and especially at Jamaica, "the people's track," where Hirsch Jacobs based his stable and where Stymie made himself at home.

From the moment he kicked off his 1946 campaign before 30,000 Jamaica faithful who had braved a windy early-spring chill to see him easily win a featured weekday allowance race, Stymie was fast making a nickname for himself as "The People's Horse."

It wasn't hard to explain his rising popularity. His against-all-odds career path and his come-from-behind racing style served as a perfect metaphor for the struggles that everyday Americans had to face as the nation made its way through the bumpy recovery to a peacetime economy. This was especially true for millions of GIs who had shipped out with barely a high school education. Now that they were back home from war, they were trying to figure out a way to forge a new and better life, how to achieve their American dream.

They were looking for inspiration, for proof that it was possible to start from the bottom and work your way up. There couldn't be more-visible role models than Stymie and Hirsch Jacobs, who through hard work and drive had both clawed their way to the top.

On the racetrack, nobody worked harder than Stymie and his fellow handicap horses. They were indefatigable iron horses that took on every challenge of weight and distance and one another, banging heads week after week and year after year.

It was the climax of a bygone era when the Triple Crown races were still viewed as spring training that prepped three-year-olds for a long career in the major leagues of the handicaps. Whirlaway and Count Fleet may have captured America's imagination with their Triple Crown glories of the early '40s, but injury turned them into shooting stars gone too soon. Left in their wake were the durable handicap horses like Stymie and Armed, forging careers long enough to become part of the permanent firmament. Previous decades saw the likes of Exterminator and Seabiscuit, beloved iron horses whose stars burned brighter with each passing year. Only time would tell whether the current generation might yield another horse for the ages.

* * *

On the first Saturday in May, with much of the nation focused on the Kentucky Derby, 42,401 New Yorkers jammed Jamaica to see Stymie run the first stakes race of his five-year-old season. Defending his title in the Grey Lag Handicap, he had to carry the field's top weight and an unfamiliar jockey on his back since Bobby Permane had a Derby mount. No matter, it was classic Stymie. He dropped to dead last, falling twenty-five lengths back in barely a quarter mile. Then, with a burst of speed that electrified the crowd, he drove past the entire field on the sweeping stretch turn, grabbing the lead as he hit the straightaway and pulling away to win by two lengths and to equal the track record for a mile and an eighth.

It was a promising way for the 1945 Champion Handicap Horse to open his title defense. And it set the stage for his first meeting of the season with his chief rival for the 1946 championship: Armed.

For their showdown six days later at Pimlico, Armed came into the Dixie Handicap so sharp that he had to spot Stymie six pounds. The weight advantage didn't help Stymie, who lagged behind as Armed ran away from him to open more than six lengths. Unleashing his drive, Stymie flew past everyone else but could only come within three and a half lengths of the odds-on favorite. Jacobs could make no excuse for his prized colt. On this day, Armed was simply the better horse.

Stymie didn't have to wait long for another shot at Armed. They met again in his very next race, the Suburban Handicap on Memorial Day at Belmont. There, Stymie could enjoy the advantage of seven pounds and of 60,631 hometown fans, the largest crowd ever to pass through the turnstiles at a New York track. They made Armed the even-money favorite, with Stymie the second choice at 3-to-1. As Armed cruised along just behind the frontrunner, Stymie lugged dead last, trailing by twenty lengths. Slinging off the turn,

Armed flew into the lead and kept opening ground with every stride. Stymie followed and circled horses around the curve, but he had unleashed his drive later than usual and could get no closer than within three lengths of Armed. As if that wasn't demoralizing enough, Stymie got overtaken at the wire and nosed out for second.

With Armed leaving no doubt that he was the new king of the iron horses, Jacobs decided to steer Stymie away from Calumet's "Golden Gelding." The problem was, the handicap division was so competitive that Stymie next ran smack into another tough rival: Gallorette, the queen of the iron horses. A sturdy chestnut filly standing well over 16 hands, Gallorette was bigger than many of the colts she faced—especially Stymie—and faster than most of them as well. A speedy frontrunner who dared them to catch her if they could, she presented Stymie with the consummate challenge of contrasting styles.

Never was that starker than their duel in June's mile-and-a-quarter Brooklyn Handicap. Despite the ten pounds that Stymie had to concede her, the Aqueduct horseplayers made him the odds-on favorite. None of them could be surprised or worried to see Stymie take up his usual place in the rear, twelve lengths back, while Gallorette easily drafted off the frontrunners. When he kicked into gear heading into the turn, they let out a sustained roar that amplified with each horse he flew past until he hit the stretch with only Gallorette in sight. Within a few strides, the commanding lead that Gallorette had grabbed at the top of the stretch was gone. Stymie pulled even, put his nose in front, then forged ahead by half a length. Gallorette surged back and the pair dueled head-to-head for the final furlong. As they flew under the wire, Gallorette had a neck in front.

The cheering crowd was struck dumb. They had never seen Stymie overtaken in the stretch. Once he snatched the lead, they were so sure of the outcome that they were already reaching into their pockets for their betting tickets to cash out.

Stymie was mired in a prolonged losing streak that would stretch for seven races over three months. The slump hit its nadir in early August when Stymie took fifth in his Saratoga debut, the first time in nearly a year that he had failed to finish in the money. A couple of days later, Jacobs stopped by for his evening visit with Stymie and stepped inside the stall. The trainer stood for a while watching Stymie eat and tried to figure what was going wrong with his champion. When Stymie paused for a moment and looked over at the trainer, Jacobs asked, "What's the matter, big fella?" Stymie, of course, did not answer. But later that night it came to Jacobs that a jockey change might make the difference. He reached out to Basil James.

Like millions of young American men whose lives were dramatically changed by World War II, Basil James had put his career on hold for four years to serve Uncle Sam. He spent most of the war stationed at the U.S. Army Remount Service's largest depot, Fort Robinson in Nebraska, breaking horses and pack mules.

Until then, James had been enjoying a star-studded career as one of America's premier jockeys. He had burst into national prominence as a sixteen-year-old apprentice leading all jockeys with 245 wins in 1936, most of them out West where he had been raised. By 1939, he topped the money list too. And by the spring of 1942, he was piloting Alsab to fame and unlikely fortune in the Triple Crown races.

Purchased at the Saratoga yearling sale for a bargain-basement bid of $700 by Al Sabath and named after his new owner, Alsab surprisingly outran his lackluster pedigree to capture the juvenile championship. But he struggled through the first three months of his three-year-old campaign, flailing in the Kentucky Derby preps, under five different jockeys. Two weeks before the Derby, James got the mount. On the first Saturday in May, he piloted Alsab to a fast-closing second behind Shut Out. In the Preakness a week later, Alsab drove from next to last to win going away. Soon after guiding Alsab to a runner-up finish in the Belmont Stakes, James was drafted. He was in the army that September when Alsab reached his greatest glory: in a heavily hyped match race with Whirlaway, the two courageous closers dueled all the way down the Pimlico stretch, trading the lead back and forth, until they flew under the wire with Alsab in front by a short nostril.

For the duration of the war, James rode no Alsabs, only the many horses he broke daily at Fort Robinson as well as the few he rode at county fairs in the odd wildcat race while on leave. Now that James had traded in his olive-drab army uniform for brightly hued jockey silks, Jacobs was enlisting him to wear Ethel's emerald-green and salmon-pink colors. Before the war, Jacobs liked to put James on horses that needed an especially balanced rider with sensitive hands. James's reputation as a peerless stretch rider made him the perfect choice for Jacobs's peerless stretch runner.

When the Saratoga paddock judge called "Riders up" for the Whitney Stakes, Jacobs felt confident hoisting James onto Stymie's back and sending them off for the mile-and-a-quarter feature. As usual, Stymie started slow and settled in at the rear, but James opted to change things up a bit. The jockey was careful never to let Stymie drop too far back, keeping him within five or six lengths of the frontrunners. Then James moved him up a little earlier than usual and put him on the lead before they had even reached the quarter pole at the top of the turn. Stymie took it from there, romping through the mud for an easy two-length win. For first time in three months, he got to continue on to the winner's circle, where he collected $19,350 in prize money.

That purse brought Stymie's career earnings to $360,710. Thus had Stymie supplanted Alsab as the biggest bargain in the annals of horse racing. Alsab had parlayed the $700 pittance paid for him at auction into a $350,015 windfall, retiring with more purse winnings than all but three horses in history. Now Stymie had turned a $1,500 investment—the most profitable claim of all time—into a bigger fortune that would only continue to grow with each passing race. What made Stymie such a worthy successor to Alsab was the blue-collar way he had earned all that money: "Both," Grantland Rice wrote, "worked their respective beats like two honest cops."

Every time Stymie raced, sportswriters found new ways to characterize his storybook rags-to-riches rise that had transcended the confining "king of the claimers." Newspapers from coast to coast called him everything from "the bargain-basement horse" to the "bargain-baby horse." Many took to labeling him "the Cinderella horse." Call him what you will, Stymie was making Hirsch Jacobs look like the shrewdest bargain hunter since Peter Minuit bought Manhattan for $24.

One evening a few days later, Damon Runyon was walking back to his lodgings after an afternoon at the track when he heard a voice murmuring in his ear: "Tempus fugit." Runyon knew instantly without turning around that the voice had to belong to the erudite Izzy Bieber because, as the newspaperman later wrote, "no one else among my acquaintances in Saratoga Springs would be likely to use that kind of language or even know what it means." Runyon was all too aware what "tempus fugit" means—Latin for "time flies"—because the phrase had taken on a certain poignancy in the nearly three years since he had been diagnosed with throat cancer. The day after his larynx had been removed, he'd scribbled a note to his doctor asking, "When do I get out of here? I have races to win." Surgery had permanently robbed him of his speaking voice, but not his writing wit. That summer around the stables, he could converse with his buddies Beeb and Jacobs only by scribbling notes.

Runyon still loved spending time at the track even though he no longer owned any horses for Jacobs to train for him, having given his entire racing stable to Patrice in their separation agreement that spring. In a Runyonesque irony that was not lost on him, he was holding court at his usual table in the Stork Club one June night when he learned from a story in the hot-off-the-presses bulldog edition of his own newspaper that his divorce had become final on the very same day that his ex-horse Scribe, named in his honor, had won a race at 8-to-1. "What a day this has been for me," he forlornly scribbled on his notepad to show his companions, who nodded sympathetically. "Yes, what a day," he continued in a second note. "My ex-horse, Scribe, came in at Jamaica. Paid $10.20."

In the years since Runyon had lost his speaking voice, Jacobs found himself missing all the time they used to pass talking horse. For his part, Bieber missed all the time they used to spend quoting the classics to one another—though not so much the smell of cigarette smoke that always announced Runyon's presence. Beeb, who was so antismoking that he refused to consort with anyone who fouled the air with tobacco and avoided his own big brother because he couldn't abide Herman's cigar habit, made an exception for the chain-smoking scribe.

Sadly, this Saratoga summer would be the last time that Jacobs and Bieber got to spend time with their famous friend. For the past two years, Runyon had been penning regular newspaper columns philosophizing about death, mortality, and his own terminal illness. He even mused about the afterlife, regaling readers with the tale of the wager he made with a wise guy on his favorite Broadway sidewalk: he had bet $10 to win $1,000 that he would return after his death. Given his candid columns and rapidly declining health, nobody could be shocked that December when headlines reported Damon Runyon's death at the age of sixty-two. A week later, his friend Eddie Rickenbacker, the legendary World War I fighter ace now running Eastern Air Lines, flew over Broadway and fulfilled Runyon's deathbed request that his ashes be scattered over his favorite spot on earth. With the DC-3 transport plane cruising north 3,000 feet over Times Square, Captain Rickenbacker tilted the bronze urn out of the cockpit window and poured Damon Runyon's ashes along his beloved Broadway. Upon hearing about Runyon's wish for his final resting place, his racing pals felt it would have been just as appropriate to scatter his ashes over Jamaica or Saratoga.

Stymie's Saratoga finale should have been his easiest race of all. Because every horse had to carry the same weight in the Saratoga Cup, all the competition except Trymenow had been scared off. Knowing that Stymie had already overcome an eight-pound handicap to whip Trymenow in the mile-and-a-quarter Whitney, Jacobs figured this mile-and-three-quarters marathon would be a cakewalk for his distance-loving router and stayer who could run all day. When the trainer left for the track in the morning, he was humming happily, anticipating Stymie's easy victory that afternoon.

But by midmorning, Jacobs's mood darkened. Racing officials had told him that Trymenow had been scratched, which meant that the Saratoga Cup was going to be a walkover—in other words, an uncontested one-horse race. At lunch, his anxiety brimming over, he told Ethel that he was thinking of scratching Stymie too. He reminded her how much Stymie abhorred being by himself. In the mornings, he explained, Stymie always had to be sent out to the track with a target or two to chase in his breezes and plenty of company to travel with on his gallops; and if the horse ever found himself alone, he would pull up and stubbornly refuse to move. There was a good chance, Hirsch said, that instead of taking an easy canter around the track this afternoon, Stymie would break from the gate, notice he was the only horse running, slam to a stop, wheel around, and run back to the barn. "I don't know if Stymie can get around the track by himself," Jacobs concluded.

If Stymie didn't make the full lap and a half, then he would lose both the race and the purse. When Jacobs told James about his concerns, the jockey assured the trainer that Stymie would finish the race. In a surreal scene, the starting gate snapped open, Stymie emerged alone, and James put him into a slow canter. Three minutes and a mile and three-quarters later, Stymie had earned an easy $5,975 and a gold-plated cup.

Ever the fierce competitor, Stymie much preferred chasing down frontrunners and battling rivals. Waiting for him back in New York his next time out was an eight-horse Aqueduct field that promised another showdown of the sexes with Gallorette. The pair had met each other seven times already, but only once had they dueled head-to-head—back in the spring when Gallorette had won by a thin neck in what her jockey proclaimed "the best race of her life." Now Stymie needed to avenge that loss.

For the mile-and-an-eighth Edgemere Handicap, James employed the same surprise tactic that had worked the first time he had ridden Stymie. For starters, the jockey kept Stymie in contention early, staying within three lengths of the leaders. Then James moved him a little sooner than usual, going into third place on the backstretch as Gallorette drafted in fourth on the outside. Coming off the turn in second place, Stymie cut loose and ran down the frontrunner by the middle of the stretch, with Gallorette still a couple of lengths in his wake. Without any urging from James, Stymie drew off and won by nearly two lengths over the filly.

Now that Stymie had gotten revenge against one old rival, he was primed to take on a new one.

He was about to meet the rising-star sensation who had galvanized the nation and the sport in the spring by sweeping the Triple Crown: Assault.

CHAPTER 15

ASSAULT ON THE
RECORD BOOK

Ever since Assault's birth in the same Texas foaling barn as Stymie's a couple of years earlier, the two colts had been on a collision course.

So striking were their similarities that they seemed predestined to eventually face off against each other: Both had been bred by Bob Kleberg at the King Ranch. Both were chestnuts, though Assault's coat was a dark liver to Stymie's bright copper. Both were small for their breed, though Stymie was a couple of inches taller. Both had been dismissed as poor yearling prospects by King Ranch trainer Max Hirsch. And both would need to summon supreme heart to surmount the longest of odds.

As unlikely as Stymie's saga was, Assault's odyssey was even more improbable right from the start.

While romping through the King Ranch pasture as a suckling, Assault had stepped on a surveyor's spike hidden in the tall grass. The sharp stake ran through his right forefoot and came out the front wall of the hoof, leaving the little colt lame and in pain. The injury was so severe that Kleberg, who had bred this son of 1936 Kentucky Derby winner Bold Venture out of an unraced Equipoise daughter named Igual, made the difficult decision to have him destroyed. Before carrying out the order, though, the ranch's long-time veterinarian, Dr. J. K. Northway, decided to give the colt a chance. He performed a risky operation that wound up saving the colt's foot and life.

Watching the plucky colt stumble and sometimes trip in his paddock while relearning how to carry himself, Kleberg's wife bestowed a name that evoked both his fighting spirit and the patriotism permeating wartime America. In time, the press would give Assault a nickname that was less complimentary: "The Clubfooted Comet."

While the "clubfooted" part was never exactly accurate, the injury had left his hoof deformed and shrunken. Because the hoof wall was so thin and brittle that it was difficult to find room to anchor a nail, he had to wear a specially designed shoe. While he was still in pain as a youngster, he got in the habit of favoring the foot and trying to protect the hoof. As a result, he developed an awkward gait and wound up with a permanent limp at the walk and at the trot.

The first time Max Hirsch saw him while checking out the yearling crop at the ranch, the trainer shook his head in resignation. "When he walks or trots, you'd think he was going to fall down," Hirsch observed, automatically crossing the colt off the list.

When the top yearling prospects were shipped to his winter training base in South Carolina, Hirsch was shocked to see Assault among them. The trainer didn't think there was any chance of ever getting him to the racetrack but decided to give him a shot anyway. Simply walking to the training track, the colt would often stumble, sometimes even fall. Once on the track, however, he ran with surprising grace and efficiency. The faster he galloped, in fact, the smoother his movement became.

That smooth stride didn't help Assault much through his

uninspiring two-year-old season. He managed to win just one juvenile stakes, by a photo finish as a 70-to-1 longshot on the day
America dropped the atomic bomb on Hiroshima. More than two
dozen juvenile colts and fillies ranked higher heading into their
three-year-old campaign, and although Assault started coming
around at just the right time in the spring, he still was given little
chance in the Triple Crown series.

Defying the odds as an 8-to-1 shot in the Kentucky Derby,
Assault came streaking off the stretch turn on the rail to grab the
lead and run off with the roses by an astonishing eight lengths, a
margin of victory unsurpassed in the seventy-two-year history of
America's marquee race. A week later in the Preakness, he pushed
the pace too hard in taking a four-length lead into the stretch and
then had to hang on with whatever he had left in the tank to survive by a neck. With that fading finish scaring off the betting public
in the Belmont Stakes, Assault reverted to his familiar role of underdog in his pursuit of Triple Crown immortality. Playing it safer,
jockey Warren Mehrtens waited until the final furlong before asking his mount to move. Assault responded with an electrifying burst
of speed, shooting into the lead for a commanding three-length
coronation.

His Triple Crown triumph was hailed as the embodiment of the
same courageous spirit upon which America had relied during the
war. When Mehrtens called him the little horse with "the heart of
a giant," he was speaking of a will to win seldom seen on the racetrack. The words could just as easily have referred to Stymie. The
two little chestnuts, as gritty and gallant as they come, were kindred spirits. And they were about to become the best of rivals.

For any three-year-old, the transition from the spring into summer
and fall is often difficult. In the spring, all the youngsters are run-

ning against horses their own age and carrying the same weight. Before long, they will be expected to run against mature and accomplished older horses. It's like getting called up from the minor leagues to the majors. And for many, it's a shock to the system.

For Assault, it would be no different. In fact, it would probably be even harder, for he would have to contend with as strong and deep an army of iron horses as ever had graced the handicap division. That meant facing the likes of Stymie, the reigning Champion Handicap Horse from 1945, and Armed, who had already established himself as the odds-on favorite to wrest the crown for 1946. His Triple Crown glory notwithstanding, Assault would have to beat the handicap heroes to have any chance of being considered for the coveted title of Horse of the Year.

In its pursuit, Max Hirsch wasted no time putting Assault back to work against fellow three-year-olds to steel him for the iron horses to come. Racing again just two weeks after the Belmont, Assault easily won an Aqueduct stakes. His next time out, he ran listlessly in the Arlington Classic and finished dead last. Shortly after the race, Hirsch found him lying in his stall sweating profusely and quickly called a vet, who diagnosed a kidney infection that would sideline the colt for six weeks.

Returning from the forced layoff in a September stakes at Aqueduct, Assault came from way back but couldn't get closer than third. A week later in a Garden State stakes, he charged from behind to grab the lead in the stretch only to be overtaken by a deep closer who beat him by half a length. While his fans wondered whether he could regain his spring form and his detractors maintained he simply wasn't a star to begin with, his trainer entered him in his first handicap against older iron horses.

Hirsch did not make that decision lightly. Waiting for Assault in the Manhattan Handicap would be none other than Stymie. It was to be the first time that Assault would ever face Stymie.

Before they could share the same starting gate, theirs was already a fierce rivalry. It was a rivalry not just because of what these two stouthearted colts promised on the track, but more because of the baggage carried by their human connections.

For Max Hirsch, it couldn't get any more personal. He could never escape the constant reminders of his inextricable link to Stymie. He was, after all, Stymie's breeder of record, thanks to King Ranch's clerical error. Every time he glanced at Stymie's *Daily Racing Form* charts for each of the horse's ninety-one races and counting, he couldn't miss the boldfaced line "Breeder, Max Hirsch." Like a festering sore that wouldn't heal, it forever reminded him of that fateful day three years earlier when he had dropped Stymie into a cheap claiming race and lost him for keeps. Sure, he had happily pocketed the $1,500 claiming fee that day. But the man who paid him the $1,500 was now the proud owner of "the bargain-basement horse," the cheap claimer that had already earned him $390,985.

When reporters asked Hirsch about that claim, he would often just shrug and say, "Those are the hazards of racing. You win some, you lose some." Other times, he was quick to remind them that Jacobs didn't protect Stymie any better than he had, running him back ten times in claiming races. Hirsch fumed every time he saw himself identified in the papers as "the trainer who let Stymie get away." And he bristled at all those stories by turf writers pronouncing Jacobs the smartest and shrewdest horseman of his age for claiming the future stakes-winning champion. So did Hirsch's friends on the backside. "It makes me sick every time I read one of those stories," a trainer friend of Hirsch's told the *Saturday Evening Post*. "If Jacobs thought he was getting a stake horse when he claimed Stymie, do you think for one minute he'd have run him back in all those claiming races? Stymie just fooled everybody."

Everybody, that is, except Jacobs. For his part, Jacobs never gloated, remaining his humble and reserved self. If there was any bad blood between the two camps, it was limited to his partner Bieber's relationship with the King Ranch trainer. Bieber was always spoiling for a fight, and in Hirsch he found an equally opinionated curmudgeon who could hold a grudge. Hirsch had never forgotten Bieber's role in preventing the King Ranch trainer from purchasing Assault's sire, Bold Venture, a decade earlier. The Stymie-Assault rivalry would only fan the flames of their feud.

Jacobs quietly stayed above the fray. He had a respectful relationship with Max Hirsch, and they remained the friendliest of rivals. Jacobs would be the first to agree with Hirsch's rationalization that the Stymie transaction was just part of the win-some-lose-some caprice of the claiming game. Jacobs had made his share of bad claims, once paying $2,000 for a horse that broke down and had to be euthanized before the trainer could halter him from the race. And he had lost his share of good horses in claiming races: Marriage, a gelding he had claimed for $1,400 and then lost for $5,000 in 1941, went on to win over $200,000 for his new owner. So he could easily empathize with Hirsch's predicament over the one that got away.

Besides, Jacobs couldn't afford to focus solely on Hirsch's latest star in Stymie's upcoming race. The Manhattan Handicap presented many more serious challengers than just Assault, the only three-year-old in the eight-horse field. Chief among them was Pavot, the 1945 Belmont Stakes winner who had beaten Stymie twice in the summer of '46. Stymie would be giving weight to all of them, shouldering 126 pounds to Pavot's 121 and Assault's 116. The Belmont bettors sent Stymie, their hometown hero, to the post as the even-money favorite. They made Assault, the Texas interloper returning to the scene of his Triple Crown coronation, the second choice at 2-to-1.

In the Belmont paddock area, the very place where Jacobs had first spotted Stymie in the King Ranch colors three years earlier, the trainer paid no attention to the horse that Max Hirsch was now saddling in a nearby stall. Jacobs was too focused on tightening the girth on his own horse. As he hoisted Basil James onto Stymie's back, Jacobs felt no need to give the jockey any instructions. Having ridden Stymie for five straight races, James had found that he had the most success when he didn't let his mount drop too far back. Today's addition of Assault to the handicap ranks only strengthened James's resolve to keep Stymie within striking distance throughout the full lap of the mile-and-a-half oval.

Right from the bell, despite Stymie's usual sluggish break from the gate, James did just that. Sensing the pace was too slow to set up his mount's customary closing drive, the jockey quickly moved him into fourth barely three lengths behind the leaders as they headed into the clubhouse turn, with Assault hanging in fifth. When the track announcer called out Stymie's name in third before he had even rounded into the backstretch, the crowd let out an audible gasp. Before the fans could recover from the shock of seeing Stymie so close this early in a race, they gasped anew when he began his one big run earlier than usual. On the far turn, Eddie Arcaro sent Pavot shooting to the lead and James asked his mount for more speed. Stymie immediately picked up his head and his pace, circling the one horse between them and stalking Pavot from about a length behind. With Assault mired back in fifth, all eyes focused on this unexpected duel developing up front. Whipping off the turn, Stymie quickly ran down Pavot, forged ahead in the upper stretch, and refused to let him pass as they drove through the final furlong. When Stymie flew under the wire, he was almost a length in front. So loud was the sustained roar for his stretch drive that no one noticed Assault finishing four lengths back, his consolation prize a dead heat for third.

The first-place purse made Stymie only the third racehorse in history to surpass $400,000 in career earnings, joining Whirlaway and Seabiscuit in that exclusive club. More than that, Stymie had not only drawn first blood in his budding rivalry with Assault but also shown the veteran handicap horses that he was back in top form.

In Stymie's next race, the Jockey Club Gold Cup at Belmont, James got a little too cocky with his mount and got outfoxed by Arcaro. In a ploy to steal the race from the prohibitive 3-to-10 favorite, Arcaro slyly pulled the frontrunning Pavot farther and farther back until James had to choose between slowing Stymie to a crawl or putting him on the lead. James opted to scrap Jacobs's prerace instruction, which was to stalk Pavot until it was time to unleash Stymie's one big run. Instead, he put his mount in front halfway through the two-mile marathon. When the stalking Pavot pounced on the final turn, Stymie was too spent to summon his usual drive and trudged home five lengths behind.

Needing to redeem themselves in the New York Handicap, Stymie and James reverted to form with a sustained drive that carried them to an easy win over two and a quarter miles of Belmont mud. That set Stymie up perfectly for his second meeting with Assault, in the Gallant Fox Handicap over a mile and five-eighths of Jamaica dirt.

With its $75,000 purse, the Gallant Fox drew such a strong field that neither of those two stars was the favorite. That honor belonged to Lucky Draw, who had whipped Stymie three times and smashed six track records in his previous eight races. The Jamaica bettors made Lucky Draw the odds-on favorite, leaving Stymie as a nice-priced overlay for a change at 5-to-1.

Right out of the gate, Lucky Draw grabbed the lead and controlled the pace through the opening mile, with Assault stalking close behind and Stymie dropping ten lengths adrift at the back of the eleven-horse field. Then Assault made his bid, drawing clear as Stymie gradually worked his way forward. On the final turn, James lifted the whip so his mount could see it. Stymie's head came up and he gathered himself to make his move. With an explosive burst of speed, he shot past Assault and quickly opened up a five-length lead. At the eighth pole, James stole a peek back and couldn't believe how fast Stymie had opened all that daylight. The jockey eased his mount and they cruised under the wire three lengths in front, with Assault five lengths in his wake in third place. Even after being eased up for the final furlong, Stymie still broke the track record for a mile and five furlongs.

With his $59,050 first-place purse, Stymie became only the second horse in history to win over half a million dollars, his $516,285 in career earnings bringing him within $44,876 of Whirlaway's all-time record. Jacobs couldn't put a value on the priceless performance he had just witnessed. Normally so reserved that reporters couldn't get much more than shrugs and platitudes out of him, the trainer was positively bursting with pride over his prized horse's best race of the year, maybe even of his whole career.

Jacobs was so fired up by the spectacular performance that he started thinking Stymie might actually have a shot at winning Horse of the Year honors. A couple of days after the Gallant Fox, Jacobs decided to improve his horse's chances by entering the prestigious Pimlico Special, a November 1 race he had initially planned to skip because it was less than a week later. No sooner had Stymie's eleventh-hour entry been announced than Max Hirsch decided to send Assault to the party as well.

Suddenly, a third Stymie-Assault showdown loomed. It was in the Pimlico Special that Seabiscuit had outdueled War Admiral in their celebrated 1938 match race. So it seemed only fitting that, eight years later, another Champion Handicap Horse was about to take on another Triple Crown winner in the same event.

There was much more at stake in this winner-take-all showdown than the $25,000 purse. There always would be whenever Stymie and Assault clashed and whenever Jacobs and Hirsch matched wits.

Jacobs had every reason to be supremely confident in the wake of the Gallant Fox. And that confidence only continued to build as Stymie prepped for the Pimlico Special. On the eve of the race, Jacobs told a reporter, "Stymie is good now. And when he gets good, he gets rough. Boy, is he rough right now! It's all we can do to get him out and back in the mornings. He really wants to run."

The bettors would mirror Jacobs's confidence, making Stymie the 7-to-10 favorite. Despite Assault's longer odds of 3-to-1 and six-race losing streak, Hirsch sounded even more assured than his counterpart. He had blamed the Gallant Fox defeat not on the colt but on the jockey, convinced that Warren Mehrtens had sent Assault to the front too soon and taken too much out of him for the stretch run. Hirsch decided a jockey change was imperative. He called on The Master himself, Eddie Arcaro.

After hoisting Arcaro onto Assault's back in the Pimlico paddock, Hirsch gave the jockey firm orders. "This horse can beat Stymie at any distance: a mile, two miles, four miles," Hirsch told him. "Never mind those other horses in the race. When James makes his move, you move with him. Stymie will outrun you for an eighth of a mile, maybe, but no more. After that, he's yours."

At the break, Arcaro followed his orders and dropped Assault way back with the slow-starting Stymie, content to let the two longshots in the four-horse field set the pace. While the two pacesetters dueled a good fourteen lengths ahead, Assault led Stymie up the backstretch, separated by a few lengths. Heading into the turn, Stymie came with his big run on the outside, quickly closing the seven-length gap with Assault. At the top of the curve, Stymie caught Assault. Arcaro had heard Stymie coming up behind him and asked Assault for more speed. The two chestnuts ran together stride for stride for a full furlong as they moved up on the two frontrunners. As they rounded into the stretch, Arcaro spotted a hole along the rail and shot Assault through it to take the lead while Stymie was left to go the long way around. Arcaro slapped his mount several times with the whip, and Assault pulled away to a commanding six-length triumph. Stymie placed second, but in this winner-take-all event, that was worth nothing.

Jacobs couldn't wait to avenge the loss. He entered the Westchester Handicap eight days hence so that his horse could get another shot at Assault—and, more important, a chance at closing the gap on Whirlaway's career money-winning record.

The only one who seemed more anxious for this shot at redemption was Stymie himself. To Jacobs, Stymie looked to be in top form, "rough" and ready for the Westchester. But in the days before the race, a hard knot appeared on Stymie's left foreleg. It was very sore. Though it was not career-threatening, it was enough for Jacobs to scratch him from the race and shelve him for the winter.

After closing out his own season with an easy win in the Westchester, Assault was crowned Horse of the Year. Armed dethroned Stymie as Champion Handicap Horse after winning both of their showdowns and earning $288,725. Stymie had earned $238,650, helping to propel Jacobs to the top of the trainers' money list for the first time with $560,077. In twenty-eight starts, Stymie had failed to finish in the money only once, winning eight times with seven seconds and four thirds.

Stymie had run ninety-six career races and was still sound. And Jacobs planned to keep him that way. He sent Stymie back to Virginia so his horse could get a good, long rest and prepare for the hard handicaps looming ahead.

CHAPTER 16

THE RICHEST
RACEHORSE EVER

With Assault's stunning upset of Stymie in the Pimlico Special, the battle had been joined. Right out of the gate in 1947, the arrival of Assault as a fully mature four-year-old promised to turn the spotlight on the handicap division to an extent that horse racing had never seen. For the past couple of years, Stymie and Armed had dominated the handicap ranks with a dynamism and durability that established them as enduring stars. With Assault joining the fray to turn their rivalry into a "trivalry," this peerless trio of warhorses combined to elevate the level of competition and excitement to unprecedented heights.

Week after week, on tracks across the country, their handicap races—and especially their showdowns—took on an electricity usually reserved for the first Saturday in May. Adding to their mass appeal, the stakes literally couldn't be higher—as all three were in hot pursuit not only of one another, but also of Whirlaway's all-time earnings record.

Heading into 1947, Stymie had already locked horns three times apiece with Assault and Armed. And the trivalry was just heating up.

It wasn't long before there was considerable clamor for a three-horse race with Stymie, Assault, and Armed. Plain Ben Jones was willing to send Armed, Calumet's Golden Gelding, into such a battle royal. And Hirsch Jacobs was eager to give Stymie, his Cinderella horse, the chance to run them both down. But Max Hirsch quickly scotched any idea of a three-way race that would include Assault, his Triple Crown hero.

One day, Grantland Rice cornered Assault's trainer and asked him why he so vehemently opposed a three-horse showdown. "Grant," Hirsch replied, "I'll run against either of those horses, but not both together. A come-from-behind horse will beat a sprinter every time. Why stick Assault in there to beat himself whipping a fast horse like Armed only to get nailed from behind by a plodder like Stymie?"

Those contrasting styles are precisely what made the trivalry so interesting. Stymie may have lacked his two rivals' speed and versatility—being a one-dimensional closer who needed a long distance and a fast pace in front of him to set up his rousing come-from-behind stretch runs—but he proved himself the toughest and sturdiest campaigner of them all. Entering his six-year-old season, he had already run a staggering total of ninety-six races and was showing no signs of slowing down.

Rice, channeling all the horsemen who analyzed Stymie's style for him, summed it up this way in his syndicated column: "He is always good, but he is better when he has to follow a fast pace where he can cut down the leaders through the stretch. He isn't a Man o' War, a Count Fleet or a Whirlaway. But he is still Stymie, which is something—and usually it is enough. He's tough, game, well conditioned, durable, consistent, and he can run. Stymie has been beaten often and he can be beaten again. But it will take good running to head him off. He's as tough a horse as we've seen in a long time, and in Hirsch Jacobs he has one of the best trainers the track ever knew."

With Max Hirsch ruling out any chance of a three-way show-down, Jacobs had to settle for taking on Assault and Armed one at a time. Since Stymie was a classic stayer who excelled at the longer distances—the longer the better—it was highly unlikely he would ever again face Armed, who never raced beyond a mile and a quarter. No matter, his budding rivalry with Assault would keep his race card full. Max Hirsch was eager to take on Stymie anytime, anywhere, at any distance—just so long as Armed wouldn't be there to push the pace and set up Stymie's patented stretch run.

Fans didn't have to wait long for the first Stymie-Assault showdown of 1947. On the first Saturday in May, the same day as The Run for the Roses, the 1946 Derby winner was making his four-year-old debut in the Grey Lag Handicap at Jamaica against the hometown handicap hero. Assault's graduation to the heavyweight division meant he would no longer be getting the multipound advantage he had enjoyed for their three 1946 meetings. For the first time, Assault would have to carry the top weight, 128 pounds to Stymie's 126. Countless three-year-old sensations before him, Derby and Triple Crown winners included, had buckled under the unforgiving weight of the handicapper's impost and had flamed out. That didn't scare the Jamaica bettors from sending Assault to the post as the even-money favorite, with Stymie at 2-to-1.

When the gates clanged open, the speed horses raced to the front, while Assault and Stymie lagged behind together. It looked like a replay of the Pimlico Special, with both favorites making their moves as they neared the far turn. As Assault sped along the rail, the horse on Stymie's left reached over and tried to take a chunk out of his neck. Basil James had to use his whip to back the offender off and somehow managed to keep pace with Assault around the turn. Heading into the stretch, Assault and Stymie caught up with the leaders at about the same time and swung to the outside to pass. As they surged past the frontrunners, one veered out and bumped Assault into Stymie, throwing him off his stride. Stymie dropped back as Assault shot forward, grabbing the lead in the final stride and winning by a neck. Stymie finished two and a half lengths back, in fourth.

Despite the troubled trip and the legitimate excuses, Jacobs could see that Stymie hadn't yet reached peak condition. The trainer decided to race him into shape a week later in the Metropolitan Handicap at Belmont. Stymie made quick work of the mile stakes, coming from way back, roaring past good horses like they were standing still, grabbing the lead in the deep stretch, and winning by a widening length. It seemed like a perfect tune-up for his upcoming rematch with Assault in the mile-and-a-quarter Suburban Handicap.

The Memorial Day matchup drew 60,122 to Belmont, and they sent Assault off as the even-money favorite. Once again, Eddie Arcaro dropped him back to fourth place, six lengths behind the pacesetting Natchez, with Stymie loping sluggishly along in fifth. Rounding the stretch turn, Assault made a big move and James tried to send Stymie with him. As Assault cut into Natchez's lead with every stride down the stretch, Stymie drove up to third but then started to fade. At the eighth pole, Assault flew past Natchez and then under the wire a commanding two lengths in front. Ten lengths back, Stymie was fading to a fourth-place finish. Adding to the disappointment, the winner's purse brought Assault within $3,865 of Stymie's career earnings.

Another trainer might have thought his horse was tired and needed a breather, but Jacobs's diagnosis was that Stymie simply needed more racing. Just three days later, the trainer entered him in the Queens County Handicap at Aqueduct. As was his wont, Stymie dropped to the back early on, made his move passing all the other competitors, and when he hit the stretch in front, the horse, his jockey, and his fans all figured the race was won. But inexplicably it seemed that Stymie had lost focus, allowing Gallorette to power past and win by a neck. Jacobs could only hope that this final tune-up for the all-important Brooklyn Handicap would sharpen Stymie enough to catch the streaking Assault.

In the Brooklyn Handicap, a lot more was at stake than winning a race, a trophy, and a purse. Whoever won, Stymie or Assault, would be the one to break Whirlaway's all-time career earnings record. Assault came into the race on such a hot streak that the handicapper saddled him with a career-high 133 pounds and the Aqueduct crowd of 33,634 made him the 1-to-2 betting favorite.

Once again, Arcaro followed Max Hirsch's script and dropped his horse back to fourth, a few lengths in front of Stymie. Arcaro bided his time until he heard James urge Stymie on heading into the far turn. Arcaro clucked to his mount, and Assault responded, lengthening his stride and closing fast on the leaders. Stymie, just a length back, was moving up too. Assault caught the leader just past the eighth pole, with Stymie still a length behind him. As they powered toward the wire, Assault widened his margin with every smooth stride. At the finish line, Assault was three lengths out in front.

With that victory, Assault dethroned Whirlaway as the all-time leading money-winning champion of the world. His $38,100 winner's check brought his career winnings to $576,670, breaking Whirlaway's five-year-old mark of $561,161. Stymie's $10,000 piece of the purse left him third on the all-time list at $556,435.

Not content with third place, Jacobs entered Stymie in the Questionnaire Handicap at Jamaica just a week later. Back to his old form, Stymie dropped behind everyone early on and powered to the front in the stretch to win easily. The purse moved him past Whirlaway into second place on the all-time earnings list with $574,660, just $2,010 shy of Assault's week-old record.

Stymie was so close to the money mark that Jacobs could almost taste it. He was so impatient that he couldn't wait the two weeks until his horse was scheduled to go head-to-head again with Assault in the Butler Handicap at Jamaica. So he decided to ship Stymie down to Delaware Park to run in the Sussex Handicap, which would be held a week before the Butler and a week after the Questionnaire.

"I'm going to try to make him king for a day, anyway," Jacobs explained with a smile.

To achieve that in the mile-and-a-quarter Sussex, Jacobs made sure to give his new jockey, Conn McCreary, one instruction: let Stymie run his own race. McCreary did. Instead of dropping all the way back this time, Stymie stayed closer to the leaders, in fourth for the first half mile and third for the next half. Then at the quarter pole, McCreary urged Stymie on without ever even showing him the whip. Stymie blew by both frontrunners and drew away for an easy three-length win, a track record, and a $20,850 winner's purse.

With that, Stymie had indeed become king: the richest racehorse of all time. He had dethroned Assault and run his career winnings to $595,510, which was $18,840 more than Assault. What no one knew, of course, was how long the new king would reign.

Waiting back home in New York was Assault. As impatient as Jacobs had been to wrest the record from Assault, Max Hirsch was just as anxious to reclaim it from Stymie in this high-stakes game of one-upmanship. Hirsch wouldn't have to wait long since Assault was set to face Stymie seven days hence in the $54,000 Butler Handicap.

The handicapper made sure it wouldn't be easy, saddling Assault with a backbreaking 135 pounds to Stymie's 126. Despite having to haul the heaviest impost of his career for a mile and three-eighths, Assault was sent to the post as the 1-to-2 choice by the Jamaica throng of 32,395.

Once again, Assault and Stymie lurked at the back of the field all the way until the final turn. Both made their move at the same time. As they came up on the leaders, Stymie swung wide and pulled alongside Gallorette. That trapped Assault behind the two of them as they hit the stretch. For a moment, Arcaro wasn't sure whether to go wide around Stymie on the outside or try to go on the rail and risk running into slowing horses. Neither option looked very good, so he smacked Assault, hoping his mount would somehow bull his way between Stymie and Gallorette. As a tired Gallorette gave way, Assault and Stymie kept dueling through the last seventy yards. At the wire, Assault had a head in front.

With a stunning finish that left witnesses gasping for breath, Assault had reclaimed the world money-leading crown from Stymie. The $36,700 prize raised Assault's career total to $613,370. Stymie's $10,000 second-place purse boosted his total to $605,510, just $7,860 behind Assault.

Stymie wouldn't have to wait long for his shot at leapfrogging back to the top: their next showdown was only seven days away.

CHAPTER 17

STRIKING GOLD

Long before Stymie and Assault stepped into the starting gate, the $100,000 International Gold Cup was already being built up as *the* race of the year. A brand-new event that promised all the pomp and spectacle of the Kentucky Derby, the Gold Cup offered racing's richest purse to attract the best Thoroughbreds from all over the world.

The Saturday feature, part of Jamaica's summer meeting, had been moved to Belmont Park to accommodate an anticipated record-breaking throng. Every seat in the stately grandstand had sold long before the July 19 date. All afternoon, the posh clubhouse was abuzz with socialites, foreign dignitaries, and celebrities, including the likes of Babe Ruth. The only thing that could possibly dampen the size of the crowd, it turned out, was inclement weather, but nearly 50,000 braved the rain anyway.

The race had been designed to lure the best horses from abroad to meet the finest from the United States. Over the winter, the organizers had journeyed to England, Ireland, and France to entice owners to send their best Thoroughbreds, but the Europeans, leery of the dirt track at Belmont, stayed away. In the end, the only international flavor was provided by two South American five-year-olds flown in a couple of weeks earlier. Watching their eye-opening works one morning, Max Hirsch bluntly told their South American trainers, "If you can beat our horses, despite the change in climate, the change in food and water, and that long trip by plane, it will mean just one thing: our horses are bums. And I don't think they are."

Especially the two Texas natives heading the seven-horse field: Hirsch's reigning star, Assault, versus his ex-claimer, Stymie. A week earlier, the two gallant and stouthearted archrivals had waged a stirring stretch duel that still had fans buzzing in awe and wonder. Now, the anticipation was rising to a fevered pitch as everyone waited to see which one would hit the Belmont finish line first and emerge as the world's all-time richest racehorse.

Any chance of luring the red-hot Armed into a three-way battle royal had been scotched when geldings were excluded in a vain attempt to placate the Europeans. Nevertheless, Stymie and Assault would face a formidable field led by two dangerous American colts: Phalanx, fresh off his impressive win in the 1947 Belmont Stakes, and Natchez, a speedster with enough staying power to have placed second behind Assault in the 1946 Belmont and run away with that summer's Travers Stakes. The event was weight-for-age, meaning that all entrants would carry the same 126 pounds except Phalanx, who as a three-year-old would get in at 112.

For days leading up to the Gold Cup, the Stymie-Assault showdown was hyped, debated, and analyzed like it was a heavyweight championship fight.

Stymie's army of fans pointed to the race's long mile-and-five-eighths distance that favored his staying power and closing drive. Whereas the five meetings that Assault had won ranged from one and an eighth to one and a quarter miles, Stymie's two victories had come at a mile and a half and a mile and five-eighths. A true stayer like Stymie, his fans would argue, got better every stride beyond a mile and a quarter.

Assault's backers would counter with the record: He had reeled off seven straight wins, five of those over Stymie, climaxed by the greatest and grittiest race of his career. If Stymie couldn't win the Butler Handicap with a nine-pound advantage, what chance did he have running against Assault with even weight?

Grantland Rice minced no words in his nationally syndicated column: "Assault should be a kick-in, weight for age. On three legs." Other sportswriters unanimously agreed, pronouncing that Assault was a sure thing not only to win the Gold Cup but also to put the earnings record out of reach indefinitely.

They certainly got no argument from Max Hirsch. "There isn't any use of me telling you or anyone else that Assault happens to be one hundred percent in the matter of speed, stamina, and courage," he crowed. "He can run from six furlongs to two miles, just as Exterminator could. He can carry weight—and still keep running fast and far. I've seen most of the great ones come and go for the last forty years, but I've never trained nor seen another Assault. I am trying to tell you that Assault is going to win the hundred-thousand-dollar race."

The bettors concurred, making Assault the 1-to-2 favorite. With Stymie at 5-to-1, Izzy Bieber deemed it the best opportunity he'd seen in ages and bet a bundle on his horse. Too bad his partner wasn't a betting man, because Hirsch Jacobs was even more confident in their horse. For the past couple of days, Jacobs had observed that Stymie was once again "rough," so fit and so full of energy that he could barely be walked around the stable. Not only that, but on the morning of the big race, Jacobs had seen Stymie hanging over his stall door yawning. Jacobs smiled. He was convinced from years of experience that when a horse yawns, it means he's relaxed and ready to run.

Jacobs was feeling good. He wanted the hundred-grand race almost as much as he wanted the all-time earnings record. A win in this race would prove to everyone that Stymie was every bit as great a champion as Jacobs knew he was. For luck that morning, Jacobs had given his wife a present: a diamond-studded, horseshoe-shaped pin to wear to the race.

As Stymie made his way to the paddock, the rain finally let up. The Belmont paddock area was as jam-packed as any of the old-timers could remember—certainly far more crowded than it had been that day four years earlier when Jacobs first spotted Stymie in the walking ring. Stymie, two saddling stalls over from his nemesis Assault, appeared quite unconcerned by the hum of excitement around him. Jacobs saddled him as always and tightened his girth. He led Stymie over to the walking ring, where Conn McCreary was waiting.

Small even by jockey standards at four foot eight, McCreary was one of racing's biggest stars. Celebrated for his come-from-behind tactics, he had famously piloted Pensive to within a few feet of winning the Triple Crown three years earlier. More to the point, McCreary had ridden Stymie to a couple of milestones: the colt's first-ever win and the race that sent Stymie over Whirlaway's money-winning record.

Jacobs hoisted McCreary into the saddle. His prerace instructions were simple: keep an eye on Assault. As McCreary guided his mount around the walking ring, onlookers could be overheard remarking how Stymie was the handsomest colt parading under the oaks, his coppery chestnut coat glowing with condition. They headed through the tunnel leading under the grandstand and emerged onto a track that had been made sloppy by the morning downpour.

When the gates banged open, Natchez, the only speedster in the field, darted to the front. The two South American invaders, starting from a standing position outside the gate, went with him for a while. Eddie Arcaro tucked Assault into fourth, with Stymie following about ten lengths back of the leader.

Up the backstretch, Natchez pulled even farther away from the field, opening eighteen lengths on Assault and twenty-two on Stymie in a bid to steal the race. The horses held their positions as they came around the far turn. Then Arcaro, worried that he was getting too far behind, clucked to his mount, asking Assault to make a run at Natchez. As Assault started to close the gap, McCreary urged Stymie to lengthen his stride.

Stymie's head came up and he exploded forward. His patented drive was met by a deafening roar that seemed to propel him ever faster, gaining power with every stride. As he flew down the stretch, he caught up with Assault just past the eighth pole and shot past him.

Then he set his sights on Natchez, whose three-length lead seemed insurmountable. McCreary, pumping with his arms and his heels, urged Stymie forward. From somewhere, Stymie found more strength. He exploded forward and started closing the gap. With less than a hundred yards to go, he pushed his nose even with Natchez's tail. With his next powerful stride, Stymie was at Natchez's hip, and then he was even with Natchez's girth. In two more strides, Stymie's head was at Natchez's throatlatch. As the finish line loomed, Natchez dug in and desperately tried to hang on to his lead. In the remaining two strides before they crossed the wire, Stymie surged forward. At the wire, he was a neck in front.

The thrill of Stymie's last-second charge left the crowd breathless, but only for a moment. In seconds, everyone was cheering. It didn't matter who they had bet on; they had just been treated to an amazing spectacle.

Jacobs and his wife headed down to meet Stymie and McCreary, pushing their way through the frenzied throng from their clubhouse box to the muddy track. An appreciative ovation followed Hirsch and Ethel as they then led Stymie to the winner's circle, where a blanket of gardenias was draped over his withers. As Stymie's owner of record, Ethel was presented with the solid gold cup.

The winner's purse of $73,000 shot Stymie past Assault as the all-time money winner with a total of $678,510. Assault's third-place money left him $55,000 behind Stymie.

Stymie had won over not only the crowd but also the last remaining skeptics, most notably Grantland Rice. "The amazing Stymie," Rice raved. "As Stymie cost Jacobs $1,500, it might be said that Jacobs put over a 400-to-1 shot—the golden dream of every longshot player. No horse in racing history has brought in so much for so little. On the money-winning side, imagine a $2 bet running into $800. Dream—and wake up."

Rice, the king of the mythmakers, was hardly the only sportswriter extolling Stymie in purple prose. The Gold Cup's international coverage helped spread the storybook saga of Stymie's rags-to-riches rise around the world. People everywhere were charmed by the improbable tale of the Cinderella claiming horse.

The Gold Cup—his greatest race and crowning glory—solidified Stymie's stature as a national sports star and a folk hero for postwar America.

Stymie had long been the darling of New York racing fans, as beloved as any racehorse who ever graced the city's tracks. New Yorkers deemed him the equine answer to America's most popular athletic hero of the time: Joe DiMaggio, the New York Yankees legend who transcended the national pastime as a surpassing cultural icon. As both superstars vied for headlines and column inches on the New York sports pages, "The Yankee Clipper" and "The

People's Horse" shared much in common—from the grace, style, and class that each displayed in competition to the admiration that their dignified work ethic elicited from fans and the general public alike. In the wake of his Gold Cup triumph, Stymie was now a household name in homes well beyond his New York stomping grounds.

Eleven days after the Gold Cup, when he took his thrilling show on the road to Boston's Suffolk Downs, Stymie instantly captured the hearts of the 30,000 New Englanders who bet so heavily on him that they broke the handle record and the pari-mutuel machines themselves. When he rewarded their confidence as the 3-to-10 favorite by easily winning the Massachusetts Handicap with another rousing stretch drive, they showered him with even more affection.

With the first-place purse boosting Stymie's career earnings to $719,660, it seemed like his world record as the leading all-time money winner would be safe for a long while. But then, a match race was arranged between Assault and Armed for September 27, assuring that whichever one captured the winner-take-all $100,000 purse would either break or challenge Stymie's money mark. Jacobs voiced his displeasure that Stymie had not been invited to join the heavily hyped Armed-Assault match race at Belmont. The controversy over Stymie's exclusion dominated the press coverage the week of the race until word started circulating that Assault was unsound, prompting track officials to call off all pari-mutuel betting on the special match.

More than 50,000 fans thronged Belmont that Saturday of the match race. Right from the start of their mile-and-a-quarter showdown, Armed took the lead and kept pouring it on to trounce the ailing Assault by eight widening lengths. The winner-take-all $100,000 prize that Armed earned brought him within $5,000 of Stymie's money record.

In the very next race that afternoon, the card's regularly featured $25,000 Manhattan Handicap, Stymie was upset as the odds-on favorite. The only consolation was that Stymie's $5,000 second-place purse opened a $10,000 cushion over Armed in the money race. It would prove to be a tenuous lead. By winning his next start twelve days later at Belmont, Armed shot past Stymie and wrested the money-earning crown back from him.

It was a measure of the respect accorded Stymie following the Gold Cup that he was now running under the heaviest handicap imposts of his career. Jack Campbell, the astute Jockey Club track handicapper famed for once engineering a three-horse dead heat, assigned Stymie backbreaking weights of 132 to 134 pounds in three straight races culminating with the Manhattan. When reporters asked if Jacobs was worried about Stymie's ability to carry the added weight, the trainer graciously refused to use that as an excuse. "I'll commence to worry about the weight Stymie is asked to carry when Mr. Campbell starts taking it off of him," he quipped.

That is exactly what Campbell started doing in Stymie's next races, a distant third-place finish under 124 pounds and an equally distant fourth under 125. Even under the much lighter imposts, Stymie seemed out of sorts as his slump stretched to four losses in a row.

Jacobs wasn't happy, but he wasn't sure what to do. Stymie seemed to have lost all enthusiasm for racing. "I don't know what to do with him," Jacobs admitted. "He won't work. Sometimes we can't get him on the track at all. I worked another horse with him and he ran a bad mile. He's just sour, that's all."

Jacobs decided to try one more rich stakes race, the Gallant Fox Handicap, which at a mile and five-eighths better suited Stymie's style. Besides, the slumping Stymie wouldn't be asked to shoulder the backbreaking weights he'd been burdened with after the Gold

Cup, this time carrying 125 pounds over his favored track at Jamaica in late October. With McCreary up, Stymie dropped way back as usual. Then at the far turn, in a leap of faith, McCreary asked for the big move that Stymie seemed to have recently lost. The old Stymie showed up. He ripped past the leaders and won by nearly two lengths. And the $56,350 winner's purse boosted his total to $816,060—lifting him back on top of the all-time earnings list, well beyond Armed's two-week-old world record.

Relieved and thankful, Jacobs decided to give his warhorse a well-deserved rest, shipping him once again to Virginia for the winter. Armed may have emerged as 1947's runaway handicap champion and the overall Horse of the Year, but Stymie at least got to rest on a rich laurel of his own. Stymie once again reigned as the world's all-time money-winning king.

CHAPTER 18

CONSUMMATE CLOSER

All through the winter of 1947–1948, Stymie lolled about on Jack Skinner's farm, rolling in the mud, galloping along the fence, seeking out the few remaining green blades of grass.

When Stymie had arrived at the Middleburg farm in early November 1947, the first thing Jack Skinner had noticed was a lameness in the left front leg. As soon as Stymie's shoes were pulled, Skinner discovered the cause. Stymie had a stone bruise in the sole of his foot. The farrier cut out the bruised sole and Stymie immediately started to improve. By February, Skinner thought Stymie was ready to do some work under saddle. He created a makeshift riding arena and then sent one of his riders out to work Stymie back into condition.

Not long after that, Jacobs stopped by to visit with Stymie and to see how he was doing. The last time he had seen his horse back in New York, Jacobs thought he had seemed out of sorts, which was why Stymie was sent south earlier than usual. Stymie looked good to the trainer, but Jacobs didn't want to rush his return to the racetrack. The horse was getting older and, at seven, would be more vulnerable to injury, especially since he'd be carrying heavy weights when he got back to racing.

"I am not setting any million-dollar mark for him," Jacobs told a reporter. "He will not be hurried, and if he displays a disinclination to do his best following his early races, I may send him back to the farm for a while. He himself will decide where and when he will race."

As far as Jacobs was concerned, Stymie had already paid his dues, bringing his owner an unexpected level of fame and fortune. The last thing Jacobs wanted was for Stymie to get hurt. But Jacobs was a little sad without his friend up in Jamaica. He missed seeing Stymie's head hanging over the stall door, the long stretches of time that they would stand together staring at one another in silent communion, and, of course, the exhilaration of cheering his favorite horse home.

By March, Stymie was already doing easy gallops, which eventually turned into breezes. True to his word, Jacobs didn't rush the horse back to the racetrack. It wasn't until mid-April that Stymie was shipped back up to New York, just in time to start prepping for the mile-and-a-sixteenth Excelsior Handicap. In deference to his prized horse's age, Jacobs had taken up a new method of conditioning him. Stymie would be sent out on the track for his gallops with no saddle or rider. A pony boy, Mickey Finney, would ride one of the stable ponies while grasping Stymie's lead shank and the two horses would gallop side by side. It was a way of minimizing the concussion to Stymie's legs while still getting in regular gallops.

The Excelsior, like many of his season-opening races over the years, wasn't impressive. In fact, when it was time to explode in the stretch, Stymie didn't offer much and crossed the finish line third. He would lose two more before capturing the Metropolitan Handicap for the second time, which was somewhat of a surprise since the mile distance was much shorter than he preferred.

After a first in an allowance race and seconds in the Suburban and Queens County Handicaps, Stymie was shipped down to

Delaware again for his third Sussex Handicap. Despite his age and the 130-pound impost he was carrying, fans made Stymie the odds-on favorite. Like the Stymie of old, he reached down deep and summoned his patented stretch drive to cruise past everyone and win by a length and a half, breaking his own track record from the previous year. Carrying 130 again in the Brooklyn Handicap, Stymie started his drive on the last turn but seemed to run out of gas and faded coming down the stretch, settling for third.

Jacobs next shipped him down to the Jersey Shore for the Monmouth Handicap on July 24, hoping that with easier competition Stymie might get a win. But once again, Stymie faded in the stretch and, worse, began to hobble as he passed under the wire in fourth. X-rays showed that he had fractured a sesamoid bone in his right front leg. The vet put a cast on the leg, and in a hopeful sign, the horse walked off comfortably. He was then shipped with the cast on to Skinner's farm to recuperate.

Two days after the injury, newspapers across the country delivered the headline news: STYMIE RETIRED.

The following afternoon, a Western Union telegram arrived at Jacobs's Forest Hills home. Jacobs glanced first at the sender's name and saw it was racing royalty: Jock Whitney, the aristocratic owner of Greentree Stable. Jacobs then began reading Whitney's warm words about Stymie:

LIKE SO MANY THOUSANDS OF HIS FANS I AM DEEPLY SORRY THAT YOUR GRAND CAMPAIGN IS THROUGH ON THE TURF. HIS PERFORMANCE AND YOUR HANDLING OF HIM HAVE BEEN A GREAT CREDIT TO RACING AND ESPECIALLY TO THE SPORT IN THIS STATE. I CONGRATULATE AND SYMPATHIZE WITH YOU. HOPE YOU HAVE A SEASON TO HIM FOR GREENTREE WHEREVER HE STANDS. ALL BEST WISHES=JOHN HAY WHITNEY=

Jacobs was surprised and delighted that Jock Whitney, a pillar of racing royalty and American aristocracy, was asking to buy a breeding to his Stymie. The telegram signaled the ultimate acceptance of the consummate outsiders—Jacobs and Stymie—by racing's elite.

As it turned out, the headlines that prompted Whitney's telegram might have been a bit premature. Within a couple of weeks, it began to look as if the injury hadn't been as severe as originally thought. Right after the fracture, Jacobs had assumed that the best he could hope for was to get Stymie sound enough to go to stud. Back in 1946, with the winnings from Stymie's races, Jacobs had bought a farm in Maryland—which, out of gratitude, he named "Stymie Manor." The plan then was to bring Stymie there at a later date to stand at stud. But now it was looking like Stymie's racing career might not be done. "He's tough, you know," Jacobs told a reporter. "Nothing bothers him. We're going to put him in the stud, just as we had planned, but if he's going well enough next spring, we'll bring him back."

The cast was removed at the end of August and Stymie continued to walk, and even gallop, in his paddock with no sign of pain. So, Jacobs was back to his original plan. He would breed Stymie to ten mares in the spring, and if the horse held up under light training at the farm, he would be shipped back to the track.

During the spring of 1949, Stymie had gotten six of the ten mares he'd been bred to pregnant, and Jacobs was looking forward to an exciting foaling season the following spring. The horse was looking fit and Jacobs was starting to think he might get to have a little more time with Stymie on the track. But he wanted to be cautious, making sure there were no signs of unsoundness before shipping back to New York. It wasn't until September that Jacobs finally felt comfortable racing his star again.

Stymie, whose come-from-behind charges once spurred sportswriters to call him "the comeback kid," was certainly no kid when he made his toughest comeback of all: returning to the racetrack after the injury that had sidelined him for over thirteen months. For Stymie's comeback race, Jacobs would have preferred a nonstakes tune-up but couldn't find one that September. So old Stymie would have to make his eight-year-old debut in the Edgemere Handicap, where he would meet up with his old archrival Assault for the ninth time.

In the crowded Aqueduct paddock before the race, Jacobs was watching Stymie work his way around the walking ring when Assault's owner, Bob Kleberg, sidled up to him.

"I'm eager to see your horse," Kleberg said pleasantly.

Jacobs grinned wide and replied, "He's your horse too."

They both laughed at the inside joke. Stymie was indeed Kleberg's horse in the sense that the King Ranch owner had actually bred him and raced him until Jacobs claimed him away for $1,500. And Stymie was certainly Jacobs's horse in every other respect, the owner and trainer who had transformed him from a cheap claimer into the world's richest racehorse. But more than that, Stymie was everyman's horse. That's why he was nicknamed "The People's Horse." And that's why more than 30,000 sentimentalists flocked to Aqueduct to welcome him back.

They greeted him with warm applause when they first spotted him jogging through the stretch on his way to the paddock, and again when he returned for the post parade. Alas, Stymie gave his fans nothing to cheer for during the mile-and-an-eighth race, finishing dead last, beaten by fifteen lengths. Instead, it was Assault, the betting favorite making a comeback of his own after a yearlong injury-induced layoff, who delivered the Stymie-like charge from last to grab third at the wire.

Despite Stymie's uninspiring return, racing fans remained enthralled by his pursuit of the million-dollar milestone. He stood just $88,665 short of becoming racing's first equine millionaire.

For years, newspaper accounts of every one of his races included an updated running total of his career earnings and a mention of the $1,500 claim. Now that "the bargain-baby horse" was so tantalizingly close to becoming the turf's first million-dollar baby, fans were eager to see him race again.

Jacobs went back to his tried-and-true method of tuning Stymie up, running him next in two allowance races—Stymie managed a third in each. Hoping that might be enough of a prep, the trainer put Stymie in the Manhattan Handicap, where he would again meet Assault. Once more, Stymie had trouble accessing his patented stretch run and managed to move up from last only to fourth. Assault started out in fourth and then lost ground through the race, crossing the finish line dead last.

Though Jacobs may not have been thrilled with the performance, he did think Stymie was on the right path. There was one more race he figured he could squeeze in before his ultimate goal, the International Gold Cup in November, and that was the two-and-a-quarter-mile New York Handicap at Belmont Park.

Stymie seemed to be recovering his old form. Slow out of the gate, he dawdled at the back of the field until the final turn. Then Conn McCreary asked for some speed and Stymie started moving up just as he had in the old days. By the time he hit the stretch, he was just two and a half lengths behind the leader and it looked as if he might have his first win of the season. But the frontrunner hung on and Stymie wasn't able to close the gap. The $5,000 he earned for his second-place finish brought him within $81,515 of the million-dollar mark.

Jacobs was heartened and figured they might have a shot at winning the International Gold Cup once again. But when Stymie stepped off the van at Jamaica, he was hobbling, sore on the same front foot he'd injured the year before at Monmouth. Jacobs's heart sank. He immediately called the vet to get X-rays to find out whether the sesamoid bone had been reinjured. The good news was that Stymie hadn't broken anything. But in the days that followed he remained sore on that foot. Discouraged, Jacobs told a reporter with a sigh, "He was just getting good."

Jacobs rested him in the following weeks, sending Stymie out with his groom, Joe Jones, for short strolls around the barns. By the week before the Gold Cup, Stymie once again looked sound and Jacobs decided to try putting him out on the track for an easy Monday-morning gallop. But Stymie wasn't interested. He sulked during his workout, pinning his ears, swishing his tail, and refusing to gallop. Jacobs realized it might be all over. He remembered that he had promised that Stymie would be the one who decided when and where he would race. And now, it seemed, Stymie had spoken. He was done.

The following day, Izzy Bieber formally announced that Stymie was retiring from racing. It wasn't until a couple of days later that Jacobs was ready to explain his decision to the reporters. "Some people have the idea that Stymie has broken down, that he's a cripple," he said. "That's not true, of course. I've retired him, but there's not much wrong with him. If management would like it, I'm willing to have him gallop through the stretch before the running of the Gold Cup race on Saturday to let people see that he's still pretty frisky."

When news of Stymie's retirement broke, sportswriters penned the final chapter of a saga so improbable that it would have been rejected by Hollywood scriptwriters. The newspapers recapped his rags-to-riches rise, from the humblest of beginnings to glory and gold. Stymie was not the first to be called a Cinderella horse, but after him, they figured they might as well retire the appellation.

The retirement stories dutifully summed up the mind-boggling statistics: Stymie had run a staggering 131 races—dozens more than any of the iconic warhorses, from Exterminator to Seabiscuit. He was the ultimate longshot who couldn't win a stakes race until he was four and then, as befit this real-life fairytale, transformed overnight from the ugly duckling into a swan who only got better with age. With consistency to rival his durability, he won 35 races—25 of those stakes—and finished second in 33 and third in 28.

In the end, the little $1,500 claimer was retiring as the world's all-time richest racehorse, his bankroll bulging at $918,485. That windfall, constituting a 600-fold return on Hirsch Jacobs's initial investment, made Stymie, undisputedly, the best bargain in the annals of horse racing. More than that, it put him in the pantheon of the legends that had reigned before him as the world's richest racehorse, a list graced by the likes of Man o' War, Gallant Fox, Seabiscuit, and Whirlaway.

Stymie had to earn his money the hard way, soldiering through seven grueling years on iron legs propelled by a stout heart. While the great Man o' War raced a grand total of precisely 19⅝ miles in his career, the gallant Stymie's journey to supremacy among the all-time money winners would take him 142⅛ miles. Making his prodigious total all the more remarkable, Stymie ran most of those miles slugging it out in racing's heavyweight division with the greatest iron horses of his generation.

All of which earned him the unflinching respect of the most hardened horsemen and horseplayers. One of his most ardent admirers, the celebrated turf writer Joe Palmer, explained how Stymie wound up sharing sentences with racing's greatest legends: "The racetrackers, I think, save most of their affection for the Exterminators and the Stymies and the Seabiscuits, who do it the hard way in the handicaps, pounding out mile after bitter mile, giving weight and taking their tracks wet or dry, running for any jockey, and trying with what they've got, even when they haven't got enough."

On the occasion of Stymie's retirement, Palmer put the little horse into historical perspective. "He is not a great horse in the sense that Man o' War and Equipoise were great," Palmer wrote in the *New York Herald Tribune*. "He isn't versatile. He can't make his own pace and he can't win slow races. He needs something up ahead to draw speed from the field, to soften it up for his long, sweeping rush at the end. But give him a field with speed in it, at a mile and a half or more, and horses had better get out of his way, even Whirlaway."

Stymie's record, impressive as it was, didn't tell half the story. What endeared him to hardcore horseplayers and casual fans alike was the way he did it: those thrilling come-from-behind charges that made him the darling of the New York tracks. The horseplayers quickly learned to stop tearing up their betting tickets in despair and disgust every time Stymie dropped twenty, twenty-two lengths behind talented horses. They knew to wait for the cue—the raising of his handsome head—for Stymie's one big run. That's how they would forever remember him: galloping with his head held high as he sailed majestically past his rivals.

On the first Saturday in November, New York racegoers would flock to Jamaica racetrack to salute their favorite horse for one last time. Announced with little fanfare in that morning's newspapers as Stymie's farewell appearance before his adoring fans, the ceremony was to be a combination post parade, victory lap, valedictory, and retirement party.

It was Hirsch Jacobs's idea to stage the sentimental ceremony right before the International Gold Cup, a race he had scratched

Stymie from just a few days earlier. In the two years since Stymie had kicked off that event in spectacular style with his crowning-glory triumph, the Gold Cup had lost half its rich purse and all its luster. Stymie, in contrast, had lost none of his own luster.

Back in the stable that Jacobs and Stymie had long called home, Joe Jones was brushing his charge's coppery coat to a brilliant sheen. Then the groom wove ribbons into the braids he was putting in Stymie's mane and tail—all in the Jacobs colors of salmon pink and emerald green. It had been suggested that Stymie carry a jockey wearing the pink and green silks, but Jacobs firmly said no. Since Stymie had refused to gallop the last time he was under saddle, Jacobs didn't want him to get the wrong idea and think he was being sent back to work.

It was only fitting that Jamaica be the site of the last appearance on any track for what racing historian William Robertson called "the 'people's horse' to end them all." That's because old Jamaica had always been known as "the people's track," even if the people themselves had come to affectionately call it "Footsore Downs."

From his usual perch in the Jamaica press box, Joe Palmer was watching the early races on the Saturday card while contemplating what it was about The People's Horse that so captured the public's—and his own—imagination. Stymie's thrilling come-from-behind drives couldn't fully explain his grip on the hearts and souls of hard-bitten horseplayers and hardened New Yorkers alike. Thinking back on all those times Stymie had moved him to poetry, Palmer puzzled it out in a *Herald Tribune* column destined to become a classic.

"It is thoroughly appropriate that Stymie should have his final appearance at Jamaica, because he's a Jamaica kind of horse," Palmer decided in that column. "Man o' War, Equipoise and Whirlaway all were equine royalty from the day they were foaled. Stymie was common folks."

There you had it: Stymie's special appeal to working-class folks had a lot to do with the way he started at the bottom as a cheap claimer and, through sheer grit and determination, clawed his way up to become racing's all-time richest racehorse. They saw their own aspirations in this horse, and it gave them hope. Stymie was Horatio Alger in horseshoes, the very embodiment of the American Dream.

"This is, you will see, basically the story of the ugly duckling, of Cinderella among the ashes, of Dick Whittington and his cat," Palmer's column went on, "and of all the world's stories none has ever been preferred to that which leads to the public and very glorious triumph of the oppressed and the downtrodden. Jamaica's horseplayers are to some extent oppressed and downtrodden, and perhaps in Stymie they find a vicarious success."

Which is why more than 30,000 of them turned out to salute Stymie on this crisp fall day. Jacobs had orchestrated the whole thing right down to the minutest detail. He wanted Stymie ponied all the way around the sweeping final turn and down the homestretch, so fans could see their favorite horse galloping one last time.

After the fifth race, Stymie was led by Joe Jones to the backstretch gap up by the far turn. Mounted on his stable pony, Mickey Finney took the lead shank and brought Stymie alongside. Then off they went. At first, it was a jog, then a slow canter, then a gallop.

At the sight of Stymie coming onto the backstretch next to the stable pony, the crowd broke into applause that started building like a wave as more and more fans caught on. Even without the benefit of the brightly colored Jacobs silks, they instantly recognized Stymie across the vast infield simply by the distinctively proud carriage of his high head. Many of them called to their equine hero.

More than a few, at their first glimpse of the copper chestnut, shouted the very words they used to scream whenever he would unleash his big move: "Here comes Stymie!"

As Stymie started rounding the turn that he had looped so often in those rousing charges of his, the track announcer, Fred Capossela, began reeling off a long résumé of his achievements. Hearing the announcer's call and the crowd's cheers, the horseplayers who were lined up inside at the betting windows gave up their place in the queues so they could rush back outside to catch the spectacle.

Stymie was now picking up speed as he swept off the turn in a full-on gallop, and from the sound of the roar, you would have sworn he was about to run down Assault and Natchez in the stretch once again. Riding the waves of applause, Stymie galloped down the stretch past the grandstand, fairly bursting with bloom and vigor. The original plan was to pony him down to the finish line and stop him there but, as Palmer pointed out in a news story, "the man who could have stopped Stymie on the way down could have pulled the Broadway Limited." Stymie kept barreling down the track until he ran out of straightaway. He slowed as he hit the clubhouse turn and stopped right in front of the paddock, which was just beyond the outside rail.

The pony boy handed the lead shank to Joe Jones, and the groom led Stymie in front of the pack of photographers who had been waiting for him to arrive at the paddock. As the cameras whirred and clicked, Stymie preened and puffed himself up, looking as if he knew exactly why everyone was there. His neck came straight up out of his shoulder, making him look imperious and much taller as he gazed down at his audience. He snorted and blew blasts of air through his nostrils as his tail rose and flagged.

All the while, Major Francis Sutherland's renowned Seventh

Regiment Band played "Auld Lang Syne," just as they had a year earlier at Babe Ruth's poignant farewell ceremony at Yankee Stadium two months before his death from cancer. Only this time, the song was pretty well drowned out by the cheers for Stymie that were reverberating through the Jamaica racetrack.

Jones led Stymie into the paddock and then took him around the walking ring along with the entrants parading for the featured Gold Cup. As he led Stymie back through the paddock gap onto the track, Jones paused for a moment, and Stymie turned toward the crowd, head held proudly, and stared at his fans as if he understood they were all cheering just for him.

Then Jones started to lead Stymie back around the clubhouse turn toward the backstretch and the stables. Fans standing near the winner's circle beckoned to Jones and shouted, "Bring him in here, for just one more time."

Jones declined, and Palmer couldn't argue with the groom's decision. "Probably he was right," Palmer wrote in the kicker to his classic column. "Stymie never got in a winner's circle without working for it. It was no time to begin."

Red Smith, Palmer's colleague at the *Herald Tribune*, preferred to see it a slightly different way: from Stymie's perspective. "He returned to the track but flatly refused to enter the winner's circle," Smith would write. "He had got there 35 times on merit and Stymie took favors from nobody."

Twenty-four years later, long after old Jamaica and the *Herald Tribune* had both gone the way of the iron warhorses, Smith would be covering a similar valedictory, this time a ceremony honoring the great Secretariat, and the scene in the winner's circle at Aqueduct evoked memories of Stymie's farewell. "Stymie was a showy chestnut like Secretariat," the storied columnist wrote that day in his *New York Times* column, "and although television had not discovered horse racing in his day, he was as dearly beloved by his following of thousands as Secretariat has been among TV's millions. Like his public at Footsore Downs, Stymie was common folks, a refugee from the claiming races who became a millionaire by honest effort."

On that nostalgic fall afternoon in 1949, as Stymie walked off the track for the last time, his storybook saga finally coming to a close, everyone knew that there had never been—and would never be—another Cinderella horse quite like him. He had spent his entire career as "common folks," and in the end it turned out that he was as uncommon as they come.

CHAPTER 19

THE EMPIRE THAT
STYMIE BUILT

Hirsch Jacobs wasn't content with having made it to the top as a trainer. The real challenge, he felt, was in creating elite racehorses in the breeding shed. And Stymie's winnings on the track were going to give him a chance to chase down that dream.

Stymie was still in his purse-earning prime when Hirsch Jacobs and Izzy Bieber rolled his winnings into the 1946 purchase of a 283-acre horse farm in northern Maryland and boldly branched into the breeding end of the racing game. At the farm they fittingly named Stymie Manor, the erstwhile claiming trainer was able to break into the breeding business where, he quipped, "all you need is money, money, and more money." While he lacked the kind of bank balance enjoyed by the multimillionaire sportsmen who could afford to breed and race Thoroughbreds as an expensive hobby, he more than compensated with an encyclopedic knowledge of pedigrees and a knack for combining them.

When Jacobs started seriously breeding his own stock, the same skeptics who had once dismissed him as "just a claiming trainer" now insisted he would never make it as a breeder. Because his success had been built on claiming horses that were bred and broke by others, they suggested he stick with what he knew best and leave the breeding to the Bluegrass bluebloods with centuries of experience.

Right out of the gate, though, Jacobs's homebreds started to prove them wrong. His broodmare Dolly Whisk, who had once sold for $185 before Jacobs claimed and briefly raced her, would present him with his first Derby horse. Bieber, who tended to give horses names that reflected his freewheeling take on politics, societal issues, and world events, named Dolly Whisk's 1946 foal after Israel's fight for independence: Palestinian. The chestnut colt proved yet another example of Jacobs's wizardry in bringing back horses from serious leg injuries, in this case a bowed tendon. In the spring of 1949, Jacobs entered Palestinian in the Kentucky Derby despite Bieber's vow that no horse of his would ever run the marquee spectacle he branded "a one-day ballyhoo" and boycotted. Palestinian, carrying Bieber's colors, would place in all three Triple Crown races—third in the Kentucky Derby, second in the Preakness a head behind Capot's track record, and third in the Belmont. In Palestinian, Jacobs had bred a multiple stakes winner who would earn $296,525 and whose son Promised Land would make $541,707.

Ironically, Stymie himself did not stand stud at Stymie Manor. Instead, he was sent to Kentucky to stand at Dr. Charlie Hagyard's Lexington breeding farm. Stymie's first foal crop included a handsome bay that Jacobs chose to name Joe Jones. That choice underscored the incongruity of the Odd Couple's respective naming conventions. Bieber's names reflected his strong views against allowing Germany to rearm (such as Nothirdchance, Remember History, Always Danger) and against smoking (Pufawaysister, Burnt Throat, Kansirette). In contrast, the Jacobses often picked out names for sentimental reasons (Globetrotter John, Our Patrice, Tanker Tom). When it came time to name Stymie's first offspring, Jacobs chose Joe

Jones after the dedicated groom who had bonded so closely with the horse through his racing career. Joe Jones the horse did his sire proud, winning 34 of his 175 races over eight years and earning $423,567. Paper Tiger, a product of Stymie's second foal crop, won 19 of his 114 starts over five years and earned $323,782, proving that durability, soundness, and toughness ran in the family.

Through the 1950s, all of the Bieber-Jacobs Stable's many stakes winners were homebreds—with one notable exception. That would be the one most responsible for ultimately turning Bieber-Jacobs into the nation's top breeding empire, a horse that Jacobs discovered in the same manner and in the same spot as he had found Stymie a dozen years earlier.

One afternoon in the spring of 1955 in the paddock at Belmont, Jacobs was saddling a youngster for a maiden race when he noticed a stunning brown filly in the adjoining stall. He went back to tightening the girth on his own horse's saddle, but he couldn't stop himself from repeatedly stealing glances over at the brown one next door. Sunny Jim Fitzsimmons was saddling that neighboring filly for Wheatley Stable, whose owner Ogden Phipps stood off to the side watching the proceedings.

"I see you've got another granddaughter of La Troienne," Jacobs casually said to Phipps, trying to sound as if he were just making small talk.

"Yes," Phipps replied, perking up at the possibility of a deal.

"I like that filly," Jacobs said. "Would you want to sell her?"

"Yes," Phipps blurted, the speed of his reply betraying his impatience with the three-year-old maiden's twenty losses. "I'll take fifteen thousand dollars for her—if it is OK with Mr. Fitz." When Fitzsimmons quickly nodded his head in assent, Phipps told Jacobs, "If you want her, you can have her after this race."

"I'll take her," Jacobs shot back.

He bought Searching on the spot, took her back to his Jamaica stable that evening, and then went home where he confessed to Ethel his apprehension about possibly overpaying for this one. The next morning, while trying to diagnose what was preventing the fashionably bred filly from running to her purple pedigree, he observed that when she walked, "her eyes got this glassy, sad look as if her shoes were too tight." He had his blacksmith pull her shoes and, sure enough, they found the walls of her hooves were so thin that when her previous farrier had clinched, or tightened, the nails, it pulled the shoe not only against the hoof wall but also against the more sensitive sole, causing discomfort whenever she ran. When she was reshod, Jacobs asked the blacksmith to put a piece of felt between the hoof and the shoe and to be careful not to clinch too tight.

Thus cured and transformed almost overnight, Searching broke her maiden the first time she raced for Jacobs and then went on to win a dozen stakes and $327,381 in purses. All of that was merely a bonus, for Jacobs always figured that Searching's real value would be as a broodmare. From a pedigree perspective, this War Admiral daughter out of a La Troienne daughter offered Jacobs a potent combination satisfying his affinity both for Man o' War and for his favorite dam line. Searching wasted no time asserting herself as the queen of the Bieber-Jacobs broodmares. Her first foal, sired by the 1955 Kentucky Derby winner Swaps and born in 1960, made the Jacobses so happy that they named her Affectionately.

Before Affectionately was even weaned, another homebred emerged as Jacobs's best Derby prospect yet: Hail to Reason, the product of Nothirdchance's mating with the Irish stallion Turn-to. Hail to Reason had already clinched the 1960 juvenile championship when, during a gallop on a Sunday morning that September, he stepped on a thrown horseshoe and fractured both sesamoid bones in his left foreleg. From their position across the Aqueduct track, Jacobs and his son John, serving as his assistant trainer, saw the exercise boy pull the colt up. They ran across the infield to Hail to Reason. John grabbed the reins, and Hirsch picked up the injured leg and held it so Hail couldn't put any weight on it.

When the horse ambulance arrived, the driver got out, surveyed the scene, and asked, "Mr. Jacobs, are you going to destroy him here or after we get him back to the barn?"

Jacobs shook his head and growled, "I'm not going to destroy him, if I have to put that leg back on myself!"

When they got the colt back to his stall, Jacobs dug out his first-aid kit and a bag of plaster of paris. With tears streaming down his face, Jacobs formed a cast around the injured leg. He slowly allowed the colt to take his leg back, and Hail lay down in the stall. The Jacobses' quick response most likely saved their colt's life. He would never race again, but he would be healthy enough to stand at stud.

If Jacobs could find any consolation in the forced retirement of "the greatest horse I ever had," it was that he had Affectionately to pin his hopes on. Beloved as "The Queen of Queens" by the denizens of the Queens racetracks, Affectionately would reign as a champion in three divisions (juvenile filly, handicap mare, and sprint) and become the second female ever to earn half a million dollars ($546,659). Jacobs, at the time, deemed her "the best horse I've ever trained."

Not to mention, the best horse he'd ever bred—at least up to that point. Just as Stymie had shown on the racetrack, Searching proved with each succeeding foal how Jacobs's uncanny knack for mining gold in the dirt extended to the breeding shed. For years, Jacobs carried around in his wallet a photo of Searching to show people what a real racemare and broodmare looked like. When her daughter Affectionately hit the track, he added a picture of the dark bay to his bulging wallet. "That's my little girl," he would beam.

Already acknowledged as the winningest trainer of all time, Hirsch Jacobs was now staking another claim: as the nation's leading breeder. In 1964, he reached the top spot on the breeders' list with $1,301,677 in annual winnings by the horses he had bred. The next year, he repeated as the nation's top breeder with $1,994,649, just $65,941 short of the all-time record set by the Calumet dynasty in its bygone glory days. The little "claiming stable" had finally taken its rightful place alongside the high-society likes of Calumet, Wheatley, and Greentree as a racing empire now routinely described with modifiers like "upscale," "fashionable," and "high class." And Hirsch Jacobs, the claiming king once mocked for running his cheap horses like "a fleet of taxicabs," now reigned over a breeding dynasty hailed by the *New York Times* as "the General Motors of the turf."

In 1958, at fifty-four still considered a youngster by the standards of the training trade, Hirsch Jacobs officially reached the pinnacle of his profession when he was enshrined in the National Thoroughbred Racing Hall of Fame. A stunning and singular achievement for a trainer so young, his selection ushered him into an exclusive pantheon whose nine previous members—all posthumously inducted after lengthy careers built on a lifelong association with horses—had been saddling them for many years before Jacobs was even born.

What made the honor all the sweeter was that Jacobs would be enshrined in the same Hall of Fame class alongside two living legends, Sunny Jim Fitzsimmons and Plain Ben Jones. Mr. Fitz, still actively training bluebloods for the Phippses' Wheatley Stable at eighty-four, had just added his unprecedented thirteenth win in Triple Crown races to his two Triple Crown sweeps, while Plain Ben, at seventy-five finally retired from the Calumet dynasty he had built, boasted two Triple Crowns and a record six Derbies. In stark contrast, Hirsch Jacobs, the self-made claiming trainer still running his own independent stable and working for nobody but himself, did not have a single Derby, Preakness, or Belmont winner to his credit—but he had Stymie as his claim to fame, and that was more than enough for the 2,000 sportswriters and sportscasters who voted him in.

Had Jacobs never claimed Stymie from Max Hirsch, the King Ranch trainer might well have been the one joining Mr. Fitz and Plain Ben for the ceremony inducting the Class of '58 into the Hall of Fame in the hallowed shadow of Saratoga Race Course. Instead, Max Hirsch, despite a long résumé capped by a Triple Crown and three Derby wins, would have to wait until the following year for his own induction at seventy-nine. No wonder the Stymie claim continued to fester like a sore he couldn't salve. For his part, Jacobs was always careful not to rub salt into Hirsch's wound.

Not long after, Jacobs invited a group of trainers over to his Forest Hills home for dinner and movies. In preparation for the after-dinner entertainment, he picked through his large collection of 16-millimeter films of stakes races that he loved to watch on a big screen. On top of the stack was his favorite film: Stymie's 1947 International Gold Cup win, which Jacobs had already screened hundreds and hundreds of times. When Max Hirsch accepted the invitation, however, Jacobs gave strict instructions to his son John, who regularly manned the projector, that no films were to be shown of the Stymie-Assault races so as not to upset an old friend and rival.

Jacobs understood that Stymie remained a sore spot not just for Hirsch but also for everyone connected with the King Ranch. In fact, King Ranch visitors taking the guided tour of the sprawling Texas spread would be admonished: ask any questions you want, but don't dare mention Stymie.

Still basking in the afterglow of the Hall of Fame recognition, Jacobs took dead aim at a more objective measure of mastery: the milestone of becoming the first trainer ever to saddle 3,000 winners. The New York dailies closely tracked his progression until, on April 1, 1960, Willie Shoemaker, a fellow 1958 Hall of Fame inductee, rode a filly named Blue Waters to Jacobs's 3,000th win in the second race at Aqueduct—fittingly a cheap claiming race whose $2,275 purse brought the trainer's career earnings to $9,013,182. Jacobs finished 1960 leading all trainers in money won for the first time since Stymie's heyday, with $748,349. In 1965, he again topped the trainers' list, his $1,331,628 in winnings falling just $3,177 short of Plain Ben's eighteen-year-old record.

By this time, Hirsch Jacobs had become as recognizable a figure at the New York tracks as the superhorses and the superstar jockeys. Racegoers, especially the $2 bettors who entrusted their hard-earned pay in any horse Jacobs saddled, had no trouble picking their favorite trainer out of a crowd. The years hadn't changed him much: the stout little trainer still had a twinkle in his bright blue eyes, his hair just as red and thick as ever. Though he always had an inviting smile and a "Hiya" for everyone, Jacobs shied away from the crowds and the autograph seekers who followed him through the clubhouse. Reserved and unassuming as ever, he often preferred watching races from the solitude of the infield, letting Bieber hold forth for the both of them up in their clubhouse box.

Jacobs was remarkably unchanged by all the success and money. When his old Jamaica stomping grounds was shuttered to make room for a public housing project in 1958, Jacobs moved his stable not to the chic Belmont but to the utilitarian Aqueduct, the no-frills heir as the people's track. Jacobs would always be common folk, the people's trainer whose most popular champion was "The People's Horse."

As soon as he retired Stymie from the racetrack to stand stud at Dr. Hagyard's Kentucky breeding farm, Jacobs began to miss his old friend. Jacobs never tired of reminiscing about his all-time favorite horse. With a twinkle in his eyes punctuated by a wink, he liked to remind folks that "Stymie Manor was paid for by a friend." Whenever anyone asked him what shade of chestnut that friend's coat was, he would sift through his change pocket, pick out the shiniest freshly minted penny he could find, and proudly hold it out. "See that nice, shiny copper?" he'd beam. "That's his color."

In the summer of 1950, Citation, by then already anointed the greatest racehorse not named Man o' War, supplanted Stymie as the world's all-time richest racehorse. Jacobs hatched a plan to bring Stymie out of retirement in an attempt not only to recapture the money-winning title but also to beat out the 1948 Triple Crown champion in the race to become the first equine millionaire. He wanted it for Stymie—and the horse's legacy—more than he wanted it for himself. At the age of nine, Stymie was still sound and, soon after arriving at Jack Skinner's Middleburg farm for conditioning, was back to his sleek racing weight of 1,075 pounds. Jacobs shipped him to California for the rich fall stakes at Hollywood Park, but it quickly became clear in morning workouts that Stymie wasn't interested in racing anymore. In the end, Jacobs decided against staging the comeback bid and returned Stymie to stud, while Citation went on to surpass the million-dollar mark and reign as the world's all-time richest racehorse for six years.

For all the acclaim Stymie earned for his rags-to-riches Cinderella legend as The Little Claimer That Could, his place among racing's all-time greats was won strictly on the democratic merits of his performances on the track. As behooves a celebrated closer who only got stronger with age and distance, Stymie created an enduring legacy. The Stymie Handicap, inaugurated in 1956 as a $25,000 stakes at Belmont, has been run since 1976 at the blue-collar track that befits its namesake's work ethic—Aqueduct. In 1975, the same year as the Hirsch Jacobs Stakes was inaugurated at Pimlico, Stymie was selected to join his trainer in the Racing Hall of Fame. At the turn of the millennium, when the *Blood-Horse* magazine polled experts to select the "Top 100 Racehorses of the 20th Century," Stymie ranked forty-first on a list led by the consensus trifecta of Man o' War followed by Secretariat and Citation. Had the *Blood-Horse* list been compiled at midcentury, Stymie would have ranked eighteenth—and, among the crowd-wowing stretch runners, second only to Whirlaway. As the magazine's longtime editor-in-chief Kent Hollingsworth defined his legacy in the book *The Great Ones*, "Stymie became an epic hero whose mighty stretch runs moved Jamaica fans to unabashed cheers, Grantland Rice to poetry, and Jacobs into the breeding business."

In the spring of 1962, Dr. Hagyard called Jacobs with the sad news that Stymie had suffered a heart attack. On the other end of the phone, Jacobs could hear the venerated veterinarian crying as he reported that Stymie was fading. Jacobs's first inclination was to rush down to Stymie's side at Hagyard's Kentucky farm, but Doc Charlie talked him out of it, saying it would be better not to see him in that condition. "If that's the way he is, I don't want to see him," Jacobs agreed reluctantly. "I want to see him in my mind the way he always was."

The day after Stymie passed away at the age of twenty-one, Jacobs choked up while addressing reporters at Belmont. "He was like one of the family," Jacobs said wistfully. "Funny thing, whenever he'd hear my wife's voice, he'd nicker. She'd talk to him and give him a piece of sugar, and he'd nicker."

Back at home, Jacobs shared with his family a sentiment that he would repeat from time to time over the succeeding years. "Everything we have," he said, "we owe to Stymie."

In the spring of 1966, Jacobs was enjoying yet another dominating season as the nation's leading trainer and breeder when he suddenly suffered a stroke. Although he would recover, his doctors ordered him to severely cut back on his business activity. In the immediate future, that meant turning over the day-to-day operation of the racing stable to his son John, who for the previous decade had been serving as his assistant trainer. In the long term, it meant dismantling much of the Bieber-Jacobs empire to ease the burden on his family. Jacobs discussed it with Bieber, who oversaw the partnership's finances but, at eighty, was also slowing down. They both agreed to reduce their vast breeding and racing empire by two-thirds, and the Fasig-Tipton auction house scheduled five one-day dispersal sales that summer and fall. While still hospitalized, Jacobs organized every detail of the consignment.

The Fasig-Tipton catalogue for the first sale, at Saratoga in August, called it simply "Bieber-Jacobs Reduction," but the *New York Times* suggested "Redhead's Revenge" as a more colorfully appropriate title. "After all," the *Times*' turf writer, Steve Cady, wrote on the eve of the auction, "with six ready-to-run $100,000 stake winners among the 55 racers and yearlings to be sold, isn't it the most dazzling night in horse-auction history? Weren't these dazzlers raised by the intruder who made Kentucky bluebloods choke on their mint juleps when he won the national breeder title in 1964 and 1965? And won't the fiercest bidding be done by the same millionaire pillars of the turf who have, over the years, looked down their binoculars at the Brooklyn-raised upstart who built his empire on cheap claimers the millionaires wouldn't have allowed in their barns?"

The evening figured to be the most bittersweet of Jacobs's long career. Because doctors didn't think he could stand the strain of seeing so many of his beloved horses dispersed in the Saratoga sales ring, they advised him to stay home for the auction and drive up the next day for the races. "I don't believe I could stand it," Jacobs agreed. "A lot of hard work and sentiment has gone into building up this stable. To see much of it torn apart in one night—well, I just don't want to be on hand to see it done." So he stayed home in the mansion his family had recently moved to in Forest Hills Gardens, a step up in class to the tony neighborhood on the uptown side of Queens Boulevard. Surrounded by four large showcases crammed with a couple of hundred gold and silver trophies won by his stable, he listened to the proceedings via telephone hookup.

What he heard left him speechless. The auction brought $1.85 million, smashing the one-day record set by Louis B. Mayer's 1947 dispersal, for fifty-three horses as well as two breeding shares in his empire's kingpin stallion, Hail to Reason. The two shares sold for a total of $323,000, meaning that Hail to Reason, with thirty more shares in his breeding syndicate, was a $5 million stallion. What was more, Admiring, the four-year-old stakes-winning daughter of Hail to Reason and Searching, brought $310,000—the highest price ever paid for a horse of any age or sex at public auction anywhere in the world. That Paul Mellon, one of racing's most respected pillars, had formed a two-man syndicate to buy Admiring as a broodmare affirmed the esteem with which Jacobs was now held as a breeder.

When the hammer fell on the last of the five Bieber-Jacobs Reductions, the nearly 200 horses they sold off for a total of almost

$4 million had brought higher averages at auction than those in the prestigious Keeneland Sales. They included eighty mares, virtually the entire broodmare band that Jacobs treasured as the cornerstone of his breeding dynasty. All that remained were approximately twenty racehorses, twenty yearlings, and the one broodmare he simply couldn't bear to part with—Affectionately.

The money itself brought small consolation to a horseman who beforehand had asked rhetorically, "When you've made a few million dollars, who needs more?" But what the money represented was priceless. The same bluebloods who once scoffed at his cheap claimers were now lining up to breed their very best mares to Hail to Reason. The prices realized for the bloodstock stood as a tribute to Jacobs's achievements and as testimony to his acceptance by the same racing establishment that had looked down its nose on him as an outsider.

In many ways, of course, Jacobs still remained an outsider. The Jockey Club, racing's ruling body populated mostly by patrician owners and breeders, had steadfastly refused to elect Jacobs to membership. Denied entry to that most exclusive clique, Jacobs threw his support behind the Horsemen's Benevolent and Protective Association (HBPA)—an organization of smaller owners, breeders, and trainers looking after the interests of nonunion backstretch workers—during a labor dispute in the late 1960s that challenged the sovereignty of the Jockey Club and the New York Racing Association.

When an HBPA boycott shut down racing at Aqueduct in the spring of 1969, Jacobs sided with the association in its attempt to force the track and the state to create a $1.3 million pension and welfare program for 3,000 stablehands such as grooms and exercise boys. One day, Jacobs was walking out of an HBPA meeting shaking his head when he was overheard muttering with philosophical resignation that the dispute was "a classic case of the bluebloods against the Italians and Jews." Although not meant for publication, the statement got traction in the press because it struck at the heart of the class and ethnic overtones of the labor dispute between the racing aristocracy and the HBPA's owners and trainers, many of whom were Italian or Jewish. In the end, the horseman's strike was crushed.

It shouldn't have been a surprise that Jacobs supported the HBPA's cause. For all his hard-earned wealth and success, he remained a champion of the little guy—from the minimum-wage stableboy to the $2 bettor.

After the stroke in 1966, Jacobs was forced into semiretirement. Throughout his first four decades in the sport, he had been the kind of workaholic whose definition of a vacation was spending the summer racing season at Saratoga and the winter racing season in Florida. That's why he had such a hard time turning the full-time reins over to his son John and why he was already back at work by the following year, though still relying heavily on John.

Hirsch Jacobs had certainly earned the right to rest on his considerable laurels. He was now a multimillionaire in his own right. He was the nation's leading breeder for four straight years through 1967. He was the most successful trainer of all time, passing the 3,500-win milestone in 1966 and leaving his closest pursuer more than 1,000 in his wake. He was the consummate horseman, the greatest all-around racing man America ever produced. For all that, however, there was still one piece of unfinished business. The only thing he hadn't accomplished in his peerless career, it seemed, was winning the Kentucky Derby or, for that matter, either of the other jewels in the Triple Crown series.

Then came the horse that offered his best hope for ending that drought: Personality, the product of his carefully planned mating between his two favorite homebreds, Hail to Reason and Affectionately. So excited was Jacobs by Affectionately's first foal that the normally low-key horseman never missed an opportunity to whip out his wallet like a proud father and show off a baby picture of "the best horse I've ever bred."

By the time Personality embarked on his three-year-old campaign in 1970, though, Jacobs had been hospitalized with a blocked artery hampering blood flow to the brain. He was gravely ill early that February when his children, visiting him in the Miami Heart Institute, handed him a photo of Personality losing a recent sprint at Hialeah. Hirsch held the photo and stared at it intently. Finally, he pointed at Personality's head and said haltingly, "No blinkers?" John confirmed that the colt had not been wearing blinkers, a hood with cup-shaped protrusions that block to varying degrees a horse's peripheral vision and for some improve focus on what's in front of them. Hirsch looked at the photo again and then looked up at John and said softly, "Do better—blinkers."

Four days later, Hirsch Jacobs lapsed into a coma and passed away at the age of sixty-five. Wearing blinkers from then on, Personality won the Wood Memorial at Aqueduct to stamp himself a Kentucky Derby favorite and, after a disappointing eighth on the first Saturday in May at Churchill Downs, captured the Preakness by a neck. Posthumously, Hirsch Jacobs had finally won a Triple Crown race, and done so with a homebred who was en route to becoming his first Horse of the Year honoree. Asked afterward how it felt to achieve something that his father hadn't, John Jacobs, tears welling in his eyes, replied, "He did achieve it. This is *his* victory. He bred this colt." Three weeks later, John sent another colt his dad had bred, High Echelon, out to win the Belmont Stakes.

Hirsch Jacobs had requested that all the Bieber-Jacobs horses be dispersed after his death and the partnership liquidated. Bieber, who would die four years later in 1974 at the age of eighty-eight, had readily agreed to his partner's request. So in the summer and fall of 1970, three dozen Bieber-Jacobs horses were auctioned off at the prestigious Saratoga and Keeneland sales. They brought a total of nearly $2 million, including the highest price that had ever been paid for a mare at auction. The final dispersal of the horses that Jacobs had bred and trained, including some significant private sales, stood as yet another testament to the legacy of the legendary horseman that *Newsweek* eulogized as "the diminutive, red-haired racing genius."

In *Newsweek's* tribute to him, Pete Axthelm, the newsweekly's sports editor, incisively summed up his legacy: "To put it simply, Jacobs was the greatest horseman in the history of American racing. As a trainer, he won 3,596 races to set a record that is unlikely to be threatened. As a breeder, he used a meticulously thorough knowledge of bloodlines to surpass far wealthier men in building his dynasty. Few of his contemporaries ever approached his ability in either field; no one even came close to doing so well in both. Perhaps more significant, Jacobs was the only figure who ever brought to life the storybook dream of all racetrackers—that of the little guy who started out with nothing and built a multimillion-dollar empire on wits and skill alone."

The day Hirsch Jacobs died, Red Smith had been hanging around the offices at Madison Square Garden, listening to the boxing mavens jawing about the upcoming world heavyweight championship bout there. They were locked in heated debate over who were the greatest heavyweight champions when suddenly word came that Hirsch Jacobs had passed away. "Oh, hell," one said. "Talk about your champions!"

In that instant, Red Smith started composing the day's

column in his head. "Talk about your champions, indeed," he would write later that afternoon. "In no sport from archery to volleyball has there ever been a truer champion than the pudgy, smiling little redhead from Brooklyn, who led the ranks of American horse trainers oftener than any other man." Smith wrote those words during an interregnum following the folding of the *Herald Tribune*. In the four years before the *New York Times* gave his prose a fittingly lofty home, America's most revered sports columnist wrote a syndicated column but struggled to find an outlet for it in New York. When Jacobs died, it was somehow appropriate that Smith's tribute to the immigrant tailor's son be published in the garment-trade journal *Women's Wear Daily*.

"It's an old story but a wonderful one," Smith wrote, "how Hirsch Jacobs started as a trainer of racing pigeons, went from birds to horses, and, racing the cheapest kind of stock against such giants as Ben Jones and Jim Fitzsimmons, was America's leading trainer in eleven of twelve consecutive seasons when he couldn't afford fashionably bred horses. Starting with selling platers, Hirsch Jacobs came to have horses as royally bred as any that carried the silks of the Jockey Club's loftiest. Yet the horse for which he'll be remembered best—and he surely would approve it that way—was common folks. The horse was Stymie."

In this fond farewell to his fellow redhead, Smith thought it only fitting that Stymie's story, so parallel to Jacobs's, be recounted in all its improbable glory from the $1,500 claim to the $918,485 gold strike.

"This was a bright red horse, a showy chestnut with a crooked blaze that gave him an almost comic, devil-may-care look," Smith began his kicker paragraph. "He held his red head high, and the faster he ran the higher he held it. Sort of like the redhead he worked for."

Thus were Stymie and Hirsch Jacobs inextricably linked for posterity: a pair of paupers who became crown princes in The Sport of Kings.

ACKNOWLEDGMENTS

This project grew out of a previous book we had written on the unrivaled rivalry between Affirmed and Alydar. While researching *Duel for the Crown* a few years back, we were so taken with the story of Hirsch Jacobs—whose daughter, Patrice, campaigned Affirmed to the 1978 Triple Crown along with her co-owner husband, Lou Wolfson—that we overwrote the section on him in our first draft and wound up having to leave most of it on the cutting-room floor. At the time, we were surprised to discover that there existed no book-length dive into the rags-to-riches saga of the winningest trainer the sport had ever known and the Cinderella horse that made him a legend.

Having endeavored to pick up those unpublished scraps and expand them into this book, we're deeply indebted to Hirsch Jacobs's three children—Patrice Wolfson and her brothers, John and Tommy Jacobs—for their enthusiastic cooperation. They graciously opened their lives to us during many in-depth interviews and shared family mementos, documents, correspondence, and photographs. As the firstborn and ultimately his father's assistant trainer, John was able to provide insights we couldn't have found anywhere else. He and his wife, Barbara, were extremely generous with their time, setting aside an hour each week to chat and reminisce. We'll miss those weekly conversations.

The list of other sources who contributed to our research is almost as exhaustive as Stymie's prodigious race record. Third-generation trainer Bill Hirsch, the son and grandson of two Hall of Famers, offered a peek into his grandfather Max Hirsch's early handling of Stymie, into Max's friendly rivalry with Hirsch Jacobs, and into Assault's fierce rivalry with Stymie (the Affirmed-Alydar of its day).

Indispensable to our research was the energetic support we received from the Keeneland Library, the nation's foremost repository of racing history. We're grateful to a host of Keeneland librarians who tirelessly dug out for us a litany of hard-to-find clippings, records, race charts, and photos from their voluminous archives: Becky Ryder, the library's director; Cathy Schenck, its head librarian until her recent retirement; and the archivists Betsy Baxter and Cathy Moore.

In addition, we'd like to acknowledge all those who likewise helped us track down information, documents, photos, and usage rights: Bennett Liebman, an attorney expert in racing law who until recently had served as New York governor Andrew Cuomo's deputy secretary for Gaming and Racing; Victoria Tokarowski Reisman, curator at the National Museum of Racing and Hall of Fame; Irwin Cohen, senior editor of the *Daily Racing Form*; Anne M. Eberhardt Keogh, visuals director at Blood-Horse Publications; Denis Blake, editor and publisher of *American Racehorse* magazine; Adam Coglianese, track photographer for the New York Racing Association; Tricia Gesner, account manager at the Associated Press.

This book would not have happened if Mauro DiPreta, the astute publisher of Hachette Books, hadn't plucked this idea from a pile of pitches he solicited after a non-racing project we were working on for him had fallen through. He took a flyer on it based on an abridged proposal with the faith that this untold Horatio Alger story of a forgotten horse and horseman could transcend the racetrack, then helped shape the manuscript through insightful big-picture suggestions. Not least, he came up with the inspired idea to take what we had submitted under the working title of *The People's Horse* and rename it *Out of the Clouds*. Throughout the marathon race that is a book, we also feel fortunate to have had Mauro's assistant editor, David Lamb, there to calmly guide us every step of the way.

Speaking of guiding us every step of the journey, Jane Dystel—the Hirsch Jacobs of literary agents—has been doing that continually through three books spanning eleven years in which we've benefited mightily from her sage counsel and dogged persistence. Like a master trainer, she shepherded and championed this project from conception to finish line, supporting us as always in every way possible along with Miriam Goderich and their consummate management team at Dystel, Goderich & Bourret.

Now that we can finally "cool out" like racehorses after crossing the finish line, we'd like to thank our families for their patience and support throughout the grueling race from wire to wire—especially Mariela, who despite her youth once again understood that Mom had homework of her own.

SOURCES

As with any work of narrative nonfiction endeavoring to transport readers back to a bygone time and place, this project was dependent in no small part on the incisive reporters who wrote the first draft of history. In that regard, we are fortunate that the intertwined stories of Hirsch Jacobs and Stymie were chronicled in real time by some of the most lyrical and literary newspapermen ever to grace a press box—from Damon Runyon, the master storyteller who counted the legendary horseman as his friend as well as his trainer, to Joe Palmer, the expert turf writer who immortalized "The People's Horse," and his pal Red Smith, the revered columnist who eloquently eulogized both the equine and the human protagonists of this book.

If the written testimony of such eyewitnesses to history gave this narrative its skeleton and flesh, then its heart and soul derive directly from the reminiscences of Hirsch Jacobs's three children—John Jacobs, Patrice Wolfson, and Tommy Jacobs. We are eternally grateful that they have been so generous with their time and their memories, patiently fielding countless inquiries and opening their lives in numerous interviews and e-mail exchanges. This book would not have been possible without all the insights they offered into their father's character and philosophy of life and of training, not to mention the memorabilia, family photos, and personal correspondence they shared to flesh out the biographical story.

As the oldest child, John Jacobs, born in 1934, naturally had the most vivid recollections of the wartime and postwar period in which his father claimed and then raced Stymie. John offered detailed memories of his trips to the track with his father while growing up and an inside look at how Hirsch ran his stable. John offered the unique perspective of a protégé who served as the stable's assistant trainer for a decade before taking over the day-to-day management following Hirsch's 1966 stroke and then the whole operation immediately upon Hirsch's death in 1970, saddling the winning homebred in two of that year's Triple Crown races. In dozens of hour-long phone interviews, John was joined by his wife, Barbara, who added insights gleaned from the many conversations she had with her mother-in-law until Ethel Jacobs's passing in 2001 at the age of ninety-one.

Ethel and Hirsch's middle child, Patrice, who was born in 1937 and named after Runyon's wife, also had some vivid memories of Stymie and of "Dad" but from a different perspective than her big brother. While her protective father insulated her from the assorted riffraff that inhabited the backside barns of the New York metropolitan racetracks, she spent countless hours talking horse with him at home, sharing an inherited passion of the horses as individuals, interviewing him for a helpful *Morning Telegraph* profile cited below, eventually campaigning a few of his homebreds (including Hail to Reason) in her own name and in her mother's salmon-pink and emerald-green colors.

The youngest Jacobs child, Tommy, born in late 1940 just four months before Stymie was foaled, developed a special affinity for the horse. One of his most vivid childhood memories is of his father taking him to the track and bringing a prancing and snorting Stymie out of his stall. Tommy grew up to join his father and big brother at the track in the family business, riding a pony to lead the stable's racehorses out in sets for their morning gallops, and came away with a unique perspective into his father's bond with his charges.

The interviews with Hirsch Jacobs's three children both supplemented and complemented the story pieced together through the sources cited in the following selected bibliography.

BOOKS

The single most indispensable reference for any project involving the history of the sport is *The American Racing Manual*—the comprehensive and authoritative annual encyclopedia crammed with statistics and a recap of the season that just concluded, as compiled each year by the *Daily Racing Form*'s experts. Seasoned horsemen and turf writers long ago turned us on to the doorstopper they deem the definitive narrative of the sport, William Robertson's *The History of Thoroughbred Racing in America*. Other go-to historical resources include Ed Bowen's books profiling the great breeders and trainers, the Jockey Club's multivolume *Racing in America* set written by various turf experts, and Joe Palmer's essays profiling each year's top performers in the annual *American Race Horses* series.

Following is a selected bibliography of books referenced:

Blechman, Andrew D. *Pigeons: The Fascinating Saga of the World's Most Revered and Reviled Bird*. New York: Grove Press, 2006.

Blood-Horse, The. *A Quarter-Century of American Racing and Breeding, 1916–1940*. Lexington, KY: The Blood-Horse, 1941.

———. *Thoroughbred Champions: Top 100 Racehorses of the 20th Century*. Lexington, KY: The Blood-Horse, 1999. [Includes spread on Stymie written by Gary West.]

Blood-Horse Publications Staff. *Horse Racing's Greatest Rivalries*. Lexington, KY:

Eclipse Press, 2008. [Includes George Bernet's chapter on the Stymie-Assault-Armed rivalry titled "Postwar Powerhouses" and Judy L. Marchman's chapter on the Stymie-Gallorette rivalry titled "The Iron Duo."]

Bowen, Edward L. *Legacies of the Turf: A Century of Great Thoroughbred Breeders.* Vol. 1. Lexington, KY: Eclipse Press, 2003. [Includes chapter titled "Bieber-Jacobs Stable."]

———. *Legacies of the Turf: A Century of Great Thoroughbred Breeders.* Vol. 2. Lexington, KY: Eclipse Press, 2004.

———. *Masters of the Turf: Ten Trainers Who Dominated Horse Racing's Golden Age.* Lexington, KY: Eclipse Press, 2007. [Culminates with chapter on Hirsch Jacobs.]

Boyd, Eva Jolene. *Assault: The Clubfooted Comet.* Lexington, KY: Eclipse Press, 2004.

Breslin, Jimmy. *Damon Runyon: A Life.* New York: Dell Publishing, 1991.

Cypher, John. *Bob Kleberg and the King Ranch: A Worldwide Sea of Grass.* Austin, TX: University of Texas Press, 1995.

Daily Racing Form. *The American Racing Manual* (Editions of 1924, 1925, 1926, 1927, 1928, 1929, 1930, 1931, 1946, 1947, 1948, 1949, 1950). Lexington, KY: Daily Racing Form, 1924, 1925, 1926, 1927, 1928, 1929, 1930, 1931, 1946, 1947, 1948, 1949, 1950.

———. *Champions: The Lives, Times, and Past Performances of America's Greatest Thoroughbreds.* Lexington, KY: Daily Racing Form, 2005. [Includes Stymie's official career past-performance chart, with an agate line for each of his 131 races.]

Denhardt, Robert Moorman. *The King Ranch Quarter Horses.* Norman, OK: University of Oklahoma Press, 1970.

Drager, Martin. *The Most Glorious Crown: The Story of America's Triple Crown Thoroughbreds from Sir Barton to Affirmed.* Chicago: Triumph Books, 2005.

Glover, David, and Marie Beaumont. *Racing Pigeons.* Ramsbury, England: Crowood Press, 1999.

Graham, Don. *Kings of Texas: The 150-Year Saga of an American Ranching Empire.* Hoboken, NJ: John Wiley & Sons, 2003.

Hervey, John. *Racing in America: 1922–1936.* New York: Jockey Club, 1937.

Hillenbrand, Laura. *Seabiscuit: An American Legend.* New York: Random House, 2001.

Hirsch, Joe, and Gene Plowden. *In the Winner's Circle: The Jones Boys of Calumet Farm.* New York: Mason & Lipscomb, 1974.

Hollingsworth, Kent, ed. *The Great Ones.* Lexington, KY: The Blood-Horse, 1970. [Includes Hollingsworth's chapter on Stymie among the seventy-six greats feted within.]

Howe, Irving. *World of Our Fathers: The Journey of the East European Jews to America and the Life They Found and Made.* New York: Touchstone, 1976.

Hoyt, Edwin P. *A Gentleman of Broadway.* Boston: Little, Brown and Company, 1964.

Kelley, Robert F. *Racing in America: 1937–1959.* New York: Jockey Club, 1960.

Lea, Tom. *The King Ranch.* Boston: Little, Brown and Company, 1957.

Levi, Wendell Mitchell. *The Pigeon.* Columbia, SC: R. L. Bryan, 1957.

Moody, Ralph. *American Horses.* Boston: Houghton Mifflin, 1962. [Includes chapter titled "Stymie—Just Common Folks."]

Moruzzi, Peter. *Havana Before Castro: When Cuba Was a Tropical Playground.* Layton, UT: Gibbs Smith, 2008.

Palmer, Joe H. *American Race Horses* (Editions for 1945, 1946, 1947, 1948). New York: Sagamore Press, 1946, 1947, 1948, 1949. [Each annual edition includes a chapter recapping Stymie's season.]

————. *This Was Racing.* New York: Barnes, 1953. [Compilation includes his much-anthologized masterpiece of a tribute column titled "Stymie—Common Folks."]

Pietrusza, David. *Rothstein: The Life, Times, and Murder of the Criminal Genius Who Fixed the 1919 World Series.* New York: Carroll & Graf, 2003.

Reeves, Richard Stone (portraits), and Jim Bolus (text). *Royal Blood: Fifty Years of Classic Thoroughbreds.* Lexington, KY: The Blood-Horse, 1994. [Includes chapter on Stymie among the fifty Thoroughbreds profiled.]

Rice, Grantland. *The Tumult and the Shouting: My Life in Sport.* New York: Barnes, 1954.

Robertson, William H. P. *The History of Thoroughbred Racing in America.* New York: Bonanza Books, 1964. [Includes section on Stymie.]

Robertson, William, and Dan Farley, eds. *Hoofprints of the Century.* Lexington, KY: The Thoroughbred Record, 1975.

Rudy, William H. *Racing in America: 1960–1979.* New York: Jockey Club, 1980.

Runyon, Damon. *Money from Home.* New York: Frederick A. Stokes, 1935.

————. *Short Takes: Readers' Choice of the Best Columns of America's Favorite Newspaperman.* New York: Whittlesey House, 1946.

————. *Slow Horses and Fast Women.* Mattituck, NY: Amereon, 1985.

————. *Guys and Dolls: The Stories of Damon Runyon.* New York: Barnes & Noble, 1992.

————. *The Racing World of Damon Runyon.* London: Constable, 1999.

Runyon Jr., Damon. *Father's Footsteps.* New York: Random House, 1953.

Simon, Mary. *Racing Through the Century: The Story of Thoroughbred Racing in America.* Irvine, CA: BowTie Press, 2002. [Includes spread on Stymie.]

Smith, Red. *To Absent Friends.* New York: Atheneum, 1982. [Anthology of columns includes his farewell tribute to Hirsch Jacobs published in *Women's Wear Daily.*]

Time-Life Books editors. *Decade of Triumph: The 40s* (Our American Century series). Richmond, VA: Time-Life Books, 1999.

Tivenan, Bill, and Cassandra Cook. *Off to a Flying Start: Horsing Around the Language.* Salt Lake City, UT: Aardvark Global Publishing, 2009.

Weiner, Ed. *The Damon Runyon Story.* New York: Popular Library, 1948.

MAGAZINE ARTICLES

Of all the magazine articles sourced below, we would be remiss if we didn't single out two that were particularly helpful: George Ryall's seminal in-depth profile of Hirsch Jacobs in the *New Yorker* from 1939 and Gerald Holland's inside look at the incongruous Jacobs-Bieber partnership in *Sports Illustrated* from 1961.

Following is a selected bibliography of magazines referenced:

Alexander, David. "Epitaph for a Horseplayer." *Sports Illustrated*, September 2, 1963.

Axthelm, Pete. "The Jacobs Legacy." *Newsweek*, August 24, 1970.

Bauer, Hambla. "He Trains Horses and Millionaires." *Saturday Evening Post*, June 26, 1948.

Haden-Guest, Anthony. "Death on the Upper East Side." *New York*, September 11, 1978.

Hirsch, Joe. "The Way to Win with Horses." *Sports Illustrated*, January 25, 1960.

Holland, Gerald. "'Sex, Slaughter and Smoke!'" *Sports Illustrated*, June 26, 1961.

Markey, Morris. "Faites Vos Jeux." *New Yorker*, May 12, 1934.

Minor, Audax. "The Race Track." *New Yorker*, September 19, 1936; August 14, 1937; February 5, 1938; January 27, 1940; December 7, 1940; April 15, 1944; September 1, 1945; July 3, 1948; September 17, 1949; April 5, 1952; April 4, 1953; April 9, 1960; February 21, 1970.

Morey, Charles. "Hooded Horses Cast Long Shadows in the Dawn." *Sports Illustrated*, December 8, 1969.

———. "The Unlikeliest Millionaire." *Sports Illustrated*, October 10, 1973.

Nack, William. "Saratoga." *Sports Illustrated*, August 22, 1988.

New Yorker. "Racing Pigeons," May 9, 1931.

———. "Pigeon Foreman." July 17, 1937.

Orlean, Susan. "Little Wing." *New Yorker*, February 13, 2006.

Reynolds, Quentin. "An Eye for Horses." *Collier's*, May 11, 1935.

Runyon, Damon. "Tight Shoes." *Collier's*, April 18, 1936.

———. "Leases on Luck." *American Weekly*, September 23, 1945.

Ryall, G. F. T. "Pigeon Man's Progress." *New Yorker*, August 5, 1939. [George Ryall wrote this in-depth profile of Hirsch Jacobs in the midst of his half-century stint as the magazine's turf columnist, penning "The Race Track" weekly department under the nom de plume of Audax Minor, as cited above.]

Time. "St. Edward of Lexington." May 7, 1934.

———. "Pigeons to Platers." October 26, 1936.

———. "$500,000 Stymie." November 4, 1946.

———. "Big as All Outdoors." December 15, 1947.

———. "Head of the Horse Factory." April 11, 1960.

———. "'A Nice Quiet Life.'" May 29, 1978.

Tosches, Nick. "A Jazz Age Autopsy." *Vanity Fair*, May 2005.

Tucker, Howard M. "Man with Horse Sense." *New York Times Magazine*, May 21, 1961.

Werner, M. R. "Workman's Compensation." *Sports Illustrated*, May 4, 1959.

TURF PERIODICALS

The *Daily Racing Form*—the bible of the sport since 1894—provided an indispensable source of news reports, feature stories, race coverage, race charts, past-performance charts, and official statistics. Other turf periodicals most heavily relied on were the *Racing Form*'s erstwhile sister paper, the *Morning Telegraph*, as well as the

Blood-Horse, *Thoroughbred Record*, and *Thoroughbred Times*. Other turf periodicals used as resources included *American Turf Monthly*, the *Backstretch*, *Thoroughbred Daily News*, and *Turf and Sport Digest*.

We are indebted to the Keeneland Library for digging out for us numerous archived clips from the *Daily Racing Form* (including official race charts for many of Stymie's starts) and from other turf periodicals, along with some chapters and sections from hard-to-find books.

In addition to news stories from the turf periodicals listed above, the following selected feature articles and columns were most helpful:

Carrell, Ruth Anne. "Jacobs-Wolfson," interview. *Blood-Horse*, April 21, 1984.
Cohen, Bettina. "Famed Claims." *Blood-Horse*, June 5, 1999.
"Death and Taxes and Jacobs." *Blood-Horse*. January 9, 1943.
Haskin, Steve. "He Did It All." *Backstretch*, July/August 1997.
Hirsch, Joe. Column on Hirsch Jacobs and the Horsemen's Benevolent and Protective Association. *Daily Racing Form*, January 17, 1968.
Hollingsworth, Kent. "A Partnership for Life." *Thoroughbred Times*, August 14, 1992.
Jacobs, Patrice. "'Our Dad' Is Champ at Track and Home." *Morning Telegraph*, April 2, 1960.
McEvoy, John. "Bieber: He Could Ruffle Feathers." *Daily Racing Form*, May 22, 1994.
Moore, Betty. "Hirsch Jacobs Was 'Greatest Horseman.'" *Morning Telegraph*, August 10, 1970.
O'Reilly, Tom. "Hirsch Jacobs 'Winningest' Trainer." *Daily Racing Form*, May 2, 1959.
———. Column on Hirsch Jacobs. *Morning Telegraph*, Spring 1960 (as later reprinted in *Chronicle of the Horse*).
Rowe, Howard A. "Hirsch Jacobs, Stakes-Winning Trainer." *American Turf Monthly*, December 1981.
Salvator. "Stymie." *Daily Racing Form*, August 1, 1945.
Sevier, O'Neil. "Trainers and Their Charges." *Turf and Sport Digest*, January 1936.

NEWSPAPERS

Of all the newspaper articles sourced, we are most indebted to the numerous columns Damon Runyon wrote about his friends Hirsch Jacobs and Izzy Bieber. In addition, we must acknowledge Red Smith not only for his inimitable prose on his favorite spectator sport in the *New York Times* and *New York Herald Tribune*, but also for occasionally turning his "Sports of the Times" column over, verbatim, to letters written to him by Bieber's kid brother Phil. A successful trainer in his own right, Phil Bieber proved a detailed storyteller of colorful tales involving his big brother.

The daily newspapers most heavily relied on for archived news stories, features, and columns were the *New York Times, Brooklyn Daily Eagle, New York Herald Tribune,* and the three New York dailies for which Runyon wrote millions of words—the *American, Journal-American,* and *Daily Mirror.* Wire services whose articles can be found in various dailies archived online and in libraries include the Associated Press, United Press, and Hearst's International News Service and Universal Service. Newspaper syndicates whose columns can be found in various dailies archived online and in libraries include King Features Syndicate, the North American Newspaper Alliance, and the Newspaper Enterprise Association.

In addition to issues of the *New York Times* archived on its website and of numerous other dailies across the country accessible through the Library of Congress and newspapers.com, the following selected columns, features, and news stories were particularly helpful:

Cady, Steve. "For Sale: An Empire." *New York Times,* August 17, 1966.
———. "Horsemen Reach Accord with State and Track, Ending Boycott at Aqueduct." *New York Times,* May 9, 1969.
———. "Everybody a Loser." *New York Times,* May 11, 1969.
———. "Hirsch Jacobs, Leading Trainer, Is Dead." *New York Times,* February 14, 1970.
———. "Late Owner Gets Credit for Feat." *New York Times,* May 17, 1970.
Christine, Bill. "Off Scrapheap, They Now Share a Claim to Fame." *Los Angeles Times,* November 3, 1999.
Comerford, Ed. "$2 Bettors Will Miss Hirsch Jacobs Most." *Newsday,* February 14, 1970.
———. "Stymie Recalled by All." *Newsday,* August 27, 1974.
Conklin, William R. "Jacobs Family Turf Tree Is Green." *New York Times,* April 20, 1958.

Daley, Arthur. "On the Dawn Patrol." *New York Times*, May 21, 1945.

———. "Waiting for the Barrier to Spring." *New York Times*, May 5, 1949.

DeFichy, Lou. "Jacobs' 'Eye for a Horse' Ranks Him High as Trainer," *Newsday*, 1957.

———. "Stymie's Still Running in Belmont Memories." *Newsday*, June 26, 1962.

Grayson, Harry. "Hirsch Hesitated and Stymie Was Lost." *Winnipeg Tribune*, August 1, 1947.

Holiber, Ben. *New York Daily News*. A 1970s letter to the editor of the newspaper's "I Remember Old Brooklyn" column in which the writer, a longtime plumber who was Hirsch Jacobs's supervisor in Frank Ferraro's steamfitting shop, reminisced about the teenager he called "Red" cutting pipe in the garage and flying pigeons on its roof.

Isaacs, Stan. "Personality: The Spirit of Hirsch Jacobs." *Newsday*, April 20, 1970.

Lipsyte, Robert. "Get Out with Jacobs." *New York Times*, June 6, 1970.

———. "Rerun." *New York Times*, June 15, 1970.

Palmer, Joe H. "Stymie Wins Gold Cup, Raising Earnings Record to $678,510." *New York Herald Tribune*, July 20, 1947.

———. "11 Go to Post Today at Gold Cup at Jamaica." *New York Herald Tribune*, November 5, 1949.

———. "Adile Wins Gold Cup by a Nose at Jamaica." *New York Herald Tribune*, November 6, 1949.

Pegler, Westbrook. "Death Ends Strange Career of Phocian Howard, Editor." *Chicago Tribune*, September 1, 1933.

Rice, Grantland. Columns syndicated by the North American Newspaper Alliance and published in various U.S. dailies. (Because dailies across the country ran them under different headlines and sometimes on varying dates, the columns are identified here by subject and by either the dateline when applicable or the date when most papers published them.)

———. New York–datelined "Sportlight" column interviewing Hirsch Jacobs. September 24, 1945.

———. Baltimore-datelined "Sportlight" column advancing Stymie's Pimlico Special race. October 31, 1946.

———. "The Sportlight" column on Assault following his Pimlico Special win. November 20, 1946.

———. "The Sportlight" column on the three-horse competition to break Whirlaway's all-time earnings record. February 2, 1947.

———. "The Sportlight" column advancing the Stymie–Assault showdown in the Butler Handicap. July 12, 1947.

———. "The Sportlight" column advancing the Stymie–Assault showdown in the International Gold Cup. July 18, 1947.

———. "The Sportlight" column on Hirsch Jacobs's conditioning philosophy. August 19, 1948.

———. "The Sportlight" column assessing the three-way rivalry among Armed, Assault, and Stymie. August 27, 1947.

———. Another "Sportlight" column on the three-way rivalry. September 8, 1947.

———. Column interviewing the Jacobs brothers on the family business of training racehorses. May 20, 1953.

Robertson, Orlo. "Hirsch Jacobs' Sale Is Expected to Be Richest in Racing History." *Lexington Herald-Leader*, August 14, 1966.

Runyon, Damon. Columns written for Hearst's New York newspapers—the *American*, the *Daily Mirror*, and the *New York Journal-American*—and syndicated first by Universal Service and later by King Features Syndicate for distribution by the International News Service. Because dailies across the country ran them under different headlines and sometimes on varying dates, the columns are identified here by subject and by either the dateline when applicable or the date when most papers published them.

———. Saratoga-datelined column on Runyon's first opening day at Saratoga. July 31, 1922.

———. Saratoga-datelined column on E. Phocian Howard. August 16, 1933.

———. Miami-datelined column introducing Hirsch Jacobs. January 5, 1934.

———. Saratoga-datelined column on Isidor Bieber and the B. B. Stable. August 13, 1934.

———. Main story covering James Braddock's upset of Max Baer for the world heavyweight championship. June 14, 1935.

———. Miami-datelined column on Hirsch Jacobs as nation's winningest trainer. December 27, 1935.

———. New York–datelined column on Isidor Bieber. August 20, 1936.

———. "Damon Runyon Says" column on Hirsch Jacobs. September 16, 1937.

———. "Damon Runyon Says" column on Isidor Bieber. November 28, 1937.

———. Column on Isidor Bieber's Broadway bar. August 25, 1939.

———. "The Brighter Side" column on Action. September 25, 1940.

———. "The Brighter Side" column on Hirsch Jacobs. January 1, 1941.

———. Column on Phil Bieber. April 25, 1941.

———. "The Brighter Side" column on ticket speculators, including Isidor Bieber. June 27, 1945.

———. Column on the Bieber-Jacobs partnership. August 20, 1946.

Smith, Red. "More Hay Money for Assault." *New York Herald Tribune*, June 22, 1947.

———. "Without Martinis." *New York Herald Tribune*, April 24, 1952.

———. "This Is a Horseman." *New York Times*, May 7, 1972.

———. "The Winner's Circle for the Last Time." *New York Times*, November 7, 1973.

———. "Sonny Boy at the Race Track." *New York Times*, September 29, 1974.

———. "A Horse Lover Is a Horse in Love." *New York Times*, December 6, 1974.

———. "Score It Martin to Bieber to McGraw." *New York Times*, April 23, 1975.

———. "A. Rothstein and the World Series." *New York Times*, October 10, 1975.

———. "Little Beebe's Claim-Box Caper." *New York Times*, February 2, 1976.

———. "In the Bookies' Hall of Fame." *New York Times*, February 18, 1976.

———. "A Bet on the Old Coach." *New York Times*, March 21, 1976.

———. " 'Nice and Quiet and Relaxed.' " *New York Times*, May 17, 1976.

———. "On Horsing Around with Nature." *New York Times*, August 9, 1976.

———. "The Dice Game on 47th Street." *New York Times*, December 31, 1976.

———. "The Fox in Phil Bieber's Past." *New York Times*, February 14, 1977.

———. "The Biebers' Double Sawbuck." *New York Times*, March 2, 1977.

———. "What They Talk about at Saratoga." *New York Times*, August 15, 1977.

———. "Beauty and Chivalry." *New York Times*, April 2, 1978.

———. "Streetfighters—Beebe to Duran." *New York Times*, April 28, 1978.

———. "It Reminds Phil Bieber." *New York Times*, November 26, 1978.

Vreeland, W. C. "Jacobs, Leading Trainer at Hialeah, Learned Speed Value in Pigeons." *Brooklyn Daily Eagle*, February 5, 1933.

———. "Angelic, Bought for $700, Rated One of Best Fillies at Hialeah." *Brooklyn Daily Eagle*, February 27, 1934.

———. "Hirsch Jacobs Works Miracle in Bringing Action to the Fore." *Brooklyn Daily Eagle*, September 20, 1936.

West, Gary. "Stymie Was a Singular Horse Who Didn't Want to Be Alone." *Dallas Morning News*, October 4, 2000.

INTERNET

Of all the websites visited for source material, background research, and historical perspective, none was more indispensable than the *Daily Racing Form*'s. The venerable racing newspaper's online archive was accessed continually at drf.uky.edu, and its main website at drf.com offered a helpful archive of blog posts. Also relied on for authoritative information was the website of the National Museum of Racing and Hall of Fame. Other websites used for source material and background included those of cited publications and of American Classic Pedigrees, Brooklyn Public Library, Brooklyn Backstretch, Colin's Ghost, Equibase, Jockey Club, Kentucky Derby, National Thoroughbred Racing Association, New York Racing Association, and Paulick Report.

The following selected blog posts were particularly helpful:

Brooklyn Public Library. "There's No Place Like Home." June 25, 2012, bklynlibrary.org.

Goldberg, Ryan. "The Golden Era of Brooklyn Racing." November 11, 2010, drf.com (*Daily Racing Form*).

Gooley, Lawrence P. "One Smart Bird: The Homing Pigeon in N.Y. History." July 31, 2012, newyorkhistoryblog.org.

Haskin, Steve. "The History of Drugs in America." July 1, 2012, bloodhorse.com.

Kerrison, Patrick. "Big Stakes on Sure Things: Arnold Rothstein's Saratoga and the 1921 Travers Stakes." August 2, 2010, saratoga.com.

Sachar, Howard. "Jewish Immigrants in the Garment Industry." myjewishlearning.com, reprinted with permission from *A History of Jews in America* published by Vintage Books in 1993.

DOCUMENTS

Court reports: *Richards v. Bieber*, New York Supreme Court, Appellate Division–First Department (1938). This 1938 court report for Isidor Bieber's 1937 appeal of his libel lawsuit features more than 600 pages of trial transcripts and exhibits that provided anecdotes and insights into the operation of the Bieber-Jacobs partnership's early years.

Certified genealogical records obtained from the State of New York: birth certificate for Hirsch Jacobs (1904).

Genealogical records for Hirsch Jacobs retrieved from ancestry.com and familysearch.org: immigration passenger list and ship manifest for his father, Jacob Jacobs (1871); U.S. Census for the family headed by Jacob's father, Morris Jacobs (1880); U.S. Census for the family headed by Jacob Jacobs (1900, 1910, 1920, 1930, 1940); New York State Census for the family headed by Jacob Jacobs (1925); New York State Census for the family headed by the future Theresa Jacobs's father, Harris Singer (1882); birth records for Hirsch's brothers Irving Jacobs (1899), Albert Jacobs (1906), and Sidney Jacobs (1908); marriage license for Hirsch Jacobs and Ethel Dushock (1933); World War I draft registration card for Irving Jacobs (1918); World War II Army enlistment record for Sidney Jacobs (1943); cemetery records for Jacob Jacobs (1959), Hirsch Jacobs (1970), and Ethel Jacobs (2001).

Genealogical records for Ethel Jacobs (née Dushock) retrieved from ancestry.com and familysearch.org: U.S. Census for the family headed by her father, Joseph Dushock (1920, 1930); New York State Census for the family headed by Joseph Dushock (1925).

Genealogical records for Isidor Bieber retrieved from ancestry.com and familysearch.org: U.S. Census for the family headed by his father, Morris Bieber (1900, 1910, 1920); U.S. Census for

Isidor Bieber (1930); New York State Census for family headed by Morris Bieber (1905); passport applications for Morris Bieber (1912) and for Isidor Bieber (1919); World War I draft registration card for Isidor Bieber (1942); New York City Municipal Death record for Morris Bieber (1935); U.S. Social Security Death Index record for Isidor Bieber (1974).

Racing documents: The Jockey Club Certificate of Foal Registration for Stymie (issued to Max Hirsch c/o King Ranch on November 1, 1941, and transferred to Mrs. E. D. Jacobs on June 2, 1943); measurements of Stymie (taken in August 1947 by Dr. Manuel Gilman, the chief examining veterinarian for the New York Racing Association).

CORRESPONDENCE

Letters: Damon Runyon's typewritten letters to Hirsch Jacobs dated December 6, 1942; December 3, 1943; and November 23, 1945; Isidor Bieber's handwritten letter to Hirsch Jacobs dated February 2, 1955.

Telegram: John Hay Whitney's July 27, 1949, telegram to Hirsch Jacobs reacting to newspaper reports that Stymie had been retired due to injury.

Handwritten notes: Hirsch Jacobs's six-page summary of the 1947 racing season written late that fall.

PHOTO CREDITS

INDEX

Index

Index

Walker, Jimmy, 51, 71, 91
Walters, Johnny, 59–60
War Admiral (horse), 129, 132–133, 138, 157, 234, 271
War Relief Days, 168–169
Wheatley Stable, 270, 273
Whirlaway (horse), 169–170, 185, 186, 188, 189, 204, 213, 216, 220; 234, 236, 238, 239, 242, 243, 248, 262, 264, 277
Whitney stable. *See* Greentree Stable.
Whitney, Cornelius Vanderbilt, 151
Whitney, John T. ("Jock"), 256–257
Whitney, William C., 28, 31
Willard, Jess, 47, 49
Wilson, Woodrow, 51
Window washing rigging, 70–71
Womeldorff, Red, 143
Women's Wear Daily, 284

Wood Memorial, 190
Woodmere Claiming Stakes, 64
Woodward, William, 117, 124
World Series 1919, 50
World War I, 22, 31, 48, 57, 66, 188
World War II, 3, 6, 157, 167–170, 187–188
  atomic bombs dropped, 206
  Battle of Okinawa, 200, 206
  Battle of the Bulge, 197
  D-Day, 192
  racetracks closed, 195–199
  V-E Day, 199
  V-J Day, 206
Wright, Wayne, 131

Yankee Stadium, 54–55